Critical Acclaim for

THE LUNATIC EXPRESS

"Carl Hoffman . . . has done a great service by reminding us, in *The Lunatic Express*, of this abiding truism: that the world's ordinary traveler is compelled to endure all too much while undertaking the grim necessities of modern movement . . . making this book both extraordinary and extraordinarily valuable . . . . It is a wise and clever book, too, funny, warm, and filled with astonishing characters. But it also represents an important exercise, casting an Argus-eye on a largely invisible but unignorable world. It is thus a book that deserves to be read widely."

—Simon Winchester, *Wall Street Journal*

"A compelling, thought-provoking read." —Jim Benning, *World Hum*

"This book is fabulous. Hoffman opened my eyes to the off-the-grid traveler, clearly most of the world, and made me cry. The last pages struck home; the duality of escape and harbor are the blessing and curse of life."

—Keith Bellows, editor in chief of *National Geographic Traveler*

"Hoffman . . . could probably sell a book about pretty much anything thanks to his beautiful writing. He served up one hell of a read." —Jenna Schnuer, WETA Public Television and Radio

"Carl Hoffman . . . takes us into the frantic fear and pitiless extinctions that punctuate the simple struggle to get from home to anywhere, for so many of the world's people. But it also takes us into the heart of the writer: and that journey, with its beauty and compassion, its conscience and courage, is so thrilling that we hope the ride never ends." —Gregory David Roberts, author of *Shantaram*

"With adventure, danger and self-discovery in one insightful package, *The Lunatic Express* is *Eat, Pray, Love* for men. But don't worry. Women will enjoy it, too."
—The Lost Girls, LostGirlsWorld.com

"Don't try this at home! That's the lesson we can take from Hoffman's adventure book, a crazy cross between *Top Gear* and *MythBusters*." —*New York Post*

THE LUNATIC EXPRESS

ALSO BY CARL HOFFMAN

Hunting Warbirds

THE
LUNATIC EXPRESS

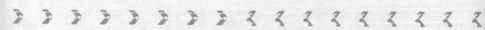

Discovering the World . . . via Its Most Dangerous
Buses, Boats, Trains, and Planes

CARL HOFFMAN

BROADWAY PAPERBACKS

New York

BROADWAY

Library of Congress Cataloging-in-Publication Data
Hoffman, Carl.
The lunatic express / Carl Hoffman.—1st ed.
p. cm.
1. Voyages and travels.   2. Hoffman, Carl—Travel.   3. Transportation—
Evaluation.   I. Title.
G465.H66 2009
910.4—dc22   2009021477

ISBN 978-0-7679-2981-3
eISBN 978-0-307-59012-1

Printed in the United States of America

DESIGN BY AMANDA DEWEY
MAP BY DAVID LINDROTH, INC.

5 7 9 10 8 6 4

First Paperback Edition

For my mother and father:
Diane Hoffman and Burt Hoffman

Our Nature lies in movement; complete calm is death.

—Pascal

We shall not cease from exploration. And the end of all one's exploring will be to arrive where we started. And know the place for the first time.

—T.S. Eliot

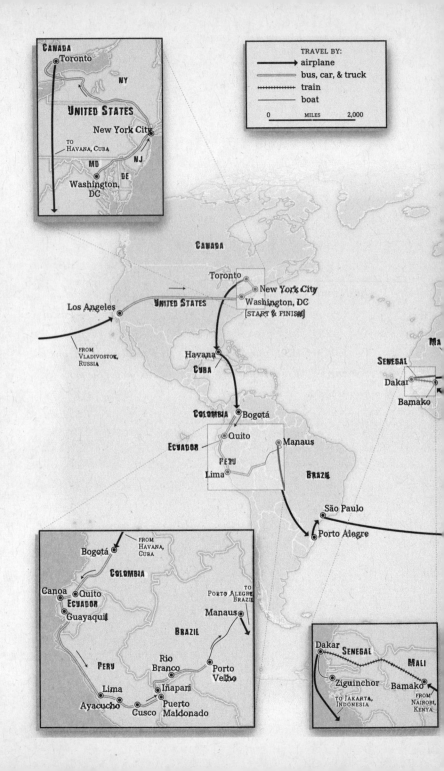

Inset: Northeastern United States / Canada

CANADA

Toronto

NY

UNITED STATES

New York City

TO
HAVANA, CUBA

MD

NJ

DE

Washington,
DC

Legend

TRAVEL BY:

airplane

bus, car, & truck

train

boat

0   MILES   2,000

Main map

CANADA

Toronto

New York City

Los Angeles

UNITED STATES

Washington, DC
[START & FINISH]

FROM
VLADIVOSTOK,
RUSSIA

Havana

CUBA

COLOMBIA   Bogotá

Quito

ECUADOR

Manaus

PERU

Lima

BRAZIL

São Paulo

Porto Alegre

MALI

SENEGAL

Dakar

Bamako

Inset: South America

Bogotá

FROM
HAVANA,
CUBA

COLOMBIA

Canoa   Quito

ECUADOR

Guayaquil

TO
PORTO ALEGRE,
BRAZIL

Manaus

BRAZIL

PERU

Rio
Branco

Lima

Porto
Velho

Ayacucho

Iñapari

Cusco   Puerto
Maldonado

Inset: Senegal / Mali

Dakar   SENEGAL

MALI

Ziguinchor

Bamako

TO JAKARTA,
INDONESIA

FROM
NAIROBI,
KENYA

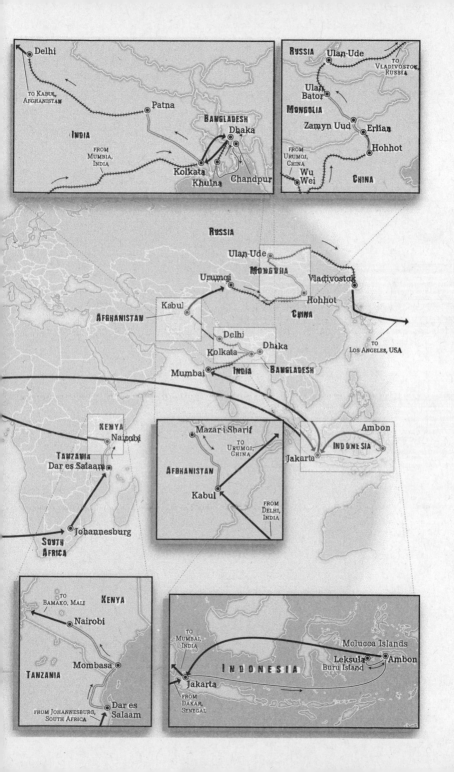

Contents

PART THREE

ASIA

THE LUNATIC EXPRESS

Time for Prayer

OUTSIDE OF PUL-I-KHUMRI, the bus shuddered to a halt on the dusty roadside and couldn't be restarted. Khalid, my traveling companion, sighed. Fretted. I rose to go outside and stretch my legs like everyone else, but Khalid stopped me. "This is bad," he said in a whisper. "It is a dangerous place. It is the home of Gulbuddin Hekmatyar. He is the most dangerous man in Afghanistan. Very religious, the leader of the Islamic Party of Afghanistan. It is the party of violence and killing of innocent people. He is not Taliban, but just as bad. He lives in exile now, but his people are here." Khalid, I knew, was right. Hekmatyar had been politically all over the place, but since the fall of the Taliban he'd been violently opposed to both the Karzai government and the American presence in Afghanistan. He'd been officially labeled a terrorist by the United States. I suddenly had a terrible feeling. A feeling of dread, worse than at any time since I'd left home months ago to journey exclusively around the world on its most dangerous and crowded and slow-est buses, boats, trains, and planes. My knife was taped to my arm and I was dressed in a grease-stained salwar kameez, with a hat pulled low over my head and a week's growth of beard covering my face, but out here what good would it do if we had to stop moving for a day? Where would I go? Where would I flee? There was no taxi to jump into, no government ministry or five-star hotel in which to hide. Outside were brown fields. A few mud houses. Bare trees. What if the bus couldn't be restarted? What if we had to get off and wait in town and I was discovered? I was crazy for trying to ride a bus across Afghanistan in the middle of a war; idiotic. What had I been thinking? I closed my eyes and tried to fall asleep, to think about nothing.

Khalid prayed.

PART ONE

AMERICAS

A Russian-made Cuban commercial jet smashed into the side of a mountain near the Venezuelan city of Valencia on Saturday night, killing all twenty-two people on board, authorities said today. There was no immediate explanation for the crash, the second major accident in less than a week for the state-owned airline.

—New York Times, *December 27, 1999*

ONE

Go!

"GO, GO, GO!" yelled a Chinese woman in front of the New Century Bus office, a yellowed, basement room in an old federal row house on H Street Northwest, in Washington, D.C.'s anemic Chinatown. The bus was around the corner. It was leaving. Now. It was cold and bright and my children and Lindsey, my wife, ran with me and we hugged and a Chinese man in a black leather jacket barked "Go!" and the next thing I knew I was alone, rolling down K Street on a so-called China bus to New York City. My phone chirped. A text from Lindsey: "I wanted a picture of all of us!" There had been no time. It seemed like a voice, fading, from up a river on which a current was sweeping me away.

The weather was unsettling, as it always is in the first weeks of March. The day before had been hot and cold and sunny and rainy and cloudy and windy all at the same time. Walking down Columbia Road with ten hundred-dollar bills fresh from the ATM in my pocket, squinting into the sun and clouds and trying not to get blown away by the gusts, I even got hit with hail the size of peas. Stop signs whipped back and forth, and a *Washington Post* news box crashed to the ground. I had a lump in my throat. My chest was tight. I hadn't slept well for weeks. In the morning I was leaving home.

For twenty years I had been a stable husband and father, and then I'd snapped. My life suddenly didn't seem to fit anymore. I was middle-aged, with a wife and three children whom I loved but hadn't been living with for almost a year. A long journey seemed the best solution. The classic move was to leave the world for the exotic to be born anew: Gauguin shipped himself off to Tahiti, Wilfred Thesiger to the Empty Quarter; the New York artist Tobias Schneebaum literally shed his clothes by the Madre de Dios River and walked naked into the Peruvian Amazon. Its opposite—the search for raw pleasure—had long been popular, too: food and cafés in Rome for Henry James, and for Liz Gilbert, the spiritual groove of Bali's Ubud.

As I fought my way through the wind down Columbia Road to finish packing in my barely furnished apartment, I had something different in mind: to escape not out of the world but right into its messy heart. To experience travel not as a holiday, but as it is for most people: a simple daily act of moving from one place to another on the cheapest conveyance possible. A necessary part of life, like brushing your teeth or sleeping or making love.

The idea first struck on a flight from Kinshasa to Kikwit in the Democratic Republic of Congo, while traveling on a magazine assignment. The thirty-year-old, eighteen-seat Short Skyvan was full, hot as an asphalt roof on a summer's afternoon and buzzing with flies, and there was some doubt about when it would leave or if it would leave at all. Planes in the

Congo were crashing with alarming regularity; my worry wasn't whether I'd get a meal, but whether I might live or die. And we were lucky; we were flying. Below us was a country the size of Western Europe, with just three hundred miles of paved roads on which hordes of people were packed into thirty-ton trucks traveling on dirt tracks.

By road or by air, none of the people moving around the Congo were tourists. My fellow passengers in the Skyvan were sweaty and nervous, but resigned to delays and waiting and discomfort. Maybe that was how all travelers had once felt, I thought. For most of human history, travel, after all, was an arduous necessity. The word itself comes from the French *travailler*—to toil or labor, reflecting the difficulty of going anywhere in the Middle Ages. Aside from a few freaks like William Lithgow, a Scotsman who wandered through Europe, the Near East, and northern Africa in the early seventeenth century, people traveled not for the pleasure of it but because they had to—long journeys by foot or horseback or wagon or sailing ship that were uncomfortable and unpredictable and scary. Roads were bad. Ships sank. Today, however, we think of travel as joy-seeking, the pursuit of pleasure, a vacation, and tourism is the largest industry on earth, generating $500 billion a year in revenue. But tourism is a relatively new phenomenon, barely three hundred years old. As a journalist who frequently ended up in some of the world's oddest corners and crevices, I gradually began to realize that the big numbers of today's tourism industry obscured a parallel reality, excluded a whole river of people on the move. Excluded, in fact, *most* of the world's travelers, for whom travel was still a punishing, unpredictable, and sometimes deadly work of travail.

After that Congo flight, wherever I went I saw it, this pulsing artery of these people, moving within cities and between countries and across oceans, people who didn't show up on the tourism statistics and didn't earn frequent-flyer miles. A largely rural planet of villages had, in the last fifty years, become a rapidly urbanizing and interconnected world. Fifty-five percent of Brazilians lived in cities in 1970; by 1995 that number was almost eighty percent. Pick a country in South America or Africa or Asia and the statistics were similar. On cars, minivans, buses, boats, trains, and planes—not to mention the most pitiful of all, packed into shipping containers or trudging through the Texas desert with their coyote guides—people moved from village to city, from country to country, between continents, largely invisible in the world's travel statistics. Only in 2008 came the report from Dilip Ratha, a renegade economist at the World Bank and the first person to seriously study remittances (the money migrants send home to their families). Until Ratha's research, most economists saw remittances as small sums insignificant to international development. But Ratha unveiled some 200 million migrants worldwide sending home $300 billion a year, three times the world's combined foreign aid. That's 200 million roofers and landscapers and dishwashers and construction workers and babysitters on the move, and most of them weren't relaxing on United or Singapore Airlines.

Reading the paper, I noticed the macabre shadows of their travels: BANGLADESH FERRY SINKS; MANY DIE, burped a typical small headline buried deep within the *Washington Post*. In the poor, watery world of Bangladesh, more than 20,000 passenger ferries were the only option between Dhaka and its outlying districts. In the last twenty-six years, 496 sinkings, killing more than 5,000 people, have been reported. Ditto Indonesia, where 400 drowned in January 2007 when an overcrowded ferry sank on a nineteen-hour passage between Java and Kaliman-tan. Which was nothing unusual for weary travelers in the archipelago: it was the second ferry to sink in two days, and the fourth loss of over 500 people on Indonesian passenger lines since 1999.

Wherever I looked, I saw them. With an eye peeled for those little news clips, they were never-ending: Amazon passenger boats capsized and sank. Airplanes in Africa crashed. Trains in India derailed or were attacked by mobs. When the *New York Times* ran a piece in 2007 about the discomforts of air travel, its website was swamped—298 angry, bitter, indignant comments poured in. "I will go to the ends of the earth to avoid air travel," wrote Isabella from Palo Alto, California, in a typical note. But those comments were largely about domestic U.S. air travel, where only one fatal crash occurred on a major scheduled airline between 2006 and 2009. Crowded (but clean) airplanes, unsympathetic flight attendants—so what? You could book your flight on the web, get a bag of mini-pretzels, and arrive. African aviation was a different universe altogether, home to fifty of the ninety airlines banned as "flying coffins" by the European Union, and where you were twenty-five times more likely to die than on an American carrier.

In *The Naked Tourist,* Lawrence Osborne writes that "travel itself is an outmoded conceit. . . . Travel has been comprehensively replaced by tourism . . . and the modern traveler has nowhere left to go." I knew what he meant, but I didn't agree.

Travel in the oldest sense of the world was still right under our noses, I thought. On all those buses plunging off cliffs and sinking ferries and crashing planes, people were unself-consciously making arduous and unpredictable journeys every day.

Once I started seeing all those deathtraps out there, I couldn't shake my curiosity. I wanted to jump on and circum-navigate the planet on that unseen artery of mass transit. I wanted to know what it was like on the ferries that killed people daily, the buses that plunged off cliffs, the airplanes that crashed. I wanted to travel around the world as most of the people in the world did, putting their lives at risk every time they took off on overcrowded and poorly maintained conveyances because that was all they could afford or there were no other options.

A long journey invites the unexpected, and I decided to take small hedges where I could. Inflatable life vest. Waterproof, battery-operated strobe light. A half-joke canned survival kit my sister had handed me on Christmas morning. A pile of orange plastic vials: Cipro if things turned "watery," said my doctor, "but if you see blood, seek help." Zithromycin for respiratory infections. Tylenol with codeine for really bad pain, "two every four hours as needed." Malarone for malaria. Sterile needles and suture thread. I'd tried to double my life insurance, to no avail: two different insurance agents had come up empty-handed, even though I'd conveniently forgotten to mention most of the really bad places and conveyances on my tentative itinerary. My "travel exposure," as the guy from AIG Insurance said, was just too great. I was pumped up with every vaccine imaginable: hepatitis A and B, and Japanese encephalitis; yellow fever and typhoid; tetanus and cholera. There was nothing more to prepare for.

. . .

Escaping was something I'd gotten good at. In my twenties I'd started writing and traveling. For me, the two were inseparable. For my first national magazine assignment I profiled the captain of a 600-foot chemical tanker sliding down the Atlantic coast. Leaving home to meet the tanker in New Haven, Connecticut, I was so nervous all I wanted to do was puke. Three weeks later an editor called and said, "How'd you like to go to the Canary Islands for two weeks?"

Lighting out was hard in those days. I'd fallen in love with Lindsey the summer I'd turned twenty-two; we'd married five years later and we were both self-employed, so we were together all the time. Leaving, walking down the Jetway for some distant place, I'd suddenly feel naked. I can remember leaving for St. Lucia once and getting choked up as I boarded the plane. I called home every day.

I don't know when or how things changed; they did so slowly, bit by bit. Over the years I grew comfortable out on the edges of the world. I was never so focused—all of my energy every day and night bent to the single task of getting the story, getting into other people's lives. I could sacrifice myself to that task, and go hungry or suffer through heat or cold in a way that I never did at home. For me, each story was like life and death, a journey to the edge and back, and in many ways I felt I could go so far precisely because I had an anchor so firmly planted in the sand of home.

I was paid to sate my curiosity about the world. I hung out with flying missionaries in the jungles and mountains of New Guinea, and with mercenary pilots in southern Sudan. I ate reindeer marrow with the last remnants of a tribe of herders in Siberia. On a 150-foot ship off the coast of southern and eastern Greenland I learned to drink whiskey with a man who'd once been imprisoned in a three-foot-square metal box in the Solomon Islands and roamed the world with a life-size cardboard cutout of John Wayne. The adventures were addictive. Instead of choking up when I walked to my next flight, I started craving that moment of setting out. To get on the plane was to roll the dice, to look up at the sky and think, here I go! What would I experience? Whom would I meet? Would I get the story and bring it home? Would I even live? And I got to plunge into other people's galaxies, see life through their eyes. That was the greatest privilege of being a journalist—to live for a time in someone else's world, to be subsumed in otherness and make it yours, wrap it around you like a new identity. The more borders I crossed, the more strange places I dropped into, the more I couldn't abandon the thought that right now, at this moment, there were Polar Inuit whipping their dogs across treeless deserts of ice and snow in Greenland, Dayak women weaving baskets in longhouses in Borneo, Mayans worshipping strange gods in smoky ceremonies in Guatemala. Once I understood that otherness was out there, I couldn't leave it alone.

Home became ever more strange to return to. The two lives were jarring; one day to be in southern Sudan in a war zone in heat and flies amid gunshot victims, the next at a PTA meeting. One day drifting down the Amazon, the next vacuuming the house and buying milk at Safeway. I told my tales—they were eagerly awaited—but I didn't tell anyone how difficult it was becoming to straddle those two worlds. I was ever more open to the world and ever more closed at home . . . until the time that I looked forward to most was walking down that Jetway, rather than coming home.

One day my body just reacted, as if I had a simmering flu. I was fully functioning, but tired, lethargic, barely able to get off the sofa and seemingly never able to get enough sleep. A year passed and the doctor could find nothing wrong with me. Then, as so often happened in my life, the phone rang and a week later I was gone—this time on a ship in the middle of the Pacific Ocean for two months, writing about a quixotic search for Amelia Earhart. My lethargy evaporated on the very first day of royal blue sea and flying fish and the flukes of sounding whales. Eight weeks later I was home again, sickness gone, but conscious for the first time of a deep unhappiness, profoundly disconnected from the life I'd thought unshakable.

IN THE OPENING PAGES of the first book I ever loved, Arthur Ransome's *Swallows and Amazons*, the vacationing Walker children discovered a dinghy in the boathouse of their rented farm on the shores of a lake—and then spotted an island. "All four of them at once were filled with the same idea," wrote Ransome. "It was not just an island. It was THE island, waiting for them. It was their island. With an island like that within sight, who could be content to live on the mainland and sleep in bed at night? With a lake as big as a small sea, a fourteen-foot dinghy waiting in the boathouse, and the little wooded island waiting for explorers, nothing but a sailing voyage of discovery seemed worth thinking about."

Written in 1930 by a roving correspondent who covered the Russian Revolution, married Leon Trotsky's secretary, and cruised the Baltic in a twenty-foot catboat, that passage captured the birth of wanderlust better than any I've read since. A boat. An island. A journey. The idea arises unbidden. It takes hold and you can't shake it. Nothing else seems worth thinking about. "Why are you doing this?" asked my friends. They couldn't fathom it. They saw my journey as some sort of masochism, and the conveyances as a self-imposed death sentence. People stopped calling me days before I even left. They didn't offer condolences or sympathy or even good luck. They just hid, as if I'd gone nuts, as if they were embarrassed for me and didn't know what to say. "Poor Carl," I could imagine them saying, "he's so lost he's gone off to kill himself the slow way."

But I had a sense that the timing was right, the moment had come. Accelerating after the Amelia Earhart expedition, I'd traveled more and more; my days had become a series of flights out and back, each one leaving me ever more comfortable in strange places. Now I needed to do something huge, to jar myself out of my life—and that was what long journeys did best. There remained so much I still wanted to know and see in the world, and I hoped that I might come home with fresh eyes.

As the bus lurched through D.C. traffic and the industrial wasteland of far eastern D.C.'s New York Avenue, my anxiety began to lift, like the passing of a summer squall on the Chesapeake Bay. Ahead of me was possible misery and maybe danger, but also adventure, the unknown, a feeling that I was about to live deeply. I realized how lucky I was. I was bracing for anything and everything and, who knows, there was the chance a long journey on the worst conveyances might transport me to somewhere altogether new.

I was starting slowly on a circuitous route that had me heading north before going south. I wanted to get to South America, and one airline stood out: Cubana Airlines, which had one of the worst safety records in the skies, with a "fatal event rate" almost twenty times higher than Southwest Airlines. But the closest Cubana flight took off from Toronto, and the worst option for getting there was first the so-called China bus to New York and then Greyhound to Toronto, both of which had plenty of tales of breakdown and catastrophe. And I liked the idea of starting from home on familiar highways, roads I'd taken a hundred times that would lead me from the exits of the New Jersey Turnpike to the peaks of the Andes and the plateaus of Asia, a continuous chain of machines and expanding experience and stories that would ultimately bring me back home.

Shaking loose from home took time. I broke my first night rolling through New York State in discomfort, opening my eyes to the sun edging over the horizon above Lake Ontario, frozen solid into a sheet of white. It was fourteen degrees, the city glittering and steaming, with snow three feet deep piled along the streets and sidewalks, and pillars of steam rising from vents and buildings under a hard blue sky. We were an hour late, twelve hours from Manhattan, but I had the feeling of the world sliding past beneath me.

My four-hour flight to Havana on one of the world's worst

airlines was surprisingly easy. An hour before landing, the stewards and stewardesses brought out their luggage and started rifling through the plane, packing anything that wasn't screwed to the bulkheads. Fistfuls of napkins. Doggie bags of chicken and iceberg lettuce salads. Great handfuls of plastic cutlery. Rolls of toilet paper. Disposable salt and pepper shakers. Prepackaged toilettes. They went through the plane like they'd never see another plastic fork again and maybe never get another meal, which finally made sense when I emerged from the airport. A light rain was sprinkling down on Havana. Five hours before, I'd been in a frigid world of sparkling glass and escalators, but there it was hot. Steamy. Dark, the kind of darkness that only exists in the crevices of the world where there are just enough streetlights to illuminate nothing, each a weak oasis for thousands of frantic, flying insects. Giant puddles were everywhere, Havana's streets and curbs broken and potholed. Emerging from customs, I'd accepted the hustle of a gypsy taxi driver, and he led me to a Toyota with darkly tinted windows and no door handles. I didn't like to lose sight of my luggage, but he popped the trunk and insisted it had to be hidden. *"Policia,"* he said. "Eleven million Cubans, five million police!"

I don't know how he got the car started, but he did, amid great coughing and choking and the thick smell of oil and gas. It had no muffler and we sputtered and roared out of the lot into the dark humidity on three cylinders, past an endless line of people plodding along the pavement like zombies in the darkness and drizzle. "You like reggaeton?" he said, cranking the tape deck so high the distorted music vibrated the door panels. "You pay me now!" he said.

"No," I said. "When we get to the hotel, I'll pay you."

"No gasoline!" he said. "Pay me now."

"No," I said again. My luggage was in the trunk; now he wanted his money up front. It didn't look good.

"We don't have gas!" he said. "We won't make it!" I leaned over to look at the gauges. "Broken," he said. They were all broken, the needles motionless. And he sounded pitiful.

"OK," I said, "half now, half when we get there." He swerved into a desolate-looking gas station, poured ten dollars in the tank, and off we roared into the wet blackness of a city that shocked me. It wasn't the Spanish colonial buildings of the old city turning to dust and being eaten by mold. It wasn't poverty or people's lack of material possessions; it was their lust for them, a lust so powerful they'd turned Havana into a city of pimps and prostitutes, a hustler on every corner.

"Hello," said a young girl named Martha, who appeared next to me on the street in front of the Parque Central the next morning. The sidewalks were crowded, shoulder-to-shoulder, with people stepping gingerly over broken curbs as '57 Chevys and late-model Chinese motorcycles swirled past. "Where are you from?" she said. "Is this your first time in Cuba?" She was twenty-one and could have been my daughter. In her modest T-shirt and shorts and clean white running shoes, she looked more wholesome and innocent than ninety percent of the women her age on prime-time television. "I teach dancing at a hotel," she said, "and I like to practice my English. Do you like salsa?"

I said I did.

"There is a most important salsa festival at a famous place, the Rosario Castro, nearby. Would you like to see it?"

"Absolutely!" I said. I followed her around the corner, down a block, and around another corner to an ornate colonial building with a wooden doorway big enough to drive a truck through. We skipped up a broad flight of stone stairs into a bright, airy atrium balcony overlooking a courtyard, with a few plastic tables and a bar. It was noon. Behind a set of glass doors lay an open room, perfect for dancing. But it was empty, the doors locked. "The salsa has not started yet," she said. "Want a mojito? They're the best here."

A woman appeared out of the bathroom. She was short and shaped like a barrel, with a prominent gold tooth and a jagged scar on her wrist. "My friend!" Martha said. The girls hugged and kissed each other's cheeks. "Buy us a mojito!" Juliana said. "Please!"

We sat down at a table and Martha ordered three mojitos. "Don't worry," she said, "since it's so early I'll order them weak."

"You think Martha is pretty?" Juliana said, pinching Martha's cheek as the mojitos arrived. I wasn't quite sure what to say, so I said nothing and took a sip; the sweet icy lime and mint was delicious, but the drink contained enough rum to satiate a Marine after a tour of duty in Iraq.

"You want to fuck her?"

Martha smiled. Juliana smiled. "Fucky-fucky!" Juliana said.

"Um, no thanks," I stuttered, suddenly feeling a little cornered.

They both frowned. "But don't you think Martha is pretty?" Juliana said.

I nodded; I shook my head. "Yes, she's very pretty," I said, "but no thanks."

"OK, but we're hungry!" Martha said, sucking air from the

rapidly depleted mojito through her straw and ordering another round.

I was curious about them, so I bought them a plate of grilled fish and rice to share. They wolfed it down like they hadn't eaten since last week. Juliana rolled cigars—one hundred a day—and earned 240 pesos a month, ten dollars at the official exchange rate.

"America is great!" they said, shoveling spoonfuls of rice into their mouths. "How about another mojito!"

"Yeah," I said, "but you get free health care."

"Ha!" They both almost spit their food out. "*Nada* free! My baby needs an operation," Martha said. "You gotta give the doctor perfume, shampoo, souvenirs, or else you'll wait on a list for years. The list is long! There are always people on the list! And the police! They make eight hundred pesos a month and another forty in convertible pesos, twice what a doctor earns." They wanted more. More money. More mojitos. And: "You sure you don't want any fucky-fucky?"

In the land of free health care and free education and Che and Fidel on every wall, the Cubans were bobbing and weaving around the system in a desperate quest for convertible currency. I couldn't relax; if I paused at a bench in a park or slowed my pace along the street, someone tried to sell me her body. Or their sister or girlfriend, or a box of cigars. I couldn't make sense of Cuba, couldn't even really see it, and the problem was home and time and the magic of the airplane. Cubana Airlines had plucked me from the icy streets of Canada and plopped me down in Havana a day after leaving home. My body was there but my mind wasn't. That was the trouble with the typical one- or two-week vacation, especially to anywhere foreign: it took time to wear away that protective sheath, and it was something other people could sense, intuit, in the way I walked, moved, looked, talked. It was like I had a neon sign on my forehead that said DAZED AND CONFUSED. It was why, careful and alert to the world as I thought I was, it was only in Cuba that I got suckered into a currency exchange that left me suddenly standing alone in a market holding a wad of useless Cuban pesos. Which was okay; to get into the world, to meet it, didn't happen overnight. It required a transition of time and space, and in Cuba I was just sort of simmering on the stove.

After four days I was antsy to move, to get deeper in. I was happy to board the Cubana Ilyushin Il-62 bound for Bogotá. Which was crazy: three of the eight Cubana crashes had occurred on flights to Central and South America, one of them on an Il-62 that crashed on takeoff into a Havana neighborhood two miles from the airport, killing all 126 passengers and crew as well as fourteen people on the ground. Not to worry, though, as Cubana's in-flight magazine addressed the issue head-on, in English. Sort of. "It is like a corollary, which does not have to be demonstrated, for it is deduced from experience: before a plane flight you were concerned. . . . Perhaps you heard that a hurricane is crossing this or that region has put you on guard and fired the mechanism of the silenced, discreet fear that does not show before others but makes you tense. So it is clear that safety is the issue of concern. However that concern is due to your lack of knowledge about the means of transportation you are using and the crew in charge." Relax, the article said. Cubana's crews had "been duly certified by prestigious aeronautical institutions," and the plane itself was "a novel mechanical gadget equipped with . . . the best systems developed by the human

mind, able to laugh at hurricanes or any other atmospheric dis-
turbances." Never mind that I was heading to a country the
very mention of which brought gasps to my family and friends.
Guerrillas. Narcos. Kidnappings. But just as flying on the world's
most dangerous airline was oddly pleasant, I suspected the
dangers of Colombia were overblown. Americans always thought
of their country as the richest, freest, safest place on earth, and
of the rest of the world, especially the developing world, as a
miasma of despair and crime, a Hobbesian universe of poverty
and assaults and bombings and kidnappings and people eking
out a living in garbage dumps. I believed it was an exaggerated
worry, which was the point, I thought, as I settled into my seat
on the Ilyushin, of traveling as I was.

The old Soviet-made airplane's armrests were cracked and
peeling, and my seat-back wouldn't go forward. The flight attendants weren't svelte and beautiful like they'd been on the
marquee Toronto flight; half were bald and overweight men,
and they didn't give a safety briefing. A guy in back fired up a
cigarette before we left the ground. But the Soviets had designed
airplanes without profit in mind, and I couldn't complain: every
seat had three feet of legroom, the aisles were wide, and the gal-
ley in the center of the plane was twenty feet long. Even better,
it was almost empty. The pilot hammered the throttles forward,
an overhead bin popped open and a pile of first-aid kits crashed
to the floor, and three hours later we slammed onto the pavement
of Bogotá. A minute early—and time, I felt, for the real journey
to begin.

LIMA, Peru—At least forty-five people died when a packed passenger bus plunged into a ravine in Peru's southern Andes despite a new campaign by President Alan Garcia to reduce fatal road accidents, police said on Tuesday.

The bus skidded off a mountain road in Peru's border region with Bolivia late on Monday night and crashed into a 1,640-foot-deep gorge, probably because the driver was speeding, police officer Julio Apaza said.

—Reuters, December 5, 2006

TWO

Hope for Buena Suerte

THERE IS NO PLACE like a South American bus terminal; they feel like the town square because, in a way, they are. At Bogotá's Terminal Terrestre, I slipped through a metal detector, showed my passport to soldiers in combat fatigues, and passed into a model of low-cost efficiency. Modern, big-city airports always felt sterile, generic, unconnected to place. But here, boys were zooming toy cars across the floor. Short, dark campesinos in cowboy hats looked shy and mystified, and women in heels clicked imperiously across the tile, under the gaze of soldiers and private security guards fingering submachine guns as ticket sellers poked their heads out of little windows touting buses and destinations in rapid-fire, singsong voices. *"Ipiales! Ipiales! Ipiales!"* they shouted, so fast it was one slurred phrase.

"Cuenca! Cuenca! Cuenca!"

In South America there wasn't much middle ground: few owned cars and only the rich flew. Buses were king. In Bogotá alone, dozens of private companies offered service to every town and village on the continent, a travel network cheaper, more efficient—and far more dangerous—than anything in America.

I felt impatient. I was still on Washington time, still on a fast-paced, get-it-done ethos, used to calls and e-mails and texts, a constant stream of problems and invitations and other people's needs. It was always like that, I knew, when you set out on a long journey; the classic two-week vacation was never enough time to slough off the dead skin of regular life. In some ways, I'd discovered during years of traveling, home life was like an insulating callus you had to wear off before you could even properly see and absorb the new world around you. I knew that would happen eventually, but meanwhile I had the idea I just wanted to make tracks, to knock back the miles, to go without stopping straight into the heart of the world.

Quito, Ecuador, sounded good, and getting there would take me straight through Colombia to the border of Ecuador, a twenty-hour ride to Ipiales across the Andes and Revolutionary Armed Forces of Colombia (FARC) guerrilla country. Avoid traveling at night, the Lonely Planet guide warned, which made traveling at night seem more interesting—and how could you avoid it on a twenty-hour journey? A complex war had been raging for years in Colombia involving leftist guerrillas, right-wing death squads, narcos, and American contractors, but things had rapidly improved and the country was blossoming. Just the week before, soldiers had stormed into Ecuador near where I'd be crossing to attack a FARC base, killing one of its senior commanders. Though six tourists had been kidnapped a few months before on the Pacific coast, the guerrillas were on the defensive. And my sense was that when it came to political disruptions and danger, the crowd knew best—the buses were leaving, people were traveling, and it was a big country.

Worse than guerrillas, though, was the possibility of crashing. The World Health Organization rated Latin American roads the most dangerous anywhere, with 1.2 million people a year killed in road accidents—nearly 3,000 a day. The buses of Peru, Ecuador, and Bolivia were particularly legendary for horrific crashes, often involving coaches plunging off cliffs, like the one in Peru in December 2006 in which a packed bus plunged into a 1,640-foot gorge, killing forty-five of the forty-seven passengers. At least Colombia had been making an effort: since 2004, its bus companies were required to post accident and fatality statistics in public view, supposedly making its riders informed consumers. Continental SA, the operators of my bus, had, in the first three months of the year, suffered eighteen accidents with eight injured and six dead. That seemed a lot. I bought a ticket and settled down with a plate of steaming curried chicken and rice and cornmeal wrapped in a banana leaf.

My seatmate out of Bogotá was a round-faced girl named Maria, wearing a white hair band and dangling silver earrings, so shy she could barely look at me. She'd traveled twenty-four hours for work, spent two days in Bogotá, and was now repeating the twenty-four-hour journey home. "I couldn't fly," she squeaked, "too much money."

We rose and fell and swirled through green, rugged, and steep mountains under gray skies that dribbled rain, on well-paved two-lane roads full of *curvas peligrosas*—dangerous curves—and every once in a while I'd catch Maria squeezed against the window staring up at me with as much fright and wonder as if she were sitting next to the Easter Bunny. Between my bad Spanish and her shyness, my attempts at conversation went nowhere. In the middle of the night the rain came harder, pelting down in pitch blackness, and I figured any guerrillas out there in the cold jungle, on land so steep you could barely stand, would be hunkered down. But what if we did hit a roadblock? The FARC had a long habit of taking hostages, from local politicians like Ingrid Betancourt to American contractors to tourists. The thought stuck in my head as we passed an army patrol fanned out along the winding road, armed with M-16s. Maybe I could hide behind luggage in the overhead rack. Would the other passengers rat me out? What if the guerrillas set the bus on fire, as they had done before?

At 4:00 a.m., Maria slipped away, and as it got light I noticed the man across the aisle staring at me. And then, just as we passed another *curva peligrosa*, I saw his hand vigorously moving up and down over his crotch. I turned my head. Guerrillas, mudslides, accidents—it seemed like sex was the only real threat.

AT THE COLOMBIAN BORDER I had my passport stamped below a wall of wanted posters of FARC commanders, walked across the San Miguel River into Ecuador, and ten minutes later was seated on a rundown bus bound for Quito, with blue-and-white bunting and dangling tassels over the windows. Over the next six hours two guys in the seat across the aisle sucked down a fifth of Suiza tequila, as *Rambo*, dubbed in Spanish, played on the TV in front of the bus, cranked out over speakers above my head. The bathroom was locked—only for the ladies, said the driver—and mortars flew and bodies exploded and Rambo kicked guys' heads in. Chick flicks did not play on South American buses, ever, I would eventually learn. As the hours fell away, my body ached and my head pounded from the altitude and no coffee. I was hot, dirty, slimy, hungry, and lonely, and Quito, twenty-six hours after Bogotá, didn't help. We crawled through raw ugliness, mile after mile of square concrete boxes piled on each other like a modern Anasazi city, amid choking traffic and acrid exhaust, a growing city stretching, cracking open like a stretching, peeling lobster.

I didn't linger. Quito's terminal covered three stories, with eighty gates of buses pulling in and out every few minutes. Ticket agents sang their refrains.

"Cuenca, Cuenca, Cuenca!"

"Pedernales!"

The smell of exhaust and gas filled the station, the sounds of clanking horns. In an hour I was on a bus with the Statue of Liberty painted on its side, barreling back into the mountains again, bound the long way to Guayaquil via the coast. The hours passed: the curves, the dips, the climbs, the sudden braking. The constant music and explosions from the television stupefied me and everyone else. There was nothing to do, nowhere to go. No one read, and passengers barely spoke; on a bus your seat holds you prisoner. My seatmates were a string of Marias— people traveling unbelievably long rides for short visits with family or for work. Vendors swarmed on board at every stop, hawking grilled corn and hot sodas and Rubik's Cubes. *"Jugo! Cola! Esta bien!"* A stream of salesmen got on, talked and talked, holding up bottles of little green pills or small pieces of candy. "My product is better!" they all said, walking down the aisle, now filled to standing room only, passing out samples, talking some more, then collecting a few coins or taking the samples back. The thought of selling penny candies or medicines on a moving bus was impossible to imagine; day after day after day, the same spiel, all for pennies.

But I was starting to see something, to understand why there was always a bus to take you wherever you wanted to go, and why those buses were always plunging off cliffs. It wasn't some inborn South American recklessness, some wild and literal leap of faith for people draped in crosses and bracelets of the saints. It was simple economics. American roads were paved and lined with signs and guardrails because America spent billions of dollars on its infrastructure, money collected in taxes. American buses had good tires and fresh brake pads because regulations required them to, and Americans paid commensurate fares. But, relatively speaking, none of my fellow passengers had any money; they couldn't afford good roads, good tires, good brakes. If they'd had money, they would have flown. But there were a lot of them, and they were on the move. To make money from people who had none, buses went without maintenance and squeezed every person aboard they could. Drivers drove for hours on end; they fell asleep at the wheel, they drank, they hardly saw their families. The police weren't paid much money, either; they took bribes from bus companies and drivers instead of forcing them off the road, or even prosecuting reckless drivers. Danger, more than anything else, kept fares low. A week later, five British women would be killed on this same route when a truck sideswiped their bus at dusk. The driver didn't even shut off the engine; he just fled.

There was no respite. PELIGRO! REDUSA SU VELOCIDAD AHORA! read yellow signs that the driver ignored, careening around corners with no guardrails on the edge of 200-foot drops, and mudslides tumbling into the road. Time was money and the amounts were so small here, so hard to come by, death was a risk worth taking.

I had been gone a week, had been on buses for almost fifty consecutive hours, and as the bus descended from the mountains into the hot, humid coastal plains, a world of banana trees and cycads and thatch and sand roads, I felt like I was beginning to wake from a long sleep, the veil between me and the world beginning to fall away. These early buses between big cities were a practice run for later, and I suspected they were easy, a picnic before getting into more remote areas. But they were doing the trick—they were breaking me down, opening me up. I was starting to relax, to feel a rhythm, to surrender that illusion of control; the road was whatever came my way, and that was okay. No, it was more than okay; it was good.

THE DEEPER I TRAVELED on these South American buses, the more in harmony I was starting to feel. And I was starting to trust the efficiency of this whole ad-hoc, unregulated system. In Canoa, a sleepy fishing village on the Pacific coast of Ecuador, I stood on a muddy street for only five minutes before a bus scooped me up, depositing me two hours later by a pier in the dusty town of San Vicente, all unpaved streets and unfinished concrete buildings. Twenty of us piled on a long wooden *panga,* paid thirty-five cents, and motored across the bay to Bahía de Caráquez, where I stepped into a waiting pedicab that dropped me five minutes later at a bus departing in minutes for Guayaquil. Though slow and statistically dangerous, travel at this level was as cheap and available as bread. Competition was so fierce, regulation so absent, there were always more buses than you needed, always pedicabs or taxis angling for another fare; you never had to wait, and you never had to worry about food or thirst because there was always a vendor selling something.

From Guayaquil, I rode a single bus twenty-eight hours to Lima. Five hours to New York on the China bus had seemed long, twelve hours to Toronto forever. But twenty-eight hours straight was starting to seem as normal to me as it did to my fellow passengers. And I was hardly even noticing the bus's condition: torn upholstery, bald tires, heat and humidity and crowds—that was all of a piece with the surrounding countryside. I was still reading Lawrence Osborne, who wanted to find "the end of the earth, a place of true adventure." Here, on these buses, I was anywhere but at the end of the earth; I felt right smack in its crowded heart, surrounded by everyday people. I was traveling via a series of veins and arteries that didn't show up on most of the developed world's anatomy charts.

We tore past flooded fields under a pewter sky, Brahmin cows with long horns and humps standing in water up to their chests, on roads of packed sand and ribbons of blacktop yawning with craters and dirt roads covered in shimmering puddles. In the station that morning I'd noticed a clearly middle-class family seeing its two daughters off; they'd hugged long and hard. Marina, a twenty-four-year-old "food engineer" whose favorite dish was spaghetti, clutched her cell phone while her twenty-one-year-old sister, Vivien, hugged a Latin American edition of *Cosmo*, and they sat across the aisle from me. Marina's father was from Ecuador, and he owned a shoe factory in

Guayaquil; her mother was half Chilean and half Peruvian. They'd had visa problems, and after living twelve years in Lima, her parents and younger siblings had relocated to Guayaquil while Marina and Viviene had stayed behind with their grandmother. They thought nothing of taking the bus twenty-eight hours between cities. "It's cheap," Marina said, "and I like to look at the world." It was a world both big and tiny; my friends and most Americans I knew would be horrified at the idea of such a long bus ride between countries. Yet beyond this marathon slog over mountains and bad roads, she'd seen almost nothing. She'd never been to Cusco, Peru, or Quito, Ecuador, or anywhere else beyond the road we were now on. And to her I was a strange interloper in their little world, and she and her sister peppered me with questions. Was I married? Did I have children? Where was I going? What was America like?

Which was even odder, because Hollywood's version of America was right there in front of us for hours and hours and hours, on the bus's TV screen. America was anything but an abstraction. It was literal, vivid, reinforced every time a South American went to the movies or turned on the TV. It was a constant tease, this magical place where everyone was rich and beautiful (not to mention violent), and I tried to imagine what it would be like to watch a daily stream of Colombia—how powerful the idea of that place would become. We watched eight movies, including *Armageddon* and *Resident Evil III*, while inching through the crowded market town of Huaquillas (six-foot-tall plastic flowers; quail eggs, four for a dollar; stilettos and skinny jeans and a whole pig upside down on a hook), and rain in Chiclayo so driving it flooded the streets up to the curbs. In the morning we paused in the hot sun and washed our hair in a concrete trough by the side of the road. "Only seven more hours to Lima!" roared one of the drivers, shaking the water out of his hair like a dog after a bath, before lathering up his armpits. Known as *conductores* in Spanish, the drivers had gold teeth and faded, mystical tattoos on their shoulders. They traded the wheel every five hours and slipped the bus through its seven forward gears like it was all they ever did. Which was true: they drove twenty-eight hours to Guayaquil, spent the night, then returned to Lima before going on to Puno, Bolivia another twenty hours south, before turning around and doing it all over again.

"Lots of accidents," they said, laughing. "Do you have a driver's license? You want to drive?"

We passed through broken-down towns of tiny, garage-sized brick houses and sun and wind and Internet cafés, a weird world that had so many layers of culture it sometimes felt, in a way, nowhere at all. When she picked up a cell tower, Marina chatted on her cell phone; the Bee Gees crooned on videos between flicks; sheep and donkeys wandered in the dusty road.

In Lima, I made my break. I needed to go deeper; I'd been on too many highways, too many long rides between big cities. These buses were beginning to feel too civilized. East of Lima rose the Andes again, and deep within them lay Ayacucho. It was there, in one of the poorest areas of Peru, that a sociology professor named Abamael Guzman had started the Maoist Shining Path movement in 1980, which had risen to become one of the most violent and ruthless guerrilla armies in South America. I'd always been fascinated by the brutality and longevity of the Shining Path, and I'd long wondered how guerrilla movements were so hard to stamp out even when, in Peru's case, soldiers and militias and right-wing death squads had been everywhere. I wanted to get to Cusco; via Ayacucho it would take thirty-six hours to cover the 450 miles.

Back in Washington it was spring break, and I invited my seventeen-year-old daughter, Lily, to come along with me. She'd be going to college next year, and I wanted her to get some sense of what my life was like. And after days and days on beat-up buses, I no longer had any concern about anything happening during our five days together. I picked her up after midnight and dragged her to the bus first thing the next morning. As we boarded, a little man videotaped us, marching up and down the aisle shooting each passenger. "What's up?" I said.

"In case someone steals something or there's an accident," he said.

"So there are a lot of accidents?"

"Oh no!"

"A lot of thefts?"

"No!"

"Anyone killed lately?"

"Oh no!" he said.

Ayacucho was only a few hundred miles as the crow flies from Lima, but it took ten hours to get there on a freshly paved road. The mountains were steep, high, relentless, and I realized I had miscalculated. I was used to the endless hours squished on buses, used to the twists and turns on the road and uncertainty of the whole enterprise—I had done it for years. But Lily had been chatting with her high-school friends one day and was being crammed on a bus through the mountains of Peru the next, with no transition. She was dizzy, exhausted after the long day, and her Spanish was good so the political graffiti shouting

"Assassins" unnerved her. Cusco was another twenty-four hours away, and there were only two choices: a bus at 6:30 a.m. or a bus at 6:30 p.m. "But don't take the night bus," the hotel clerk warned. "It's dangerous."

So on the bus we were again, at six thirty the next morning. And immediately it was clear why it took twenty-four hours, why the night bus was dangerous, and why it can be so hard to dislodge festering guerrilla movements in the mountains and jungles of South America.

There was no road. Or what was called the road was a one-lane dirt track that rose and fell thousands of feet in altitude, full of switchbacks and cliffs and eroded sections that dropped straight down steep mountainsides. Looking out of the windows, it felt like flying, albeit in slow motion through turbulent skies. Mountain ridge after ridge, valley after valley—traveling ten miles took hours, through villages of adobe mud and thatch, atop high, treeless mountain plains where there was nothing but sheep and alpaca and round, waist-high thatch shepherd's huts. We passed a truck with no windshield, its front crumpled from a recent crash; we jerked to a halt on a hairpin turn inches from crashing into a truck filled with watermelons. We plunged into river valleys that were hot and humid before climbing back up above the trees, all at the speed of a walk. This was the highway; anyplace off the road, and there was only one way to get there—walking in brutally steep country. Every six hours or so we'd stop and we men would pile out—sixteen of us pissing on the side of the road. The women didn't budge.

At a small village we paused for a quick break and I snapped a photo of the rugged landscape. "Are there no rocks in the U.S., gringo?" said a woman. Lily was quiet. I ate whenever I was hungry, as vendors piled in with hot, waxy corn with kernels the size of quarters, and chunks of fried bread filled with warm cheese, but Lily wanted nothing. I worried about her, but it was nice to have her along, not to be alone.

At dusk we pulled into Andahuaylas to change buses. The station was wild, dirty, almost medieval, full of feral, begging dogs and piles of dirt and women in bowler hats and twin braids. Carleton, a mid-fifties Indian-Canadian and the only tourist I'd seen in days, was freaked out. "I promised myself I wouldn't take any night buses," he said, "but the rest of the journey is at night. I'm really scared! I had to turn my eyes away a few times on those cliffs."

I didn't feel any danger. I'd taken so many overloaded helicopters and airplanes in the past few years, I'd learned to resign myself to fate, or fate mixed with preparation; you controlled what you could (hence my excellent first-aid kit), kept your eyes open and your wits about you, but then you just rolled with things. Carleton couldn't eat; I wolfed down a quick meal of rich, gamey chicken soup ladled from a pot big enough to throw a couple of toddlers inside, sitting on a on wooden bench the width of a single two-by-four under a ragged blue tarp. Lily didn't want any, but the chef could spot a hungry, nervous girl and brought her a bowl, insisting that she eat, which she did under the pressure of a mother, even if it wasn't her own. Then, as church bells pealed, we piled on an even older bus. "Aren't you afraid you'll get sick?" said Carleton, shaking his head. "I'm starving, but there's no way I'm going to risk eating that!"

I looked at Lily and we laughed. "See how brave you are!" I said, secretly praying she wouldn't get sick. As soon as the sun went down, roaches swarmed out of the curtains; they fell into

Lily's lap, crawled into my coat, scurried under our feet. It was black outside, the bouncing headlights illuminating dirt road and sheer drop-offs. Lily was scared; I felt bad for her and proud of her. I hoped she'd love the journey, but even if she didn't, at least I knew she'd remember it and feel, perhaps only later, strengthened by it. That she'd learn that the world was big, rich, complex, sometimes dangerous, always interesting. That you could hide from it or explore it and embrace it in all its complexities.

The bus stopped every few miles, quickly filling to standing room with people who were so brown and withered they looked like canned mushrooms. Soon a dog joined us, and then an old man dressed in a black suit and so small and frail he looked like a marionette puppet.

All this time on buses was odd time—time in sort of a suspended state. With no light, we couldn't read. We were in the heart of things, but removed, too; I wanted to climb out of the bus and be in places and not just passing through. And it was physically painful—the seats were close together, there was no legroom, and the bus was so crowded we couldn't stand to stretch our legs. At some points I got Zen-like, just succumbing to the pain in my knees and my aching neck. It was out of my control, and I rose out of that suffering into a state of grace, totally surrendering, my mind dancing to distant places. It was easy for me to do, but harder for Lily; she sank into lethargy, though she never once broke down. She smiled, kept her cool, learned to trust her instincts and to open herself to experiences beyond her usual boundaries. She was being transformed only by learning the strengths she already had, who she already was:

someone capable and confident, and sometimes scared and happy, even at the edges of the world. I'd fall asleep and wake up confused, shocked to find myself on a bus in South America with my daughter.

When we got to Cusco we spent two days wandering, eating on balconies in the sun, forgetting, in a way, the journey I was on. So quickly she had to go, and I took her to the airport and she disappeared through security and I sat waiting for her plane to take off and cried. Five days hadn't been enough time. I couldn't tell if she'd enjoyed the trip or not, couldn't tell if she'd gotten to know me more or had liked what she'd seen. And it was easier for me to feel content the more distant my home and family became; having Lily with me and then not left me feeling empty, deeply conscious of what I'd left behind. I missed her and felt guilty for not being more normal, for pursuing a life that took me so far away, for needing to experience the intensity of loneliness and danger and discomfort.

IT WAS TIME to move on. From Cusco, my plan had always been to travel by bus to La Paz, Bolivia, there to ride the World's Most Dangerous Road and then take a train to the Brazilian border, known as the Train of Death. Both sounded tempting. But a new road had been built, bypassing the World's Most Dangerous Road, which had become a staple of tourist mountain bikers who wanted to experience a taste of danger in an organized package. And in Cusco, Lily and I had run into a stringy-haired British computer programmer who'd just taken the Train of Death. "It was sweet, dude," he said. "No problems at all and there was a great bunch of other backpackers on it." It wasn't that I was a snob about backpackers; I had been one, too. Authenticity was a buzzword in travel, but what exactly did that mean? At its purest form you could make the argument that the only really authentic places were ones that had never seen contact with the outside world at all. There were still a few of those left—in the Amazon, perhaps in Indonesian New Guinea. But they were hardly representative; they were freakish vestiges of a changed world, and authenticity was simply everywhere; it was all authentic in one way or another. But if you were on a train with a lot of backpackers, it got too easy not to meet locals, not to get lonely, not to feel scared, and I wanted all of those things.

Which made the road to Puerto Maldonado, in the Peruvian Amazon, sound like heaven: "According to Peruvian road engineers, this is Peru's worst road between two major cities," warned my guidebook. "It takes two and a half days in the dry season and longer in the wet. Don't take the trip lightly; the journey requires hardiness, self-sufficiency and loads of good luck. Fatal accidents are not uncommon." The book was outdated. Immigrants were pouring into Puerto Maldonado to seek their fortunes, so of course a bus company had stepped into the void and Expreso los Chankas didn't seem worried. Seventeen hours if it didn't rain; twenty dollars; buses left daily at 3:00 p.m.

The road was the last key piece of the Carretera Transoceanica—a 6,000-kilometer highway linking the Atlantic and Pacific Oceans from Brazil to Peru. More important, though, it would tie one of the last great remaining pristine rain forests of the Amazon basin to ports on the Pacific coast. Gold. Mahogany. Uncontacted tribes. Puerto Maldonado was said to be a seething boomtown on the banks of the Madre de Dios River; only two weeks before, a researcher had been shot there after reporting on an illegal load of old-growth mahogany.

ALL STARTED WELL. The bus was old, with cracked armrests, and it smelled of urine, but was freshly swept, and I had an aisle seat with no one next to me. And the road, it turned out, had been paved in December, two lanes of smooth blacktop snaking up the Andes into a cold, largely treeless world of llamas and adobe houses, with smoke pouring from chimneys in thatch roofs.

The clouds were ominous, though. And a couple of hours out, as we started descending the Andes' eastern flanks, everything changed: the pavement ended. Harsh white lightning ripped through the skies and torrential rains poured down. The bus filled; the air turned humid and thick. The seat next to me was taken by a peasant in rubber boots and thick sweaters. His three-year-old son coughed like a wounded guinea pig and puked into a plastic bag and pissed out of the window throughout the long night. The rain fell in heavy, big drops and the driver, thirty-two-year-old Juan Luis, fought to keep us on the road. All through the night we jerked and bumped and slid, big blobs of water leaking onto my head. We forded dark frothing rivers so deep I thought we'd get swept away. We stopped, backed up, waited, inched past trucks and cliffs so close I could touch them out of the window. "It is heavy," Luis confessed to me on a bathroom break, during which forty people pissed on the side of the road in the rain, and a trillion frogs croaked. "And very tiring. The road is clay and very slippery."

The journey was twenty hours of torture. But hardship brings rewards: as dawn broke in pouring rain, we bounced and jerked into a wet and glistening terrarium. Sopping jungle and red mud roads and one-room wooden shacks from which candles flickered—I had, at last, passed into a new set of arteries, smaller, more remote; the world I was entering felt fertile and fresh.

Puerto Maldonado might be the beginning of the end of Peru's rain forest, but I liked it the minute I stepped off the bus. It was all frontier prosperity and dynamism: dirt and mud streets filled with motorcycles and Indian auto rickshaws right off the lot, and wooden clapboard gold-buying houses and open-air restaurants dishing out thick soups, against the banks of two big, khaki-colored rivers half a mile across. I spent hours walking through its muddy streets, just soaking up the energy. Houses were springing up, new mud streets reaching ever farther into the bush. Immigrants were pouring in from the Andes to work its timber and gold; when the road was paved and the Madre de Dios River bridged, the place would explode. Which could happen tomorrow or never—two concrete pilings stood on either side of the river for a steel bridge that had been stored in a nearby warehouse for the past decade.

Along the muddy shores of the river, fifty-foot longboats jostled for passengers and wooden one-car ferries with outboard motors pulled in and out. Lumberyards with rusty cranes unloaded stacks of jungle hardwood; it was along this river that the artist Tobias Schneebaum had walked naked into the forest, where he found tribes that still practiced ritual cannibalism. Even now, some of the Amazon's last uncontacted people lived up the river's tributaries in Peru, and just five hours downstream lay Bolivia. I wanted to know more, and found Joseline Vizcarra tending her newly opened Internet café. She agreed to take me down the river.

"I don't know what all these people will do when the bridge is built," said Vizcarra, dickering for a boat and captain. A pretty, brown-haired woman wearing Teva sandals (a mark of her travels outside of Puerto Maldonado), she waved her hand over the ferries and longboats as we slid into the current of the swollen river, the air heavy with humidity and the smell of smoke. The daughter of a high-school principal, she'd grown up in a village twenty-five miles east of Puerto Maldonado, but had been shipped off to live with an aunt in Lima for high school and college. "When I was little," she said, "there was nothing here. It was a wild town and the road was terrible; it took us five hours to travel the twenty-five miles from our village to town." We were going downstream and stayed where the current was strongest, right in the middle. The river was high, flooding banks tangled and overhanging with scrub, full of tree limbs and whirlpools. "Now, every day, more people come. We call them colones. All this, when I was little, was still primary forest cut with little trails where native people came to fish." It was a disappearing world; loggers had taken the trees, and cattle ranchers had moved in afterwards. "There's no mahogany left," she said, as heavy, widely spaced drops of rain fell. "When I was little my father and I would walk through the forest looking for Brazil nuts, but now you've got to go seven hours upriver to find primary forest."

We ground down the river, the engine roaring, for two hours. After so much time on buses, the river felt free, open, a wide, silvery brown pathway under a huge gray sky. But I was seeing it at its fullest in the rainy season; during the long, hot, dry summer, Vizcarra said, "it will be covered with miner's dredges. Like a city at night." The river divided around a flat, forested island. "It is full of black spider monkeys," she said. "A man used to live on it and feed them and you could go and see them," Vizcarra said, "but then he died and now it's dangerous. The monkeys are aggressive and wild; they'll bite you. It's horrible!"

We swept around a bend, and ahead lay five gold-mining dredges rafted together, hard against the banks of the fast-moving river. Rodolfo Muñoz waved us aboard, glad, I think, for a distraction. Small and wiry and leprechaun-like, with green eyes and a helmet of black hair, Muñoz was a Bolivian who'd been going after gold for twenty-four years, since he was sixteen. The five boats shared a single cook, a woman in cut-off blue jeans, and his colleagues were from Brazil and Bolivia, all illegally in the country. His boat was sun-bleached, bare wood on two hulls—two simple beds, a one-burner gas stove and enamel basin, an outhouse, and a grinding, burning-hot, eight-cylinder diesel engine inhaling sediment from as deep as forty-five feet into the riverbed up onto a king-bed-sized sluice covered with gray carpet.

Six days a week, twenty hours a day, Muñoz worked the river, sucking up sediment and water that poured over the carpet, leaving a fine mud behind. He stopped at 4:00 p.m. on Sundays until nine on Monday morning. "On a good day," he said in Spanish, scooping up a day's sediment from a blue bucket into a rounded gold pan, "we get one gram an hour." He swirled the mud and flicked water into the pan and pointed: a speck of gold so small I would never have noticed it. "A bad day is eight grams in twenty hours. Now, gold is eighty-four *soles* ($31) a gram; in a good week I get 120 to 140 grams."

As big-headed and long-beaked banded kingfishers dived overhead, the sluices sparkled with round balls of mercury the size of skateboard wheel ball bearings. Muñoz brought out a plastic jug of the toxic metal and showed how he poured it into the bucket, mixed it with the mud, and squeezed it all through a cotton sieve—the water and mercury washing out into the river, leaving gold behind. His was one barge; it was hard to imagine how much mercury was washing into the river every day during the busy dry season. From his bunk, curtained by a sheet of blue plastic, he fished out a small piece of paper wrapped around a silvery ball: five grams of gold.

Two men worked each boat; someone else owned the mining concessions for every section of the river. "Every day is for us," he said, "except Saturday, and that day's gold goes to the men who own the concessions." Sometimes Muñoz had to dive into the underwater hole, sucking on an oxygen hose. "It's dangerous," he said, "because the hole is not wide and sometimes it collapses and you die. Only the pipe comes out, not the man. I've lost men in Bolivia, but not here." He shrugged, grew quiet, looked down at his feet.

"Ever been robbed?" I said, imagining a wild-west scene of highway—or river—robbery.

"Only once," Muñoz said. "A man stole my boat, but my friend saw it and we jumped in his boat and followed him, and I took it back."

"What did you do to him?"

Muñoz smiled. "Nothing. I knew he did it because he was poor, and I felt his shame."

The engine was deafening, and the humidity and heat were as heavy as a wool blanket. This was his life. "What else can I do?" he said. "It is peaceful here and I make eight hundred *soles* a week instead of eight hundred *soles* a month like I would if I had a job in town. We take a risk," he said, "and hope for *buena suerte*."

When the road was finished, whenever that would be, Puerto Maldonado would roar louder. More timber. More gold. More tourists to see the rapidly disappearing jungle and its monkeys. I liked it now, I thought, as we pushed back upriver in the hot sun back to town. Soon it would need all the luck it could get.

A ferryboat carrying more than 100 passengers collided with a barge loaded with fuel tanks and sank to the bottom of the Amazon River on Thursday, officials said. . . .

Rescue teams recovered the bodies of four children, five women and one man . . . and a check of the boat's passenger manifest indicated nine people were still missing.

—Los Angeles Times, *February 22, 2008*

THREE

Your Time Comes or It Doesn't

THE DEEPER INTO THE AMAZON Basin you go, the fewer roads there are, until they give out entirely; rivers take over, and buses are replaced by boats. According to my map, if I headed due east from Puerto Maldonado I'd hit Rio Branco, Brazil, and then Puerto Velho, on the banks of the Madeira River, from which I hoped to catch a ferry 660 miles northeast to the jungle metropolis of Manaus. Amazon ferries sank with regularity; in the first three months of the year more than two dozen people had died in two separate incidents. But to get to the Madeira I had to cut a hundred miles east through the Peruvian Amazon, and there was only one option for getting there: shared taxis on roads that looked none too impressive on my map.

Tiptoeing around the mud of Puerto Maldonado, I caught a three-wheeled auto rickshaw to the Imperial Car Service. Inapari, the Peruvian border crossing, was supposed to be three hours away, but "the roads are horrible," said the driver, a short fellow in a Buffalo Bills football jersey that came down to his knees. "Too much rain. Maybe we can do it in five hours." I bought some crackers and bottled water and waited for the car—a white Toyota station wagon with plastic-covered seats and a red-and-yellow lightning bolt painted on its side—to fill up. Its tires were as bald as racing slicks. After forty-five minutes there were six of us piled in hip-to-hip, plus two men huddled in the back deck with no seats—and bumped through the streets and the puddles and down a concrete ramp to the river. We stepped out as the driver backed down a slippery dirt trail and then up two wooden planks barely wide enough for each tire, and onto the ferry. We crabbed across and piled in again on the other side, accelerating along a rutted, soaked red mud road with low green scrub on either side. The air was sweet and smoky and wet, the sky filled with low gray clouds, and the car slid and swerved, mud spattering so hard and high I had to roll my window up.

My fellow passengers were mute. We killed a dog, a quick thump, and the driver laughed. We skidded past horsemen and small farms and giant ficus trees, and I spotted a hawk perched high above the road. At every river, big concrete pilings were rising from the banks, while we inched across narrow, one-lane wooden bridges. Soon, when the bridges were finished and the road paved, this would be a highway, but now it was still the outer reaches of the known world. I was happy; nothing but mud and rain and big wet sky, with no idea of where I was heading, save my vague notion of catching a boat that I wasn't sure even existed. I felt a building exhilaration, with little loneliness. It should have been the opposite, but this deep frontier fed my romantic soul. I liked the idea of a place so vast and unexplored that, as the legendary British travel writer Peter Fleming wrote in his 1934 *Brazilian Adventure*, "You can believe what you like . . . ; no one has the authority to contradict you. You can postulate the existence of prehistoric monsters, of white Indians, of ruined cities, of enormous lakes." There were people not far away who had never seen a telephone or computer. Macaws and parrots, jaguars and sloths. Who cared if I couldn't see them from the road? Just knowing they were out there felt good. This was the kind of place I'd learned to love, and feel at home in, during all my years of traveling. To be discovering a world, to be thriving in a place without connections, made me feel free. And out here I had to be alert all the time, focused, watching my back even as I roared across a dirt road with no idea where it would lead.

We pulled into Inapari at 4:30 p.m. under a light rain, after six hours of hard driving through the relentless, sticky, flying mud. The town was a single square surrounded by wooden clapboard houses and more mud; a sign announced that the Atlantic Ocean was 3,908 kilometers away, the Pacific 1,874. Alone in the middle of nowhere, I got out of the car and stood in the rain. A pregnant feral dog slinked by. Chickens pecked at the edges of puddles. I wasn't sure what to do; Inapari didn't look like much of a place to hang around. A man approached me; he looked different. Tall, broad-shouldered, but pale-skinned, with black jeans and pointy-toed loafers. "Asis?" he said. That was the name of the town across the river, in Brazil.

"Any hotels here?" I said in Spanish. He didn't understand, and I realized he was Brazilian and spoke Portuguese, not Spanish.

"Taxi?" he said, pointing to a small white station wagon. His taxi was spotless, with newspapers spread across the carpet, and before crossing the border he tanked up on gasoline siphoned from a bucket. When he offered to take me all the way to Rio Branco in the fading light, I agreed, and I fell asleep on the fast, straight, paved roads of what just two decades ago was remote Amazon jungle, foreshadowing Peru's future. In Rio Branco I caught another bus and arrived in Puerto Velho at four in the morning, falling onto the thin mattress exhausted, in a concrete room across from the bus station.

I was so tired I couldn't sleep, though, and thought of Lawrence Osborne's words: "A journey is never a simple thing. The hitches and the boredom, the missed connections and empty hours are the price for leaving one's real life and entering an unreal one." Right now I was nowhere and everywhere, alone and foreign and unsettled in never-ending movement. It was raw travel that was stripping everything to the bone and tearing away my leftover anxieties. When you travel you imagine leaving your old self behind. But hunger, fatigue, the aches and pains of life in a bus seat, only show you the real you—there's never any escape from yourself. And that's no small thing. It was just me, and over the past few years I felt like I'd gotten so twisted up in multiple lives of trying to be different for different people, it was sometimes hard to remember who I was. Out here I could just be myself, happy, self-reliant, content, exactly where I belonged. Osborne was saying this was an unreal life, and maybe it was—I certainly couldn't do it forever. But it was also the opposite, real, a reminder that happiness wasn't all the external comforts but just there, within myself.

. . .

IN THE MORNING I tumbled out of my concrete hotel and flagged a taxi. "Take me to the river," I said, "to the docks." It was hot, humid, cloudless, the sun glaring and burning on top of my head. We wound through haphazard streets and blocks and squeezed down an unpaved road as full of people as a fair, stopping at the river's edge. Literally: it was so high it overflowed its banks, muddy water lapping onto the street. As everywhere in places that were poor, I didn't have to search or wonder and I was never lost; I stepped out of the taxi and was assaulted by touts for every service I might ever need. "Manaus?" shouted a man in bare feet and a muscle shirt.

He grabbed my arm and we trotted onto a series of wooden planks over the water and mud, out to a lovely sight: Tied to rotting wooden rafts floated the *Altamonte Moreira VII,* 100 feet of wooden Amazon river boat. She was three decks tall, all elegant curves and upturned bow, with a graceful sheer-line and a low waist ending in a rounded stern. "We sail at two p.m.," said the captain, a bulky man in flip-flops and loose shorts, sitting at a folding table collecting money, as an army of men bearing crates of tomatoes and giant sacks of potatoes ran up and down the narrow gangplanks. "Seventy dollars to hang your hammock and three meals a day." The journey would take three days.

I raced back to my hotel, checked out, bought a hammock and some rope, and was there by noon. A bit late, as it turned out—the *Moreira* was filling up fast. The first deck, just two feet above the water, was one open space stacked with crates and sacks; I had to weave my way through narrow passageways between them, and they unnerved me. They must have weighed tons. The second deck, open too, was a tangle of hammocks tied to the rafters; they were next to each other and above each other; I tied mine among the tangles, only inches to spare above and next to me.

The top deck was open, except for a roofed bar area with a few tables and plastic chairs, and the party was already cranking. The sky was high and wide and epic, the breeze like a big-bladed fan on low, the double-time beat of accordion-fused samba coursing through from a pair of three-foot-high speakers. Two women were dancing, swaying their hips like their spines were worms, around a table heavy with empty beer cans. Ten little kids ran around the deck, and two played naked under an outdoor shower spigot. "What's your name? Where are you from?" asked Irma. She had long black hair, skintight blue jeans, and a belly that hung five inches over her waist.

Off to one side swayed a black cowboy with green eyes, wearing cowboy boots and high-waisted jeans with a huge metal buckle and a ten-gallon hat. He looked like he needed a horse. "This is the best boat," said Roberto, an agricultural economist in a polo shirt and loafers. "The food is good and there's a lot of it and there are a lot of women!"

It was like I'd stumbled into a dormitory on the first day of college. Irma, Val, Kleyton, Lucia, and Antonio were dancing and drinking and none of them had ever met each other before. Irma slipped off her wedding ring and slid it onto her right hand. Antonio, already shirtless, did the same. Kleyton smiled, clapped me on the back, and said, "All Brazilians think about is sex!"

"We're not leaving until seven," said Val, who had two huge dimples and was almost bursting out of her halter top.

I bought them all a round of beers and settled in, and at five the engines started rumbling and we pushed away from the dock. But out in the current we stopped, going nowhere. Aluminum johnboats sped out, full of men. "Look," said Carlos, an older man from Venezuela. "There is supposed to be a line down there, the waterline."

I peered over the rail and saw nothing. "Yes," he said, "You can't see it. We are overloaded!"

He was a former accountant from Caracas who'd taken up long river trips in his retirement. He'd been on enough ships to be worried. In late February, just a month before, the *Altamonte Montiero* (a carbon copy of the *Moreira*) also en route to Manaus, had struck a fuel barge during the darkness of a lunar eclipse. No one knew exactly how many people were on board, but the *Monteiro* rolled and sank, killing at least eighteen. Three months later another ferry, carrying eighty, overturned in a rainstorm, killing fifteen.

It took an hour to sort out; instead of offloading cargo to reduce the boat's overloading, money exchanged hands. Disaster films are filled with ominous foreshadowing: dramatic music plays; the camera lingers on, say, the payoff. But this was the stuff of everyday life. It was utterly banal and commonplace, hardly even worth mentioning. Until, that is, a storm rolls in or two boats collide and tragedy ensues. On these riverboats it was usually those sleeping in the tiny, hot windowless cabins toward the bow who drowned, as had happened on the *Monteiro*. The Venezuelan shrugged and made the sign of the cross. There was nothing to be done about it; we would be in God's hands. As the sun dipped low we finally eased down the wide, silver-brown river.

There's nothing better than the vibration of a ship's engines gently surging underfoot. It's the sound of travel, a long journey. The Madeira was a mile wide and seemed to go on forever. I had grown up sailing on Chesapeake Bay, had a sailboat on the Potomac River now, and I was struck, not for the first time, by the idea of the earth defined and dominated by water, the continents but islands in a great pool of liquid that is more the original road than any highway. From here we could float to the Amazon, from the Amazon to the Atlantic; from the Atlantic we could go anywhere. Deep in the jungle, I still felt strangely connected to everywhere. And though roads are, by definition, new constructs, rivers flow as they always have; here in the Amazon Basin, as we slid past wild green banks and forest, it couldn't have looked too different from what Francisco de Orellana had seen along the Amazon itself in 1542.

Night falls quickly on the Equator; one minute it was sunny, the next it was dark, the Southern Cross low in the sky and the Milky Way thick overhead, the blackness of the river and its unpopulated banks impenetrable. Heat lightning flashed along the horizon, and I played a simple card-slapping game with Kleyton and five kids. But after the afternoon's beer, sun, and heat, we were all suddenly exhausted. Irma and Val stopped dancing and plunked down on plastic chairs. Kleyton disappeared. And I ducked and shimmied under hammocks and swaying bodies and slid into my scrap of hanging cloth. It was a long night. Bodies above me and beside me pressed and bumped into me every time one of us shifted. The boat rumbled. My rear end touched the floor. The night grew damp and cool; I threw on extra shirts but couldn't stop shivering. In the middle of the night I awoke to find us docked, a line of men throwing whole frozen fish, one by one like cut wood, from a truck into the hold.

A Klaxon sounded at six a.m., signaling breakfast, and again at eleven and five, for lunch and dinner. We ate around a long table, twenty at a time, big bowls of rice and beans and noodles and chicken, with copious amounts of farina and homemade hot sauce, finished with black coffee as sweet and thick as ice cream. No one spoke; we shoveled it in and hurried out for the next group standing in two lines on either side of the door. We dozed in our hammocks. We paused at villages where crowds of people nearly sank the floating docks, and took on sacks of charcoal, bags of ice, motorcycles, pots and pans, and people. At one village the sound of our Klaxon was answered by a string of firecrackers. We passed miles and miles and hours and hours of nothing but a tangle of green trees. Sometimes we were but a few yards from the riverbank; at others we were midstream, amid a swirl of languid currents and floating islands of water hyacinth. The river held no buoys, no markers; navigation was by intuition and experience. We played cards and read; we drank too much beer; we baked in the sun. We observed each other. Not for one second was I bored.

There was nowhere to go, nothing to do; we drank as much as we liked. We talked, mostly—visited, as my mother would say of the long conversations people had in her native North Dakota. Kleyton was a half-Peruvian doctor from Rio Branco, being posted to a boat out of Manaus to tend to small river towns for six months. He was small, with wire-rimmed glasses and a baseball cap. Yesterday he had been all over Val and Irma, dancing with them, touching their shoulders, trying to make them laugh. Neither one had shown any particular interest, though, and now he was angry.

"Those women," he said, shaking his head and nodding

toward Irma and Val, dancing and swaying in their own world, "they are prostitutes."

"I don't think so," I said.

"No, they are," he insisted. "They are bad women! You shouldn't talk to them."

Kleyton was a man obsessed. Every conversation turned to women, as it often did throughout my journey when I talked to other men. If there was an international language between men in the world, it was about women. The truth was, we were all obsessed. "In Brazil, all the women have curvy backs," he said. "But in America, their whole bodies are curvy, right?"

We were in a bubble, the world of the boat on the river our own; it was strangely liberating. In the old days, I mused, every trip across the country by train, every trip to another continent by boat, was like this. An escape. A suspension of time, and a time for reflection.

The *Moreira* was clean—a crewman was always mopping— but there was only so much you could do with 200 people on a boat with four bathrooms. They were wet, stiflingly hot wooden rooms the size of closets, and smelled so strong I couldn't breathe. To bathe, you turned a faucet and eighty- degree river water poured from the ceiling. Communal sinks lined a wall of the hammock deck; I stood in line and shaved and brushed my teeth in front of an audience. Personal space, cleanliness, silence, safety—I was getting used to not having any for long periods of time. But I was also starting to realize they were an unbelievable luxury. In America, the richer you were the more things you had and the bigger they were—but money didn't just buy things. After so many days on crowded buses and boats, it was becoming clear that more than anything else, money bought insulation and protection. From wind and rain and heat, from other people, from noise, from pollution. The deeper I went, the clearer this became.

WE ATE, WE DOZED, we bumped against each other, the river flowed on. Once I stumbled on the captain having nits picked out of his hair. By the afternoon of the third day we passed more and more small cattle farms carved out of the green, surrounding weatherbeaten shacks on stilts near the river's edge. My hammock mates packed their bags, brushed their teeth, washed their hair, and waited. By nine, as we plowed up the Rio Negro, lights began to appear, and then more and more. They were so bright—a shocking industrial brightness illuminating huge oceangoing freighters, a world of metal and power and muscle, after nothing but wood and water and sky and green. "It's scary-looking," said Kayla, a hairdresser returning to Manaus after three months visiting her father in Bolivia. Like Marina on the bus to Lima, she, too, had seen so much and so little— nowhere but Santa Cruz, Bolivia, and Manaus and hundreds of miles of rain forest and river in between. "I've never been to Rio, to São Paulo," she said, as we averted our eyes from the blinding sodium vapor lights.

We slid past piers where hundreds of similar riverboats were berthed and tied up at the end of a floating wooden dock, and in a mad rush dispersed. One moment we were all together, the next everyone was gone, real life grabbing us by the lapels, pulling us in all too fast. For a few days I had been part of a community, and then it was gone, evaporated, and I was alone again.

. . .

I'D BEEN TRAVELING almost nonstop for a month, and it was time to go to Africa, and the only way to get there was from São Paulo, Brazil. I booked my flight from Manaus through Porto Alegre on TAM, Brazil's national carrier. While Cubana was statistically the most dangerous national airline in the world, TAM was rated the third most dangerous in Latin America—and that was before two recent crashes. The problem was fairly straightforward: Brazil was booming and it was big and its roads were terrible. Lots of Brazilians were making money; more and more of them were taking to the skies, flying on a system that was being overwhelmed and that required nearly every plane to fly in and out of São Paulo, one of the largest cities on earth, through one of the most crowded and urban airports on earth.

Delays of hours and sometimes even days were frequent at Congonhas, the oldest and busiest of São Paulo's three airports, with notoriously short runways that were surrounded by dense blocks of high-rise apartments and frequently pummeled by heavy rain. The runways at JFK in New York stretched for more than 14,000 feet; Bogotá's were over 12,000 feet. Congonhas's longest runway, however, stretched a mere 6,362 feet. In 1996 a TAM jet plowed through an apartment building on takeoff, killing all ninety-six people on board. In 2006 two Boeing 737s nearly skidded off the end of the runway (and a Gol Airlines 737 collided in midair over the Amazon with a private jet and fell to earth, killing all 154 passengers). In February 2007 a Brazilian court banned all Boeing 737 and Fokker 100 jets from taking off at Congonhas—the airport had been closed an average of three times a month because of heavy rains—citing short runways, decaying tarmac, and slippery conditions. People protested, however—the ban forced passengers to the much farther away Guarulhos International Airport—and an appeals court reversed the ruling. Soon after, the International Airline Pilots Association issued a pointed warning to all pilots flying in Brazil, citing "a lack of proper government oversight and control" of aircraft. Then, just five months after that, on July 16, 2007, a turboprop ATR 42 had skidded off the runway, though no one was injured. And the next day, TAM flight 3054 landed in heavy rain and it, too, failed to stop as the runway ended.

I booked a ticket on the very same flight. And found myself in shock when I hit the airport in Manaus, not twelve hours after stepping off the *Moreira*. The floor was nubbed rubber, clean enough to eat from. Diamonds and gold and pearls sparkled behind glass counters. Men in suits and women in skinny jeans and silver flats padded past. After a month on bad buses and in the near constant mud and dirt of mountain and jungle roads and winding rivers and wooden boats, it all looked hard, shiny, slick. I was overwhelmed by the orderliness of it all. A disembodied voice called out my flight; I handed my pre-printed boarding pass to a woman in lipstick and big hair and heels, and strolled down the Jetway to the shiny new air-conditioned Airbus 330 filled with seats upholstered in orange plastic. A stewardess passed out hard candy in individual wrappers from a wicker basket. Everything about flying, about operating airplanes, was the polar opposite of the buses and boats and cars I'd been traveling. Schedules, technology, pilot and safety training, baggage handling and tracking, maintenance, air traffic control, radio communications, and fuel management—the whole enterprise required a quantum leap in skills and organization and government intervention above the bus drivers with their gold teeth and tattoos and the river captain with nits in his hair. The wooden riverboat, the buses, they all had schedules, more or less, but not really; they left when the boat or bus was full; they arrived when they arrived. People expected no more. The schedules took a back seat to reality. Ditto with maintenance and safety: tires were bald, buses were overloaded, the system was upended with corruption. Usually the only consequence was a flat tire and a delay, and when tragedy did strike, its victims were poor, people whom no one but their immediate family and friends cared about.

Brazil's airline system was expanding by leaps and bounds—in fact, more people were starting to fly all over the world in places they hadn't ever before; planes were becoming much more democratic. New low-cost airlines were popping up everywhere, not just in Brazil but in every country that had a burgeoning middle class, from Indonesia to Nigeria to India. But the underlying systems that made flying safe hadn't caught up. In America the days of planes filled with sexy, eye-candy stewardesses were long gone, and planes themselves often felt like unkempt cattle cars. Stewardesses were more often than not stewards, who stomped down the aisles brusquely jerking your seatbacks forward on final descent. But behind the cranky utilitarianism of flying on, say, United lay a powerful statistic: at that point in my journey no regularly scheduled commercial jet operated by a U.S. airline had crashed in two years. Behind all those aged flight attendants American businessmen complained about lay decades of seniority, women and men whose real job wasn't passing out pretzels or looking good, but simple passenger safety should anything go awry.

On TAM, the old, romantic patina of flying as luxury was all there; the Brazilians had it down pat. The stewardesses wore tight-fitting blue skirts and clingy white tops with plunging necklines and four-inch stilettos, the Airbus was spotless, and they handed that candy out to us before we even took off. But as we roared down the runway and rotated up, no one checked to see if any seatbelts were fastened or the seatbacks were up. Behind the façade lay an air traffic control system run by the Brazilian military that was in complete disarray.

All of which was on my mind when I boarded TAM flight 3058, from Porto Alegre to São Paulo the next morning, nine months after the very same flight—then called 3054—had killed every passenger on board. That morning, like this one, had been completely routine. Nothing special. No prescient foreshadowing drumbeats. Just a full load of businessmen and businesswomen in dark suits and creased designer blue jeans clutching cell phones and BlackBerries and slim attaché cases. I looked around. None of us expected to die. People had meetings to get to. Families to see. The captain in his starched white shirt, four gold bars on his epaulettes, stood at the door to the flight deck and greeted everyone. Disasters happened quickly, I realized. One minute you were watching *Rambo* on the TV screen, the next the bus was diving off a cliff. I fastened my seatbelt. The woman next to me chatted on her phone; I thought of how many people on that TAM flight had talked to friends, family, and colleagues from their seats—their last conversations.

We took off. Sun streamed through the windows. Had the

same flight ever crashed twice? I wondered. I looked around. On that flight, as on this one, nothing but the usual banal movements. People leafed through their in-flight magazines. Adjusted the airflow overhead. Sipped Coca-Cola in plastic cups. Movements that meant nothing, except that on 3054 they meant everything because those passengers were doing them for the last time in their lives. I knew I wasn't going to die, that this time this flight wasn't going to crash. But, no doubt, that's exactly how they'd felt nine months ago, on this same trajectory, dropping an hour later out of the clouds over the endless acres of São Paulo's rooftops, coming closer and closer, so close you could almost see through the windows of people's apartments. On 3054 there had been one piece of information that the passengers didn't know, though the pilots did: only one of the airplane's two thrust reversers was working.

I tightened my seatbelt, looked out the window. Sun and puffy cumulus clouds; on 3054 that morning the ceiling was low, rain pouring down—that was the only difference. As far as I knew, that is. Were both of this plane's thrust reversers working? Had all its maintenance been done? I had no idea; none of us did. And that was the rub with airplanes like this one: everything looked so good. On a bus in the Andes I braced myself for disaster, but on a shiny, new-looking airplane with pilots in white shirts and stewardesses in tight skirts, what could go wrong? I knew what was happening up in the cockpit because I had a transcript of 3054's cockpit voice recorder, and because it was a closely followed script that never varied from one flight to the next.

PILOT: Flaps one.

COPILOT: Speed checked.

PILOT: Clear status.

COPILOT: Clear status. Clear.

CONGANHAS TOWER: TAM three zero five four, reduce speed for the approach, and call the tower on frequency one two seven one five, good afternoon.

A grinding sound—flaps extending and landing gear coming down.

PILOT: Good afternoon. Landing gear down.

COPILOT: Landing gear down.

PILOT: Flaps three.

COPILOT: Speed checked. Flaps three.

Sitting over the wings, I looked out the window and watched the flaps extend.

PILOT: Flaps full, standby final checklist.

COPILOT: Standing by.

The rooftops were even closer now. The woman next to me closed her magazine. I noticed a man in front of me, through the crack in the seats, checking his watch. We'd be there in a few minutes, another flight over.

"Cabin crew," said the pilot over the PA system. "Clear to land."

Back in the cockpit, the pilot said, "Auto thrust. Speed. Landing."

COPILOT: Landing.

PILOT: Okay.

COPILOT: Final checklist complete.

PILOT: Runway in sight, landing. Ask the tower about the rain conditions, the runways and if the runway is slippery.

COPILOT: TAM on final approach, two miles away. Could you confirm conditions?

TOWER: It's wet and it is slippery. I will report three five left clear, three zero five four.

PILOT: Wet and slippery.

TOWER: TAM three zero five four, three five left, clear to land, the runway is wet and is slippery and the wind three zero at eight knots.

PILOT: Checked. Is the landing clear?

COPILOT: Clear to land.

PILOT: Land green, manual flight.

COPILOT: Checked. One now, okay.

PILOT: Okay.

We touched down, the wheels making that familiar and comforting bump on hard pavement. We were safe, which is exactly what everyone thought on flight 3054. But we were still traveling at 160 mph, and the controlled but frantic ritual and dance up front in the cockpit was in full motion. Time was ticking. Our fate, the fate of 187 passengers, was sealed; we—they—were all alive, all comfortably seated and strapped in, seatbacks up, novels tucked away, watches ticking and hearts beating and lungs taking in air, everyone thinking about love and work and traffic and if they'd be able to get a taxi quickly, and they had seconds left.

COPILOT: Reverse number one only. Spoilers nothing.

PILOT: Aiii! Look this . . .

COPILOT: Decelerate, decelerate.

PILOT: It can't, it can't. Oh my god, oh my god. Go, go, go, turn, turn turn turn.

COPILOT: Turn turn to . . . no, turn turn.

Crushing noises.

"Oh no!" a male shouted.

A woman's voice screamed.

More crushing noises, and the recording ended. Silence. Flight 3054 skidded off the end of the runway, bore left, hopped over a road, and plowed into a TAM warehouse at a speed of 103 mph. All 187 passengers died, as did twelve on the ground.

I felt rattled as we slowed and taxied toward the gate. A few seconds of braking and deceleration—that's all that had sepa rated this uneventful flight from the one that killed 199. The more I traveled on dangerous conveyances, conveyances that were so like ones that had crashed, the more it seemed such a narrow line between life and death, a matter of luck and timing, or simple fate. Of course, my flight wasn't going to crash. My ferry on the Rio Madeira wasn't going to sink. My bus in Peru, crossing the Andes, wasn't going to plunge off a cliff in the night; I had dismissed Carleton's worries without a thought. But not a single person, I'm sure, had thought they were on their last bus ride or ferry ride or plane flight, either. I was playing it close, I realized. Walking through the crowded terminal I wanted to hug my family, to feel human warmth and comfort and life.

I was alone, though, and thought of what Darryl Green-amyer had once told me. Greenamyer had been a test pilot and airplane racer; he'd flown the CIA's precursor to the SR-71 Blackbird, had won the Unlimited division of the National Championship Air Races in Reno, Nevada, six times, had broken both the piston-engine airplane speed record and the jet speed record, flying a home-built F-104 Starfighter at nearly 1,000 mph thirty feet off the ground, and he'd once planned to take wing from a frozen lake in northern Greenland in a World War II–era B-29 bomber that hadn't moved in forty-seven years. He'd seen pilots die and he'd done crazy stuff and lived. "Either your time comes or it doesn't," he'd said to me, "and when it does there's just not anything you can do about it."

PART TWO

AFRICA

Police in Kenya say twenty-three people, including ten children, were killed when the minibus they were traveling in swerved off the road and plunged into a river southeast of the capital, Nairobi. The minibus was licensed to carry twenty-three passengers, but there were fifty-eight people on board at the time.

—BBC, August 16, 2001

FOUR

Agents of Death and Destruction

OF ALL THE FABLED CONVEYANCES in Africa, the train on the 600-mile line from Mombasa, Kenya, to Kampala, Uganda, stood out. Over a span of eight years in the 1890s, nearly 32,000 imported Indian coolies, overseen by British engineers, built the railroad. So many men died during its construction of disease, exhaustion, and hungry lions, it was dubbed the Lunatic Express. The historian Elspeth Huxley called it "the most courageous railway in the world;" at its finish in 1903, as Charles Miller wrote, "the Union Jack flew over 3.7 million square miles of African soil—one third of the continent's total area." These days the train only went as far as Nairobi twice a week, and it was reputed to be a long, hot, slow journey, but at least it was still running; many of the continent's trains had simply fallen into such disrepair they'd eventually stopped completely.

I hailed an auto rickshaw for the train station. Mombasa was sticky, humid, and chaotic, but I liked it. Arabs had been crossing the Indian Ocean to the East African coast for centuries, joined by Indians in the nineteenth century, and the streets were packed with women in loose, flowing, burkha-like robes called *buibui*, with ornately hennaed feet, and Indians in gold and blue saris, and men in skullcaps. But when the rickshaw dropped me off at the train station, something felt wrong. The old, one-story brick building lay behind a wall and a fence in a beaten dirt and gravel yard, and it was deserted. SAY NO! TO BRIBERY AND CORRUPTION! announced a battered blue metal sign. PLEASE DO NOT GIVE OR RECEIVE BRIBES. DO NOT NEGOTIATE FOR UNDUE FAVORS!

A guard stood at the gate. "Oh, many troubles," he said, sweating under a white shirt and tie over a second collared shirt, with pink and blue stripes. "The train is canceled now because we care too much about our customers." That was a bit too enigmatic for me, so I pressed on, and found a woman behind steel bars at the ticket office. "They have suspended service because of the kills," she said. "For the time being there is too much risk to human beings." The recent elections in Kenya had unleashed a wave of ethnic cleansing around Nairobi and the Rift Valley, which had mostly calmed. Now the trouble lay with the Mungiki, a mafia-like organization linked to Kenya's most numerous tribe, the Kikuyu. They were referred to as a sect and shrouded in myth: Mungiki sniffed tobacco standing in rivers wearing loincloths. They bathed in blood mixed with urine and goat tripe. They stripped women of short skirts in public, and forcibly circumcised them. In fact, the Mungiki received most of their income from Nairobi's *matatu* industry, the private minibuses notorious for overcrowding and murderous traffic accidents, and claimed two million members, including high-ranking members of the government and the police. Their leader had recently been jailed and then his wife murdered; the current riots were blamed on the police's refusal to let him attend her funeral. "The train was attacked last week by those Mungiki people and the tracks removed and the train capsized," the woman in the ticket office said. "It is terrible; the coaches just climb all over each other."

"So there are no trains going?" I asked.

"The cargo is going, we can pick that up and we are working on the tracks. But we care a great deal about our passengers. Traveling by air, my good sir," she said, "is much safer these days. We will review the situation on Monday."

It seemed worth waiting to find out, so I settled into the Castle Royal Hotel. A long veranda ran the width of the hotel, buffered from the street by planters with mother-in-law-tongue and hibiscus. Ceiling fans stirred the thick humidity; little groups of Indian businessmen huddled together drinking glasses of fluorescent orange passionfruit juice. When the waiter came over I ordered a Tusker beer. "White Cap!" a man sang out at the table next to me. "White Cap is the only good beer in Kenya. It's like a German beer!"

Joaquin Fechner was chubby and pale and wearing a khaki fishing vest over a pink shirt. He was sweating profusely, a Swiss native who'd been living in Africa for twenty-five years, and in Mombasa the past six. "Come join me," he said.

Fechner was having a few beers before jumping on a night bus to Nairobi, and he wasn't too enthusiastic about the train. "It's very dangerous," he said. "I would not travel on that train right now. The Mungiki are uneducated. Fanatical. Obsessed. You know what they do?" He leaned forward. A drop of sweat slid off his chin and splashed on the table. "The Mungiki will cut your penis off. With a machete!" The bus, he thought, would be okay. "The buses wait outside Nairobi and then travel into the city in a convoy."

We had another round and Fechner started to talk, to loosen up. He'd led a routine life in Switzerland, a solid middle-class citizen. Then he'd become obsessed with business books. He couldn't put them down. And one thing stood out to him: "The most successful businesses never paid taxes!" He liked that idea. He loved it so much, in fact, that he went to an accountant and asked, "How do I make money and never again pay any taxes?" The accountant told him to start an import company in one country and an export company in another, and to live in a third. Fechner bought a motorcycle and shipped it to Durban, South Africa, and ended up on Zanzibar, where he opened a dive shop in 1983.

He paused, sucked down half a sixteen-ounce White Cap, scanned the veranda. "This is the only place a respectable man like me can drink in Mombasa. Not seven hundred feet from here is the Casablanca. It's got the worst prostitutes in all of Kenya!"

On Zanzibar he became rich. "But then I lost it all! Every penny!" He laughed. "I've been a multimillionaire at least twice, but I have never, ever paid any taxes!" It was his life's biggest accomplishment. For the past decade he'd been importing used food-processing equipment from Germany into Africa, mostly the Hobart brand. "They think it's English and they pay more for it used than they would for new stuff from Korea or Japan." Before he came to Africa he spent four years in New York City. "You know what I learned in America? Five words that transformed my business: 'Take it or leave it.' I learned to say those five words and they work in every business deal anywhere in the world. You must do your research, you must know your customer's bottom line, but then you have to say those words to get the deal done.

"Oh, the tales I could tell you!" He nodded toward an African man sitting alone, impeccably dressed in a dark blue, pinstriped suit, a leather briefcase at his feet. "Those men," he said, "we call them 'headhunters' and 'air businessmen.' They are here looking for a mark. They have nothing but a briefcase and the clothes on their backs. You must be careful of them or they will take you. I know, because I learned the hard way.

"And Zanzibar. You know who lives on Zanzibar? It is filled with American mafia. There are hotels there that never have guests."

As dusk came and went and the night got black, Fechner's Conradian tale unfolded. Men like him lived in unlikely holes all over the world, in war zones and turbulent cities and jungle outposts. They lived remarkable lives of tremendous risk and adventure, and once they'd tasted it they couldn't live without it. They knew it, were aware of it, reveled in it, but were also isolated, lonely, and they would always be lonely. I understood Fechner because I was a little like him. I, too, craved adventure and even risk, and loneliness was its by-product. Usually they weren't braggarts—boastful men didn't prosper in the twisting, labyrinthine worlds in which they dealt—but when they found an appreciative listener, their stories could spill out with the force of a gusher of oil.

Half a dozen White Caps in, Fechner rattled me with his sadness. "I spent three years in Uganda before coming to Kenya, and those were the best three years of my life," he said. "In

Kampala I met a woman. It is the only time I have been in love. She was thirty-five, from the Rwenzori mountains. She couldn't read or write, but she was a born trader. She knew it deep in her blood. And she was beautiful. She said, 'Give me two thousand dollars.' I did. She traded in charcoal, and every night she arrived with a pile of Ugandan money on my table." As he talked I pictured the pale, overweight Fechner in the dim light of a Kampala apartment, admiring the piles of tattered, dirty banknotes, and I could almost feel his admiration and strange love for her; it was such an African tale. "She would be down in the dirt for me," he said, smiling, remembering. "On her knees. She cooked and cleaned and I lived like a king. But I wanted to go to Kenya to trade. It is in my blood, as it was in hers. I must trade. I asked her to come with me. 'No,' she said, 'I don't speak the language and I cannot read, and I have a brother in London.' I had given her shares, and by then she had four thousand dollars in her account. From trading charcoal! I bought her a ticket to London and she went."

Fechner paused. Wiped his brow with a damp paper napkin. Took a breath and then a long swig of beer. "If I close my eyes I can see her," he said, looking at me, holding my gaze. Memories, years, deep human yearnings, regret—I could see them in his eyes. No matter the inequality of their relationship, no matter his insistent and constant roaming, he had paused and loved for a time. "I am with her. She was so good to me." He grew silent again. Took another swig. And then said, "I heard she's married now to a British guy."

It was nine o'clock; hours had passed and Fechner's bus was leaving at ten. He had to go. "But let me tell you something," he said, leaning close. "In Nairobi I have an old rusty shipping container. I haven't opened it in two years. It sits in a yard with many other containers under floodlights and walls and towers and men with guns. I keep things in it. It is safe, safer than a bank. In Africa you must take care of everything."

WAITING ON THE TRAIN, I decided to find a beach north of Mombasa. A travel agent said one called White Sands was the closest, and the next day I was squished into the Hungry Vulture—one of the thousands of minibuses that careen through the streets of Kenya's cities and are the only public transportation for two-thirds of Kenyans. Called *matatus,* after the Swahili word for the three ten-shilling coins that a ride originally cost, they were some of the most dangerous and crowded conveyances in the world. The country's former president Daniel Arap Moi once called them "agents of death and destruction." Mombasa's streets were so thick with them you could walk around town on their rooftops. Officially known as PSVs—passenger service vehicles—their accident rate climbed so high—3,000 deaths a year and 11,989 accidents in the first eleven months of 2004—that the transport minister forced a law that year requiring speed governors and seatbelts. Just the day before, the insurance industry had rescinded a 15-percent premium break given after the law was imposed. The minister who pushed the law was gone, and the Transport Licensing Board told the *Daily Nation* newspaper that most of the matatus' speed governors had been "tampered with," and that "most PSVs were moving at speeds between 140 and 160 kmh, instead of the stipulated 80 kmh."

"Travelers on Kenya's roads," the licensing board's chairmen told the *Nation*, "are increasingly being put at risk because of the matatu madness."

Mad but efficient.

We were nine, and then in rapid succession ten, twelve, and fourteen, plus driver and boy.

"Malindi, Malindi, Malindi," the bus boy—who was a man, not a boy—shouted so fast it was all one singsong word. He rode with his head and shoulders out of the open door window, scanning the crowded streets. He wasn't just collecting money and operating the door, he was actively selling, cajoling, sniffing for the slightest sense of someone, anyone, waiting for a ride. Two hard bangs with his knuckles and the matatu swerved to the curb; the door slid open and out he jumped. A woman leapt in, stepped on my feet—wide hips and thighs pushing against my shoulders—and squeezed into the seat behind.

Two more hard, fast raps and the matatu was off. The boy swung in, slid the door forward with a bang, soiled bills folded lengthwise between his pinky and ring finger. A tap—he didn't even make eye contact—and we handed over our forty shillings, about sixty-five cents.

Had we been shot into space to a distant planet, we would have been the perfect sample of African humanity, conveniently packed into a can.

Next to me was a woman covered from head to toe in black, only her eyes darting about, her left hand covered in an intricate and graceful henna design. Behind us a dark black woman with an almost shaved head, a baby on her back, with long, dangling star-shaped earrings and red beads around her neck. In front of me a woman with her arms covered in silver bracelets and a purple turban around her head, clutching a bucket wrapped in plastic, a Rasta guy next to her, and men in ubiquitous T-shirts and flip-flops. And me. The smell of humanity as raw and acrid as a Delmarva Peninsula chicken house.

Knock, knock, swerve, open, shut, slam, knock; brake and accelerate and honk and swerve—the driver's eyes never left the road and the pace was fast; a dance times a hundred, a thousand, as matatus everywhere all around moved in frentic step, honking and braking, bus boys jumping in and out, past rows of market stalls built from sticks and plastic sheeting, and carpentry shops displaying beds and coffins, that went on for miles and miles. The third world is all about tiny margins of profit in billions of minuscule exchanges; speed and maximum capacity are of the essence. Regulation; safety; comfort—they cost money and there is no money here. Or rather, there's money, it's just like grains of sand instead of pebbles that fill your hands.

But it worked: in twenty minutes I was at the beach. Even more impressive, on my way home I had to catch a matatu from the highway and wondered how long I'd have to wait. No worries: it was eleven seconds before a matatu scooped me up and deposited me at the Mombasa post office, there to grab a waiting three-wheeled rickshaw for my hotel. Total cost: about a dollar.

I HUNG AROUND MOMBASA for four days, but the train was still not running and the woman at the station said I ought to try again in another week. This was Africa; days and weeks meant nothing. So that night I jumped on a bus for Nairobi. Fechner had said I should only take a specific company's express, air-conditioned bus. Instead I bought a ticket on a jalopy with no

AC and windows that didn't open. Every seat was taken; the bus was stifling, close, the smell of underarms even stronger than the matatu. "You must not worry about the Mungiki," said my seatmate, a farmer named Joseph from outside of Nairobi, who sold his cabbages in Mombasa every two weeks. "I am Kikuyu, like them. They only attack when someone gets in the way of their money-making. They don't mind foreigners or regular people. The problems right now are not political, but internal. The man in jail, his wife had her own kitchen cabinet. It is all about power; that's why she was killed."

Nairobi and Mombasa were the two biggest cities in Kenya, but the road between them wasn't paved. We bumped and jarred and jerked sideways through the night, and as we rose away from the coast, the temperature dropped. It was still so hot I felt like I was gasping for breath, but Joseph pulled on a heavy sweater. "I think you are used to the cold," he said. Somehow I fell asleep and woke to Joseph shaking me. "We're there," he said. "Welcome to Nairobi. Be careful."

My EXPERIENCE IN THE MATATU in Mombasa had left me wanting more. By luck I found David Wambugo, lounging in his taxi in downtown Nairobi, his feet up on the open doorway. There were thousands of taxis and they were all hustling me, but something about Wambugo caught my eye. He had shoulder-length dreadlocks and the whites of his eyes were as red as if they'd been caught by a too-close camera flash, but there was kindness in them. I hired him take me to the house where Karen Blixen, the author of *Out of Africa*, had lived, and on the way back into town I asked him if he knew any matatu drivers that I could spend the day with. Yes, he said, and in minutes he was on his cell phone and it was all arranged: he'd pick me up at my hotel at five the following morning.

It was still dark the next morning when I left my hotel, and there he was. "Come on," he said, "they have picked up the matatu and they are on their way." The streets were still empty, the air cool but smelling of smoke; we were meeting the matatu at its staging point at the Nairobi train station. But even blocks away, we suddenly hit standstill traffic. "There is a problem at the stage," he said. "Too many matatus." He swerved onto a side street, cut through traffic, taking a winding, indirect back way. "I have been awake all night, but I am very sharp!" he said, skidding around a tight corner. "We drivers eat mira"— the mildly narcotic drug known elsewhere as qat chewed throughout the Horn of Africa and the Middle East—"and this makes us alert on the road. It is not like beer. Beer you cannot take, but mira you can take and drive. You have to eat first because this juice will not let you eat until the next day. Me, I have not slept or eaten in thirty-six hours." Wambugo didn't own the taxi; he only had access to it two or three days a week, so he chewed qat and drove without sleeping as long as he had it.

Suddenly there we were—at a semicircle packed with matatus, like a thousand ants trying to squeeze into the same hole, all honking and belching exhaust into the darkness. They were all on the very same route, the 111, operating between Ngong Town and the central Nairobi train terminal. "You see, the competition has already started," Wambugo said, opening a folded piece of paper and extracting two green twigs of qat to chew, while smoking a cigarette.

Wambugo spotted a green Mitsubishi bus slightly bigger

than a minivan. "OK, there's my friend, let's go," he said, introducing me to driver Joseph Kimani and tout Wakaba Phillip. It was just getting light; hundreds of matatus, from fourteen-passenger minivans to fifty-one-passenger buses, were angling, squeezing, honking, pushing, to navigate a semicircle that they entered empty and left full. Kimani, thirty-two, with a wispy mustache and a wiry body, worked the wheel and gears, while Phillip, thirty, ran back and forth waving his arms, shouting and banging on other matatus, trying to leverage Kimani through the madness while enticing passengers. (That's not all Phillip did, but the other stuff I didn't see, never saw—it was all too quick, too fluid, too under-the-radar—and didn't even learn about until midnight, seventeen hours later.) Competition was fierce. Every matatu, after all, was angling for the same passengers.

The semicircle was 150 yards, tops; passing through it took nearly forty-five minutes—think the tank scene in the film *Patton*. Matatus with names like King of the Streetz and Homeboyz were jumping the curb onto the sidewalk, parrying, jockeying, blocking one another's doors; when we broke free Phillip swung up into the doorway and we blasted up Ngong Road, an undivided two-lane strip of cracked blacktop, with the Bee Gees—there was no escape from them, I was learning, anywhere in the world—at deafening volume.

As he worked the gears and lurched along, Kimani told me he'd been driving matatus for seven years, after a brief career driving trucks. Phillip was moving up; he'd been selling vegetables on the street until two years ago. "Business was bad," he shouted over the music. "I was very poor." Both had climbed out of bed around four this morning, and picked up the matatu in

Ngong Town, in the shadow of the Ngong hills, not far from where I had gone the day before to see Karen Blixen's coffee farm. Or what's left of it. "I had a farm in Africa . . ." is one of those famous literary opening lines, but her elegiac words recall a different, colonial Africa. When we hit Ngong Town an hour and a half later, it was a miasma of overcrowded mud and trash and corrugated shacks, with the occasional rail-thin, six-and-a-half-foot-tall Masai warrior looking like a Hollywood extra still in costume waiting at a bus stop. One man's pierced earlobe was so long it was wrapped up and double-tied through its hole. The staging area was a football-field-sized patch of mud and banana peels and cornhusks and cigarette wrappers and crushed plastic water bottles surrounded by four-foot-square market stalls.

We pulled in, Kimani and Phillip shouted, "Come, Mr. Carl, it's tea time!" and leaped off the bus. We crossed the mud, crossed the muddy road, waded through garbage, wolfed down fried dough and a somosa and sweet, milky tea in a concrete room, and hit the staging area again. That's when the complexity of it all started to hit me, the minute economic scale spread over as wide a net as possible. A small army of touts fanned out to fill the bus. "Forty, forty, forty," they called. "Fortytown, fortytown, fortytown,"—forty shillings to Town. The touts were freelance; Phillip would pay them each forty or fifty shillings for their work. And ours wasn't the only matatu; there were dozens here, all doing the same, hiring the same freelance touts, a series of ever smaller layers, both cutting into the profit and spreading it out over as many people as possible.

Back and forth from Town to Ngong we went all day as the traffic built; in places it took fifteen minutes to move two blocks—wall-to-wall, bumper-to-bumper matatus honking and flashing their lights and blasting music, some with monitors pumping out music videos. Each matatu spat a continuous, visible plume of gray exhaust, and the fumes were intense, overwhelming. Kimani kept the music at earsplitting volume, from Marvin Gaye to African melodies to Britney Spears, just as the volume had been cranked on the films on all the buses in South America. In America people flipped out if you talked too loudly on your cell phone; in the rest of the world there was so much noise, the very idea of silence was unheard of.

The road had no lane markings and barely a shoulder; for mile after mile it ran past makeshift market stalls and men hauling heavy, two-wheeled carts. Kimani rarely actually stopped the bus—Phillip was like an acrobat climbing over passengers to collect fares, hanging out the doorway to spot them and hurry them on and off the vehicle, banging on the side and whistling loudly to signal Kimani.

On it went, at a grueling pace, the economy of it all hard to grasp. A fourteen-passenger matatu cost seventy shillings to ride; in a fifteen-hour day it could make six to seven round trips, taking in 6,000 to 7,000 shillings, about $100. Riding a fifty-one-passenger matatu cost forty shillings for a vehicle that moved more slowly; it only managed five to six round trips in a day. For passengers the bigger one was slower and thus cheaper; but for the driver and tout, the bigger matatu was better, the volume adding up to more income. Still, a driver and tout like Kimani and Phillip made about KSh 600 a day—ten dollars— paid in cash at the end of every evening. Maybe. "It's a good job," Kimani said, his eyes darting from the mirrors, his feet and hands always in motion, "but to succeed, not everyone can do it. You must get up very early and work very long hours."

The speed, the weaving and honking and cajoling; at first I saw it as some form of romantic African expression. But that was wrong. It was simple economics: poor people—desperate and hungry—trying to squeeze one more passenger, one more round trip into a day that never seemed to end, a day where literally every shilling counted. On the matatu in Mombasa I'd seen it as a cool, mysterious, and exotic dance—look at those wild Kenyans and their nutty matatus! But now I saw it as it was: a mad scratching for pennies.

At noon we snapped a main front leaf spring, and Kimani sped off to the garage. But it was no garage; it was a place that boggled my mind, that stretched my imagination. It was Dickensian: block after block of mud passageways littered with garbage and upended vehicles and men sleeping on piles of tires and the sparks of welders and the smell of smoke and oil and diesel and Bondo. It was one lane wide, with two-way traffic. It was hot and glaring, a place of burning fires and braziers and hammering and music, and the mud was so dark, so black, so viscous, it was like oil. It was the worst and the most compelling place I had ever seen.

We crawled through the mud and crowds and sparks, and in front of a corrugated shack stood three boys clutching a new leaf spring, and they dove into the project like it was their last chance for redemption. They had no jack; they slithered through the mud in jeans, their leader in a gray jumpsuit and Puma soccer cleats so worn that his toes stuck out and the cleats were the barest nubs. Kimani and I plunked down on the seat of an old bus in the sun in front of a shack that sold lukewarm sodas. "I am saving to buy a matatu," he said. "Maybe in two or three years. But after the election there was a lot of trouble and people were fighting and we could not work for two weeks. We got no pay and it was a big loss." He lit a cigarette, exhaled a long plume of smoke. "Mr. Carl, can you get me a job in America?"

"A job is no problem," I said, "but a visa is."

"Can you get me a visa?"

"No."

He was silent, sweating, took his baseball cap off and rubbed his head. The heat was searing. Hammers smashed and banged and generators roared and flies landed on our arms, our faces. Children walked barefoot through the greasy mud with tubs of packages of cashews and cigarettes on their heads. A man draped in steering-wheel covers and screwdrivers and Playboy Bunny air fresheners, like a walking display case, hustled everyone in his path. Across the mud, a man welded on the back of a flatbed truck. He had no goggles, no face mask—against the eye-burning white light of the arc welder he held a shard of dark glass in front of his face. A fine layer of sanded Bondo drifted over and settled on my sweaty arms. Smoke filled the air from hundreds of fires. Broken, rusted, and smashed cars lay stacked on each other like books in a used-book store. A pair of eight-year-olds in ragged T-shirts slowly swept by, collecting bits of wire, stray nuts and bolts, which they dropped in a plastic bag. Another economic layer: the bottom, perhaps.

"Come," said Kimani, "they must be finishing." We walked back to the bus as the three mechanics slithered out from underneath it. They were black with grime and sweat. It had taken two hours, and Kimani was eager to get back out. The labor charge: 300 shillings. Five dollars split among three men.

The afternoon ground on in slow motion. More heat. More traffic. More noise and exhaust and more going nowhere.

Kimani's patience was extraordinary. Getting in and out of downtown Nairobi was five lanes of chaos, honking, and blue-black exhaust. Kimani chain-smoked and worked the wheel and gearshift with his sinewy arms as Phillip jumped and whistled and banged and gesticulated and cajoled. In Nairobi, at the train station, we literally hopped the curb and plowed along the sidewalk, scattering pedestrians. Near Ngong Town again the skies opened up and rain slammed down, snarling traffic, making the bus rank.

Suddenly we pulled over, Kimani grabbed me and we jumped out, and another man leapt into the bus and took the wheel. I have no idea how the shift had been arranged, but Kimani led me into a corrugated-roofed butchery with a dirt floor and bloody carcasses hanging from the ceiling. We washed our hands at a sink, and a man in a bloodstained white coat dumped a pile of fatty mutton onto a wooden board on our table. He chopped the meat with a cleaver, poured out a mound of salt, and slid a single bowl of ugali—corn flour—next to it all. We ate with our fingers, the mutton rich and flavorful, but inseparable from veins of thick gristle. I splurged, buying two Cokes for both of us, and they cost as much as the rest of the meal.

Fourteen hours after I'd met them, sixteen hours after they'd started their day, Kimani and Phillip were at the Nairobi train station for the last time—they'd end their day when they dropped the last passengers off in Ngong Town. I'd been planning to get off the matatu, but Phillip said, "You should come back to Ngong Town with us and stay there tonight!"

"Where will I sleep?"

"Oh, we'll put you somewhere," he said.

I was exhausted, sticky with sweat and grime, and hungry,

but it seemed an offer too good to pass up. "OK," I said, "and I'll buy you some beer if there's a place to go."

Before we pulled away, David Wambugo jumped on the matatu; he lived in Ngong Town, too, and his forty-eight-hour taxi shift was done. "I am tired, so tired," he said, his eyes drooping.

It was after 9:00 p.m. when Wambugo and I jumped out into pitch darkness and, after the downpour, a world of thick, soupy, sticky mud. Kimani said he'd drop off the vehicle, go home, get his car, and return to pick us up. Wambugo slapped and slid through the mud and the darkness, to a wall of concrete topped with corrugated tin, a metal doorway every ten feet. He banged on a steel door, locks clinked, the sound of steel on steel sliding, and the door swung open into his house: a single room ten feet by ten feet, where he lived with his wife, her sister, and their two children. There was a TV, a sofa, a one-burner stove on the floor, and behind a curtain, a narrow bed where the children slept. No bathroom. No kitchen. No running water. No windows. Posters of Bob Marley decorated the walls. Wambugo introduced me, and his wife silently brought me a steaming hot cup of sweet coffee and a bowl of *sukuma*, collard greens, which I wolfed down while watching a Nigerian soap opera about a rich man beset by bad fortune after refusing to donate money to his local Catholic church. Wambugo ate nothing. "I cannot eat," he said, as rain pounded on the metal roof. "It is the mira. Tonight I will sleep and then tomorrow I will have a big breakfast!"

His cell phone rang; Kimani was here. We slipped through the mud again and drove to a dark, half-finished six-story concrete building surrounded by more mud and darkness. The door led into a cave, literally—a ramp that wound back and forth instead of stairs, whose walls and ceiling had been covered with rocks to make it feel like a cave. Upstairs was a bar, empty but open. I was so tired; it had been seventeen hours since I'd met them at the train station. But finally, at midnight, twenty-one hours after they'd started their day, Kimani and Phillip spilled the secrets of the matatu industry over warm pilsner in the deserted Ngong Town bar. They were, in fact, nickeled and dimed at every turn. Kimani and every other matatu had to slip 200 shillings to the police at every staging area, for the "privilege" of working the stage. "There are so many police taking a piece from you!" Kimani said. "There are police at the train station. Police in Ngong Town. Police on the roads," said Kimani. "It is the best job! A policeman at the railway station makes at least 10,000 shillings a day, minimum, every day!"

"That's crazy!" I said. "Why don't you refuse to pay?"

"If you don't pay the police, they will come on board the matatu and arrest you," Kimani said, "and fine you 15,000 for something. It's cheaper to pay. And sometimes the policeman will change in the middle of the day, so we must pay the new one all over again."

"And the Mungiki is there and he finds you," Phillip said. "If you don't pay the Mungiki one hundred shillings you will have your head cut off. Yes, you will lose your head."

"How about reporting the Mungiki to the police?" I said.

Kimani and Phillip exploded in laughter. "The police are *with* Mungiki! No, you must pay always!"

Inspectors and matatu owners and robbers all demanded their share. It was Phillip's job, as the tout, to take care of everyone; even as he had been cajoling passengers on board and hiring other touts he had been keeping track of the police and the Mungiki and every other sticky finger and greased palm.

Kimani's matatu had been robbed at gunpoint three times. "Three or four men with guns get on the bus," he said, looking serious, "and they say 'move over.' So you move over and they drive the bus to a remote place in the woods and steal everything. The first time, I was very worried. The gun was pointed at my head and it was even cocked. But now, hey, I just move over and let them work." To make the robberies even worse, since the robbers stole the day's proceeds, Kimani and Phillip did not get their day's pay.

It was a vicious racket, a Hobbesian struggle to survive. Everyone was guilty and no one was innocent, not even Kimani and Phillip. The fares they charged changed according to the situation, price-gouging as art. "We double the fare in the rain," Phillip said, laughing. "The sun is bad for the matatu driver!" They boosted it at rush hour. They had their freelance touts attract passengers at forty shillings and then made the duped passengers pay sixty, claiming the freelancers were unauthorized. "If they refuse to pay, we don't let them off the matatu," Kimani said, giggling and taking a swig of Tusker beer. "They must pay!"

Finally, at 1:00 a.m., they saw me into a concrete room with no running water behind a steel gate in a world of mud. I was delirious with fatigue, beaten up, my neck, back, knees, and shoulders aching; hungry for solitude and quiet and cleanliness; my nerves frayed from the constant jangling noise and crowds. Kimani and Phillip had four more days to go before the weekend. Another seventy or eighty hours of work for fifty bucks. And Wambugo had been working without sleep or food for two days and two nights, living purely on mira. And yet they all had been in a good mood, laughing and joking and eager to have another round.

I passed out, woke, and felt an overpowering need to escape. I threw my clothes on and stumbled out into a light rain. It was still dark and I didn't really know where I was. Somewhere near Ngong Town. But, no worries. I stood on the side of the road and a pair of headlights swerved around a corner, flashed, and I held out my hand. A matatu screeched to a stop. I piled in, and there was Shakira wiggling her hips on the video. It was 6:00 a.m. The smallest bill I had was a hundred-shilling note. The tout took it and offered no change; this time I knew better than to argue. Thirty minutes later we were stuck in traffic a half mile from the train station. And I felt like I was about to snap, was snapping. The matatu stank so badly I couldn't breathe. Hips and shoulders pressed against either side of me. The DVD—now it was Diddy—was deafening. I had been in the thick of it for twenty-four straight hours, nothing but crowds and their heavy, musky odor, a constant barrage of noise and people and mud and jostling. "Let me out!" I barked to the tout, and I leapt from the minivan as if I had been held underwater for too long. And never had I been so grateful for a dim, cheap hotel room. I whipped my clothes off and lay sprawled naked across the bed. The room was silent. Still. Clean. Secure. I was alone. It was an almost unspeakable luxury.

An ocean ferry capsized in a fierce Atlantic storm off West Africa and plunged beneath the waves in minutes, trapping hundreds of screaming passengers, and rescuers said Friday that more than 760 people were believed to have been killed. Just thirty-two people aboard the ship were known to have survived the disaster late Thursday night, some by clinging to the sides of the overturned craft.

—Los Angeles Times, *September 28, 2002*

FIVE

That Train Is Very Bad

IN ONE OF THE QUIRKS of African travel, there are few direct, nonstop international flights between major African cities. Which is why, to get to Bamako, Mali, from Nairobi, I had to fly through Addis Ababa, and the leg from Addis was twenty-four hours late. Around me in the gate were the shock troops of globalization. Groups of Chinese, the new merchant class of Africa, in black shoes and white socks and formless brown jackets clutching Naugahyde briefcases. Filipinos in flip-flops and T-shirts. And ten Sri Lankan seamen, bound for a ship in Dakar, Senegal, in crisp polo shirts and ironed blue jeans. "We will land and go straight to the ship," said their leader, the first engineer. "We'll go to Poland and then the Caribbean; it will be at least seven months, maybe a year, before we see our families again."

"That must be hard," I said, thinking of my own life and family, and how despite all my travels I'd never been gone more than two months before.

"Yes," he said, "but remember: you never know when you will die, so you must be happy all the time."

We dropped into Bamako at 2:00 a.m. and even in the middle of the night it was searingly hot, baking, in a city that looked like it had been hit by a bomb. Potholes and dust and dim lights, the smell of smoke and garbage and bodies asleep on every sidewalk, in front of stores, as if they'd been out walking and had just suddenly collapsed. I'd come for a train: the line from Bamako to Dakar was legendarily bad. And the moment I stepped out of my hotel in the morning I was adopted by Guindo, one of the city's thousands of licensed guides. "What do you want?" he said. "A trek in Dogan country? Buy some masks?"

"Can you help me get tickets on the train to Dakar?" I said.

For a second his face looked blank. "Yes," he said, "it's maybe possible. But I think that train is very bad."

If the city seemed hot and ramshackle in the night, it was fifty times worse in the day. Guindo walked fast, and we skipped past piles of rubble and garbage and smoldering fires and broken-down cars filled with sand, past legless and blind beggars in 120-degree heat that was so sharp it burned my skin and mouth, through dirt streets thronged with men in pointy-toed slippers and women in silk turbans. There was nowhere to hide or to get away from the chaos and throngs. Crowds and heat and dust and noise, the streets bumper-to-bumper with crooked matatus with no glass in the windows, the smell of excrement and sweat and smoke.

The railway terminal was empty; the train wasn't here, and no one knew when it would return or depart. "No one knows anything," said a man Guindo cornered. "There are no fixed dates. Maybe it will leave on Monday or Tuesday or Wednesday. You will know when the train is here when the train is here. You must come every day. My friend, this train is very bad."

"I don't think you should take the train," said Guindo, as we walked away. "I think it's not too safe. How about a bus?"

When I insisted on the train, Guindo said he would go to the station every day and, when the moment was right, get my ticket. He wanted the money—about thirty dollars—up front, and I reluctantly handed it over back at my hotel. "You don't worry, Carl! I will call you."

It was Monday; the train was officially scheduled to leave on Wednesdays for the forty-eight-hour journey, but I figured, if anything, it would be leaving late. I called Guindo late the next morning to see if he was on the case. "No, Carl, the train is still nowhere," he said. But at 5:00 p.m. my phone rang. "The train is almost here," he said, "and it is leaving soon. Tonight. I have your ticket! You must be fast; I will pick you up right now."

Guindo arrived a few minutes later in a taxi so broken I had to hold the door shut. It was over a hundred degrees outside, and I was drenched. It hurt to breathe. This time the station was crawling with people and noise, bursting with heat. A sea of African humanity: women sitting on blankets, guarding huge piles of sacks filled with potatoes and mangoes, covered the platform, their batik *boubou* dresses a riot of blues and golds, their heads wrapped in scarves, with dangling gold earrings and hennaed feet. Men in shimmering green kaftans with bell-shaped sleeves lugged boxes filled with what looked like salad bowls. The train wasn't here and the sun was dropping. The platform reeked of rotten vegetables and fruit and sweat. Trash two inches deep covered the wavering tracks, and vendors hawked padlocks, paper fans, cheap flashlights, and little rolls of toilet paper.

Suddenly I heard a grinding, rumbling, clanging sound. "The fucking train," said Guindo, patting me on the shoulder. "Good luck, Carl," he said, vanishing into the dim, crowded evening, like he was running away from the police. The train inched slowly in. It looked a thousand years old. Like it had been thrown off a cliff, beaten up, torn apart for scrap, and pasted together again. It had rusty holes in its sides and mud spattered across its flanks. I'd asked for a second-class ticket, which Guindo had bought me. The tickets actually had seat assignments, and when I fought my way through bodies and noise and boxes and crates and bags, my seat, my row, was destroyed. The seatbacks were there, but not the seats. I looked around; there were no others. An old man, toothless, thin, desiccated-looking in a soiled shirt, grabbed me by the arm. "Follow me," he said. We climbed and squeezed out of the carriage, walked past two cars, and into one marked FIRST CLASS in faded letters. Its condition was identical to the other, except it had cabins, each with four bunks topped with a yellow, pitted, crumbling rectangle of foam.

Night had fallen. The inside of the train was pitch black, and as hot as a toaster oven. People were shouting and loading goods through the window. Mosquitoes buzzed around my face. In the lower bunk next to me sat a thin, dark man from Dakar, returning there after a trip buying dozens of big clay pots to resell in the capital. At 7:30 p.m. the train jerked, slid forward, jerked to a halt again. I leaned out of the open window in the hallway, gasping for air. More people, more shouting, more boxes and bags loaded through the doorways and windows. The train lurched forward again, and this time didn't stop. We were on our way, moving at ten miles an hour. Suddenly the power came on, the dim lights in the hall and my couchette re-vealing a world of dirt. My mattress was so stained it looked like a bullet riddled soldier had died on it. The walls were smeared with brown. Piles of dust covered the floor. Everything was bro-ken, crooked, askew. A thin man in a shimmering green robe and beard arrived, and in the room he piled ice chests and gal-lon jugs of water, a single-burner stove, plastic trash bags, and bundles wrapped in twine.

I had to pee badly, but the bathroom at the end of the hall was filled to the ceiling with boxes. Desperate, with my room-mates talking out in the hall, I slid the door of my couchette closed, turned off the light, perched on the edge of my bed, and pissed out the window.

Suddenly there was a tussle, and down the hall marched a short, stocky bulldog of a man in rolled-up blue jeans and a plaid shirt, crashing through the hallways like it was an NFL line of scrimmage. He was five foot seven, 200 pounds. "Con-fusion!" he yelled, when he burst into the room and saw me. "You speak English? Where are you going and where is your home?"

"Yes. Dakar," I said. "The United States."

"I am Papa-si!" he said, thrusting out a big, warm, dry hand, before crashing down the hall again for more bags and boxes.

I felt exhausted, dirty, overwhelmed, and lay down on the mattress, imagining malaria and bedbugs and robbers, and drifted off to sleep to the rocking and jerking.

I WOKE UP AT SIX in the morning. The night had seemed end-less. The car's passengers had been agitated for hours. We stopped every twenty minutes, and so many vendors got on and yelled and banged on the windows it sounded like ocean waves of voices crashing on the beach. Papa-si rearranged his boxes throughout the night, each time climbing up to the shelf above the hallway by boosting himself up on my bed. But as the hours passed the next day I settled into the rhythm of the clacking rails and gave myself to the heat and dirt. The sky was pure blue, the countryside desiccated brown and yellow knee-high grass dotted with leafless baobab trees, with sharp, high, flat escarpments in the distance—a hot, baked world that felt like Lucifer's anvil. The Senegalese pot trader made thick, syrupy sweet tea, a ritual of boiling and pouring and boiling and pouring in two different teapots, over the stove teetering on the floor of the room, a fur fetish strapped tightly to his bicep. We passed village compounds of conical mud huts with peaked thatch roofs fenced with upright sticks, and paused at small brick station houses that must have been a hundred years old.

At a place called Keyes, statistically the hottest location in Africa, with an average temperature in April—now—of 108 degrees, a man jumped on the train and stole a bag of charcoal; there were shouts, and a policeman emerged from the train and chased him down, returning with the five-foot-long sack on his head.

By the afternoon it felt searing, leaning out of the windows—attached to which were signs admonishing DO NOT LEAN OUT OF THE WINDOW in French, English, German, and Spanish—it felt like bending over a barbecue. *"Mon ami!"* Papa-si would yell, every time he looked at me, giving me a thumbs-up. In the morning and afternoon and evening, men prayed on rugs in the hallways. When we rounded bends I could see hundreds of boys and men on the train's roof. I wanted to go up to talk to them, but a guard on the train stopped me. Before every station they would stream off into the bush at the edge of villages; at Coulombo there were so many, soldiers and police streamed after them. They caught an unlucky few. I watched as one policeman held a man by the collar and kneed him repeatedly in the back, marching him into the heat.

As the sun dropped, I discovered two men selling cold beers out of a cooler in the next car. I bought a round and settled on the floor of the vestibule, my feet dangling out of the train. Moussa was long and lean, wearing jeans and sandals, and he was returning to Dakar with crates and crates of mangoes that filled the bathroom—a journey he'd been making twice a week for five years. Which meant that he practically lived on the train, spending at least four days a week rumbling through the heat and dust. There was no moon in the black sky, and we clanked along at ten miles an hour, the Southern Cross just out of the open door, on the horizon. A man slept curled on a plastic sack next to us; we were squeezed together, our legs touching. It was hellish and filthy. But Moussa was happy; he rifled through a burlap sack and brought out a one-burner propane stove and two green chipped enamel teapots, and the Malian tea ritual began. Boil and pour. Boil and pour, always from two feet in the air—even on the jolting train he didn't spill a drop. "The first is bitter, like life," he said, pouring the tea through a strainer. "The second is easy, like friendship. And the third—ahh, the third is sweet, like love." He made tea, two cups at a time, poured into shot glasses on a silver tray, for all of us crowded in the heat and dirt of the rattling vestibule. Free of charge, of course.

By legend, at least, this was one of the worst trains in Africa, maybe the world. It was definitely hot, crowded, and broken. But it was also beginning to feel surprisingly pleasant; the heat, dried mud, and crowds simply stopped being remarkable, stopped being a thing that bothered me. Or I should say, once I stopped fighting them and surrendered to it, it seemed like nothing. It was part of the landscape. I was covered with a layer of sweat and grime. So what? Everyone else was, too. I stank. So did everyone else. As for safety, a hot, filthy, crowded African train brought to mind thievery and assault; I'd made sure my switchblade was close at hand, open and tucked against my hip as I'd drifted off to sleep that first night. Which spoke to my own prejudices and fears more than anything else, and made me remember something my father had once told me. We were driving through a "bad" neighborhood in Washington when I was a child and it was summer, the car windows open. Suddenly I'd started to roll mine up, fearful of assault. "You don't need to worry," my father had said. "These people are no different from you and me, except they're poor. That's all." He'd been right, of course. Now I was on a barely functioning train in a place that looked and felt like Hades, but I felt safe, surrounded by people I'd known only twenty-four hours, and Moussa and Papa-si and the fetish guy in my cabin were all looking out for me, and they for each other. I was happy, losing myself in the African train and the African landscape. And hungry: whenever we'd stop I'd hop off the train and buy whatever was offered—grilled chicken and greens and bright red Baggies of frozen hibiscus juice, and sweet syrupy coffee, and never worried about my luggage, which nobody touched.

In the afternoon of my second day, I fell into conversation

with Lamine Ly, the fourth man in my compartment. The intense heat of the past two days was lessening; we were 200 kilometers from Dakar and the Atlantic Ocean, and hints of an Atlantic breeze passed through the windows every now and then. Ly was tall and thin, with a gray goatee and wearing a shimmering green kaftan, and there was something elegant about him. He was a lawyer in Dakar, he said, fingering a set of brown prayer beads, and he had a friend who worked on the train and had let him on for free. Where was I going? What was I doing? Why was I here? He was full of questions. And then, he said, "Do you believe in God?"

I'd seen him praying regularly, assiduously rinsing his feet and hands with bottled water before kneeling on a rug in the hallway. But I looked him in the eye and answered honestly. "No," I said, "I don't."

He nodded, fingered his beads, looked at me with gray eyes. "Is it true that in America homosexuals live together?"

"Yes," I said, "it's true. Some do."

"And some of them even adopt children and raise them?"

"Yes," I said, preparing myself for a tirade, assuming any Malian man in a kaftan clutching prayer beads would be violently conservative. But he only nodded, fingered his beads, and thought.

And then said, "People must live the way they must live. America must be a great country. I would like to see New York. My son is picking me up at the station in Dakar; someday I would like to take him there."

As dusk fell we stood in the hallway leaning out of the window, while the train rattled slowly into Dakar. It was a world of sand and block houses and warrens clustered together, smoke and fires and drying laundry. We inched through it all at five miles an hour for almost two hours, and when the sun dropped it was all candlelight and kerosene lamps and market stalls pressed so close to the train we literally scraped against them. Oddly, I felt sad, sad that a grimy and uncomfortable journey was ending. Except that I'd become used to it, inured to it all, had made friends, connected to people, and it had ultimately become a pleasant sojourn through Africa that I was loath to end. But end it did. Somewhere in the suburbs Ly jumped off and asked me to pass him his bags through the window, and introduced me to his son. Half an hour later we stopped. No station—just sand and fires and smoke and cool Atlantic winds and thousands of dark figures pressing in on the train. I grabbed a taxi, and the minute the door closed I was enveloped in silence and stillness, and thought of all those people out there who would never get a break from it. And a few minutes later, in my hotel, I turned the shower as hot as it would go and stood under the water sudsing myself over and over again, watching a black stream of water swirl down the drain. It was a cheap hotel room—thirty dollars—but it seemed the most luxurious experience I could ever imagine. Yet a part of me wondered, imagining Ly in a noisy, cluttered home amid too many brothers and sisters and sons and uncles and aunts, who was happier.

I'D TAKEN THE TRAIN from Bamako not just because it was so famously bad, but because it brought me to Dakar, from which a ship named the MV *Le Joola* had sailed six years before— and sunk in the second worst maritime disaster in history. The *Aline Sitoe Diatta*, its replacement, was leaving at 2:00 p.m.

the next day. Surprisingly for the Third World, things had in fact changed after the *Joola*'s sinking—you couldn't kill 1,800 people even in Senegal without people noticing. At a barred window to a room built in the twenty-foot-high concrete wall of Dakar's port, I bought a third-class ticket on the afternoon's departure. The smell of the Atlantic Ocean, mixed with peanuts roasting on vendors' carts, wafted by on a cool breeze. Reminders of the *Joola* were everywhere, I couldn't help feeling: my fellow passengers and I were held safely in a departure lounge and taken in groups of twenty by bus the 150 feet across the concrete dock to the *Diatta*, and escorted up the ferry ramp to the ship. Which was not just brand new, but spotless. Ships, all ships, are in a daily struggle against rust and corrosion, and this one didn't have a single flake of rust on her sides or rails or decks. The chaos I'd read about on the *Joola* was nowhere in sight.

I found my third-class seat—an airline-style reclining chair—three decks down, through a series of winding passageways all carpeted, and manned by stewards in white shirts and ties. Air conditioning made the room frigid, and a flat screen TV blared *"Al Hamdoulilaha"*—all praise be to God—over and over again, to revolving pictures of eagles in flight and snowy mountains and aqua icebergs and the Golden Gate Bridge at dawn. Men in *kufi* skull caps and flowing caftans, and women in turbans, plunked down and spread out, hoping to score a few extra seats. Two decks up, at the stern, I found a bar and white plastic benches overlooking the harbor, one of the busiest in the world. Tens of thousands of sacks of rice were piled on the docks, fifty feet high, and trucks were bringing more all the time; an army of men in robes and bare feet unloaded the trucks and stacked the pile higher. As the sun set, we edged away from the dock and steamed to sea. And, as everyone does on a ship, I leaned on the rail and watched its foamy wake as we rolled gently over the Atlantic.

"This ship, you know," said a man next to me, "is the replacement for one that sank. And I have ridden that ship many times." His name was Zaid Zopol. He was a wandering minstrel, a street musician who spent six months of the year in Barcelona and six months in Africa, and though he was originally from Patagonia, Chile, he could have been from anywhere. He had long black hair in a ponytail, topped with a black cap, and wore a short black beard beneath vaguely Asiatic eyes. He wore an orange T-shirt and was draped with beads of beans and wood and cowrie shells, loose, yellow cotton pantaloons, and he stood clutching the hand of his girlfriend, a six-foot-tall Senegalese beauty in blue jeans, named Animata. "She is very frightened," he said. "She cannot swim and she remembers the *Joola.*"

Zopol spoke Spanish, English, Portuguese, French, Arabic, Italian, German, and Polish. He had been a journalist for two years in Chile, "but I am free and in my country you couldn't say what you wanted," so he'd taken off. "It was in India that I was reborn. All my bags were stolen. I had nothing. Nothing. I was so poor. And India is even more fucked up than Africa." He'd spent five years wandering overland from Cairo to Cape Town, and had tried to pass from south Sudan into Uganda to see the Blue Nile. "But the border guards had never heard of Chile. They said it didn't exist, so they kept me in a room for three days." In Dakar he had met Animata. "She was eighteen, a kid. I talked and talked to her for months. Just talking. I didn't touch her for years. It was slow, so slow. But I love her so much, so deeply." Now he divided his time between Barcelona and Dakar, and the two of them were taking the ferry to Ziguinchor and then going to the beaches along the coast.

"That ship, the *Joola*, was awful," he said. "It was always so crowded. But she is so scared; she is stubborn and she won't listen to me. This ship is good, safe, but she can barely breathe!" It was a weird sensation to be, once again, traveling on the replacement of the very same conveyance that had once been a disaster. The now dark, gently rolling Atlantic waves, the lights of the ship and the stars overhead and the fresh, humid air— they were the same ones the passengers had experienced on the *Joola*, only six years ago. A hair's breadth, it seemed, was all that separated us. While I knew the basic story of the *Joola*, I didn't yet know it intimately. I had the name and telephone number of a man in charge of the organization of survivors, in Ziguinchor, and I asked Zaid if he could help me find him and translate for me. My French was passable, barely, but not nearly good enough for such a nuanced task.

"I will buy you dinner," I said, "if you'll help me."

"Deal," Zaid said, sticking out his hand. The *Diatta*'s dining room was carpeted in red, with white linen tablecloths and waiters in ties and wine glasses on the table. Animata wouldn't eat, though; she sat clutching Zaid's hand, and every few minutes had to go outside to puke. The *Diatta* was hardly moving; it was seasickness as an expression of fear. Oddly, my cell phone was working, and when Zaid dialed Moosa Sissako, he answered. They spoke in fast French, and then Zaid handed me the phone. "Just tell him again who you are and what you want. I told him, but he doesn't believe me; he thinks you are in the

U.S.A. and he wants to understand that you are next to me. He speaks maybe a little English."

I took the phone, said hello, and said I was hoping to talk to a survivor from the *Joola*. Did he know any? Could he find one for me to talk to?

"Yes," he said, "I can find one for you. You must call me tomorrow afternoon."

I tossed and turned in the night, freezing, squished in my seat, feeling that I might be better off, safer, if I wasn't so far down below. But the benches on deck were sopping with dew, so I stayed put. And in the morning we zigzagged through a narrow channel into the Casamance River, passed Karabane Island, and arrived in Ziguinchor around noon. It was steaming, oppressively hot. Dusty. A garden had been built on the shore as a memorial to the victims of the *Joola*; its gate, under a green arch, was locked, though, and it was overgrown, the concrete paths choked with weeds, the benches broken, the fountain empty. Zaid called Moossa, and we followed his directions, walking through the dirt to the back end of town, past donkey carts and piles of dust and litter. Finally we ended up at a concrete office building that seemed to be falling down. Some of its windows had no glass; the front door hinges were broken, the plaster ceiling inside was crumbling and hanging and covered with black mold.

"Wait here," a group of men said, and soon a tall man in a pink dress shirt and blue jeans arrived, carrying a notebook. "I'm Moussa," he said. "Come." We entered a closed office, piled with stacks of papers and file folders, its air conditioner humming, a man thumbing through piles of receipts and tapping at an adding machine. There was a knock at the door, and a survivor of the *Joola* named Pierre Colly came in. He was twenty-four, dark-skinned, sturdy, with an egg-shaped head and a white and blue striped polo shirt. I asked him to tell me about his trip on the *Joola*.

He looked down at the floor. Said nothing. Looked at us, and then at Moussa, who nodded. Colly started talking.

Six years earlier, on September 26, 2002, a day just like this one, he'd walked through Ziguinchor. It was painfully hot and humid. Chickens pecked in the dirt. Goats tethered to sticks nosed through piles of garbage. Under a hazy sky and a punishing sun, Ziguinchor had a forgotten, end-of-the-earth feeling—a place of unpaved lanes and palm trees covered with dust. Crumbling two-story stucco buildings with tile roofs and narrow balconies fronted the baking streets, a legacy of the town's colonial Portuguese rulers. Lethargic donkeys pulled two-wheeled wooden carts, ignoring their driver's cracking whips; the snapping seemed more habitual than insistent. He was nineteen, happy, privileged to be heading to Dakar that afternoon for another year of school with his older brother. Even better, this year they were taking the ferry up the coast, instead of making the punishing fifteen-hour overland journey packed in a battered Peugeot taxi. That trip could be harrowing: the taxis were old, crowded, and stifling, the roads unpaved and rough. And the drive required traversing the narrow country of Gambia, a gantlet of border guards and corrupt police and soldiers manning roadblocks, who routinely exacted bribes. Everyone wanted to take the ferry; Colly had spent three days fighting lines and cajoling at the ticket window. But finally he had them: two third-class seats on the *Joola*.

He and his brother kicked through the dirt streets toward

the wharf on the Casamance River, past market stalls overflow-
ing with blue jeans and T-shirts and CDs and padlocks and
enamel bowls. Near the river the smell of fish, glistening on ice
under the sun, mixed with the scents of smoke and overripe
fruit. Beyond the gates of the ferry terminal floated the *Joola*.
She was made of steel, built in Germany, 260 feet long and,
for Africa, still newborn—only twelve years old—with a high,
sharp bow and modern lines. There, Colly and his brother
found chaos. The *Joola* had a rated capacity of 580 passengers,
but thousands of people were crowding the concrete pier trying
to get on the ship; among them were some 400 students heading back to the capital for the start of the new school year.

Colly and his brother grabbed a sandwich and walked up the
ferry's ramp at the stern. On deck, a rumor buzzed through the
ship: a fisherman in a pirogue had bumped into the *Joola*'s bow,
fallen overboard, and drowned. Sudden deaths are taken as
omens in Africa; Colly had a funny feeling. He had never been
on a big ship before, and as the *Joola* swung away from the
paved mole and edged into the harbor, he leaned on the rail
feeling the thrum of the engines under his feet, feeling excited
and nervous.

For two hours the *Joola* plowed slowly up the ever-widening
river toward the Atlantic, sliding past traditional Diola fishing
villages on the beach, each a collection of thatched huts around
a large, cylindrical central hall. Porpoises played in the ship's
white, foamy wake, diving and arcing over the waves. Just a
mile shy of the Atlantic lay Karabane. The island wasn't an official port of call, but the ferry always stopped there. When the
Joola motored into the harbor, Colly watched as pirogues swept
out, laden with mangoes and coconuts for the market in Dakar,

and hundreds of people fought to board. The *Joola* listed so far to starboard that the doors on the lower side couldn't be opened, and the surging crowds clambered up the port gunwales into the ship. Some, Colly saw, couldn't make the climb and gave up. As the sun set, the *Joola* zigzagged through the twisting shallows and channels and swung north, up Senegal's Atlantic coast, carrying 1,046 officially ticketed passengers. Later counts would show that at least another 717 had either bribed soldiers for passage or simply snuck on board.

At 10:00 p.m. the Joola radioed its office in Dakar. Seas were calm; all was normal. Passengers were drinking and dancing in the bar on the *Joola*'s top deck, and Colly and his brother were there. On ships you feel removed from the world. Time stops in a way it never quite does onshore. You relax; you have nowhere to go. A feeling of freedom sets in. A Senegalese musician played and sang, but there were so many people, the bar so crowded, Colly felt overwhelmed. He and his brother bought more sandwiches at the snack bar and went out on deck, gazing at the foamy wake in the darkness. "This makes me think of the *Titanic!*" Colly joked. "Can you imagine that happening to us now?" They laughed, shook their heads. Colly mentioned the *Titanic* because, deep down, he felt that tinge of anxiety we all feel on every ship passage, on every airplane flight. Who hasn't walked down the Jetway and wondered if this flight will be his last? Who hasn't boarded a ship and thought of the *Titanic*?

It started raining, so Colly and his brother and their friends returned inside to the packed bar. Colly stood by one of its four-foot-square windows, his brother to his right, a girl he'd just met to his left. West African rhythms filled the room, every seat taken. Colly opened the window. Rain, now harder, flew in—the

Joola had sailed into a squall—and he slid the glass closed again. Around the room, lives were being lived: Music. Drinking. Laughing. Flirting. Everything was normal, except for the wind and rain outside, and even that was normal.

And then it wasn't.

Colly heard a noise. A loud CRACK! Felt a bump. Everyone heard it and felt it. *"Q'est qui c'est passé?* What's happening?" The lights went off; the hot, crowded room plunged into darkness.

Shouting.

The lights went back on. "What's happening? What's happening?" cried a hundred voices. "Are we going to die?" Colly heard a woman near him scream.

The *Joola* rolled heavily to port. Colly grabbed the window, the curtain, a seat that was bolted to the floor. From instinct he slid open the window as he watched people, bags, cans of Castel beer tumble across the floor. The lights went out again. Decks below him, the cars and trucks on the *Joola*'s ferry deck broke their chains, a sudden and massive shift in weight. When the untethered vehicles tumbled to port the *Joola* rolled faster, past the point of no return. Colly heard a noise, a noise he'll never forget: the sound of thousands of tons of rushing water. He knew only this: the water had him, it held him, and it pulled him of the window and it was night and dark and raining and he saw the sky. He reached out, felt something solid, grabbed it, thought, *I'd better stay here until it finishes*, and then he realized it already had. The MV *Le Joola* floated upside down in the darkness.

He saw something white. A light. He swam toward it, calling his brother's name. He swam and swam, and called and called, in rain and wind and rough seas. He swam for fifteen minutes, until he came to a floating fish trap. Seven people were clinging to it, and it began to sink, so Colly swam to the next one. Others were already there. *I'm lucky*, he thought. *I better keep fighting.* But it was still raining. Cold. Colly was freezing. His raftmates were losing strength. "Don't give up," he said. But one by one they slipped away and Colly was talking to no one, just hanging on to the floats telling himself over and over again not to give up.

Toward dawn, six hours later, a fisherman in a small sailboat appeared. He was frightened. "What are you doing here?" he asked Colly.

"Don't be afraid," said Colly. "We were on the *Joola* and it sank."

"That's impossible!" said the fisherman. Then he told Colly that there was a flare stored in the floating trap. Colly found it, and the fisherman lit the flare.

And then. And then the details go hazy. Colly can't remember. Other boats appeared; he remembers a different fisherman refusing to help and then he was on a pirogue with eight other survivors, and that's all, and then his life dissolved into a strange fate: of the 1,863 confirmed passengers on board the *Joola*, Colly and sixty others survived, only one of them a woman. Three hundred more people died on the *Joola* than on the *Titanic*, and nearly every single one of the dead came from the town of Ziguinchor—among them its best and brightest students. Colly lived to become something he didn't want to be, something that soon had a name: a *rescapé*.

A survivor.

I wrote, and listened for almost two hours. At times the tale rolled out of Colly, at other moments he stopped talking, said nothing, stared for long seconds. And then it was done; no journalist or investigator had ever asked to speak to him before. He had endured the sinking and then had been left alone. "I was lucky," he said. "It was God who pushed me out of the window. But . . . often the sadness comes. I am alone and I think about my brother. And what happened was a big thing for people in Ziguinchor. People look at me like I'm weird. They say, 'How could so many die and you live? It's not normal! You saved yourself and the rest died!' They give me a hard time. They call me the *rescapé*—the survivor."

Colly had dropped out of school and never returned. "I couldn't think, and my older brother had been in charge of the family, so I had to take his place." Now he was a taxi driver. Colly had to get back to work; Zaid had to get back to his girlfriend, waiting for us at the port. We climbed in Colly's taxi and lurched down the streets in a cloud of dust. "When the anniversary comes, I just want to go away from here. I want to escape; I want to leave here and find a job and start a new life somewhere else." A muezzin called the faithful to pray, the chants cutting through the heat. Colly pulled up to the gates of the port. He was silent, staring straight ahead. He had nothing else to say.

"Have you taken the ship again?" I said, fumbling for money to pay the fare.

"I have not done it, but if I had to I would. If I have to die on that ship, I will."

ASIA

A ferry carrying around 850 passengers sank in a storm off Indonesia's main island of Java and hours later only 12 survivors had been found, a military commander said Saturday. The cause of the accident was not known. Sea accidents are common in Indonesia, the world's largest archipelago nation, where boats are the main way to reach many islands. Safety measures are often poorly enforced and many craft lack sufficient safety equipment.

—New York Times, *December 30, 2006*

SIX

Jalan! Jalan!

THE HEAT FELT THICK enough to touch. Sweat dripped from my temples and I couldn't keep the flies off. Smoke from hundreds of cigarettes hung in the air like faded, yellowed lace curtains. I was three decks down, in *ekonomi*—steerage—on the *Bukit Siguntang*, a 479-foot-long steel ferry operated by Pelni, the Indonesian government-owned shipping line. The *Siguntang* officially carried 2,003 souls, all but 300 in third class, but it seemed as if every man, woman, and child in Jakarta were swarming into her belly. There were no beds or bunks—just two open decks full of knee-high, linoleum-covered platforms on which we were supposed to lie like hot dogs lined up on a grill. The bulkheads were brown, the ceiling brown, the deck white linoleum covered in ocher cigarette burns. It was an industrial holding pen with the occasional basketball-sized porthole that didn't open.

"Nasi, nasi, nasi!" vendors yelled. Babies cried. Water and chips, noisemakers and rice wrapped in brown paper cones, balloons—it might have been the circus.

"Air, air, air," water in Bahasa Indonesian.

We hadn't left the dock; I wanted to go on deck but feared leaving my bags. I was the only foreigner, hungry and nervous to be so totally submerged in otherness. Indonesia was a world of islands, some 17,000 stretching across 3,100 miles, and without ferries the nation would never hang together; they were its lifeblood, carrying not just people, but cars and refrigerators and anything and everything too big or too expensive to fly. The *Siguntang*'s route was epic: nine days from Jakarta to Sorong, in Indonesian Papua, via Surabaya, Makassar, Bau Bau, Ambon, Bandaneira, and Fak Fak. I was booked through to Ambon in the Molucca Islands, five solid days in steerage with no breaks, no bed, no door to keep acquisitive hands off my stuff, and, it was immediately clear, no way to get out quickly if we hit rough seas. And chances were good that I might have to: In 2002 and 2003 two ferries sunk, each killing more than 500. In 2006 the *Senopati Nusantara* went down in heavy seas off Java en route to the island of Borneo, and more than 800 died. Like the *Joola*, these weren't ancient rust buckets; the *Nusantara* was built in 1990 and was government-owned, just like the *Siguntang*. And those were just the big ships; thousands of small, decrepit wooden ferries plied shorter routes, and they foundered with the frequency of kids' bathtub toys. Two months after my journey on the *Siguntang*, another ferry sank and the online magazine *Slate* ran a story postulating that so many Indonesians died in ferry disasters because they didn't know how to swim. One look at the *Siguntang* reveals that claim as ridiculous. It was just crowded, and the ocean distances across which it sailed were wide and wild. Safety took a back seat; no one said it, would ever say it, but risk was just one more economic

THE LUNATIC EXPRESS ⟩ 125

calculation in a country of islands with 240 million people, great masses of whom earned only a few hundred dollars a year and lived in villages or urban slums. Everybody was just trying to make a little more; politicians skimmed big, and ship captains and lowly seamen skimmed little.

"Why aren't you flying?" asked a man who was seeing his large extended family get settled on the plank across from me. The question was rhetorical; he wasn't really expecting an answer. But flying in Indonesia wasn't much better. After a string of aviation disasters, including Adam Air Flight KI-574, which simply disappeared off the radar in January 2007 en route from Java to Manado with 102 passengers, every one of its airlines were banned from flying to the U.S. and Europe, including its national carrier Garuda. I shrugged, said I liked ships better.

"You must be careful," he said. "Sometimes the people . . . they take things. And pirates . . ."

Porters in yellow shirts humped boxes wrapped in twine— more and more boxes that they piled in the aisles, against the walls. This was no casual, quick hop to Chicago for the weekend. Whole families were on the move, armed with goods and prepared with bedding and enough plastic bins of rice to survive on a desert island for weeks. "Hello," a high-pitched voice said. I turned, and next to me knelt a teenage girl wearing skinny jeans and a Mickey Mouse T-shirt that said PIRATE GIRL in sequins. "I am Mrs. Nova," she said. "What is your religion?"

Two women wearing headscarves on the other plank eyed me. The woman to my left clutched a Koran. I was surrounded, captive. I hesitated. "Atheist" seemed too provocative. Thankfully Mrs. Nova, who was clearly not a Mrs., didn't wait for an answer. "Christian?"

I bobbled my head noncommitally.

"My hobbies are singing and billiards," she said in nearly perfect English, as if reading from a conversation book. "Mr. Carl," she continued in the third person, "Mrs. Nova likes Linkin Park and Britney Spears. Mrs. Nova is seventeen and she lives in Makassar."

That broke the ice; suddenly the family across from me cut in. Florinda spoke a little English and wore a pink headscarf, and she was with her sister and one of their sons, Kahar. They'd traveled three days from Makassar to Jakarta for a family wedding, stayed a week, and were now making the three-day hike back. Thirteen days, six of them traveling. A ramen seller came by, and I flagged him down. Mrs. Nova nearly attacked him, barking a string of Indonesian. She jumped up, fished around in her bag, and pulled out a case of ramen. "For two!" she said. "For Mrs. Nova and Mr. Carl!"

A vendor hawking thin cotton mattress pads muscled by. I waved him over; five days on linoleum wasn't going to be easy. This time the woman with the Koran barked, looked at me, shook her head, waggled her finger no. Then pantomimed picking tiny things off her ankles, and held her nose. The message was clear. The vendor scowled and stomped off.

There was another message, too: once again, the more I gave myself to the world, the more I made myself vulnerable by putting myself completely at the disposal of people and situations in which I had no control, the more people took care of me, looked out for me. At first I had thought they were taking pity on me. But over the days and weeks ahead I started to understand something else, something that had been sinking in gradually over the months. Being a white American conferred on me an automatic status. I represented power. Affluence. Vast numbers of the world were poor, watched American television and films, listened to American music, but had no real contact with westerners, and if they did it was often as chambermaids, taxi drivers, waiters—none ever sat down in their slums or ate their food. Florinda's brother's question—why wasn't I flying?—said much. It was a question I heard over and over again. Why wasn't I in first class? Why wasn't I on an express bus? Why wasn't I anywhere but here? My fellow travelers were right: I could have been flying. I could have been traveling in first class, in an air-conditioned cabin with a soft mattress and stewards. In silence and stillness. That I wasn't was like a gift to them, a mysterious one they couldn't fully understand but that they appreciated in a way I would never have imagined. And the more I shed my American reserves, phobias, disgusts, the more they embraced me. In the weeks ahead I would accelerate what had started gradually over the miles. I would do whatever my fellow travelers and hosts did. If they drank the tap water of Mumbai and Kolkata and Bangladesh, so would I. If they bought tea from streetcorner vendors, so would I. If they ate with their fingers, even if I was given utensils, I ate with my fingers. Doing so prompted an outpouring of generosity and curiosity that never ceased to amaze me; it opened the door, made people take me in. That I shared their food, their discomfort, their danger, fascinated them and validated them in a powerful way. And as Lena waved away the cushion man and Mrs. Nova insisted I share her food, I realized I was in good hands, surrounded by women with eagle eyes. I could relax; murder or robbery was the last thing I had to worry about.

Which was a good thing, since I was dying to find the head.

I got off my plank, walked through the hot crowd. Hundreds of eyes watched. At the end of the long room that stretched the width of the ship stood the bathroom. The smell hit first, like gallons of piss had been simmering on the stove for weeks, boiling down to a concentrated essence. Where once three urinals had been attached to the wall were bare pipes. The sink's drain had no pipe—it drained onto the floor, which was two inches deep in liquid. A man stood in the corner pissing into a floor drain. Behind two doors lay Asian-style toilets, rank with humanity's excretions. I rolled up my pants, tiptoed through in my flip-flops, strained to aim in the darkness of the stalls, not that it mattered. And I noticed what appeared to be large black spots. Moving. I blinked, opened my cell phone to shine a little light: cockroaches the size of half-dollars scuttled across the floor.

Sometime, I don't know when, we pulled away from the dock and headed to sea, and I lay down on my plank—Lena six inches to my left, Mrs. Nova six inches to my right—and tried to sleep. The fluorescent lights hummed brightly overhead. People coughed. Babies whined and screamed. A kid nearby twirled a noisemaker, the sound like stones grinding in a barrel. The air was still and humid and oppressive. Radios blared. And lying there, staring at the walls and ceilings, I noticed more roaches. Half an inch long, they scurried up the walls, across the ceiling straight over my head. What is the saying? For every roach you see there are a thousand you don't? Or for every one you see there are ten thousand you don't. Either way there must have been millions, hundreds of millions, of roaches on the *Siguntang.* They were everywhere, and I became convinced that one or two would eventually lose their grip and fall. But no one else took notice of them; roaches were a constant in their lives, not even worth noticing.

I pulled a T-shirt over my eyes, tried to get comfortable. It was midnight and already my hips, knees, and ankles hurt from the hard plank. I don't know when I finally fell asleep, but at 4:30 a.m. the PA system blared to the chanting of the muezzin. Dawn: time to pray. I tried to wait it out, shut it out. But all around me people began to move. Lena slid a white dress over her clothing and enveloped her head in a lace headdress, knelt, and bowed up and down, murmuring.

I got up, stiff, and went up two flights of stairs and out on deck, first light just beginning to illuminate the eastern horizon. Ten-foot-wide decks ran the *Siguntang*'s length, and there was a snack bar on the stern under green corrugated fiberglass. The air felt balmy and fresh; nothing but dark blue calm sea and lightening sky, and at 6:00 a.m., when the snack bar opened, I got a sweet coffee in a thin plastic cup. My ass hurt; there was no place soft to sit anywhere on the ship. I wandered; I stared at the sea; I returned to my plank. "Mr. Carl," said Mrs. Nova, "you must eat breakfast!" With my ticket, it turned out, I was entitled to three meals a day. I stood in a long line that wound past a window; each passenger was handed a Styrofoam box and a bottle of water. I opened my box: white rice and a fish tail, a packet of sambal—hot sauce. There were a lot of bones. Mrs. Nova sang softly to herself and then someone brought out a guitar. She took it, started singing. Lena joined her. It was melodious, beautiful, and I lay down in the heat and dozed off.

That afternoon, sitting on a rail overlooking one of the lifeboats, I met Daud Genti. He was tiny, five inches shorter than me, dressed in blue jeans and a T-shirt that read ILLINOIS

STATE, and he spoke English well, part of the army of cheap, semi-skilled laborers dispersed throughout the world, keeping their parents and their ancestral villages afloat. He was returning home to the Celebes after five years, the last six months as a seaman in Dubai. The *Siguntang*, I soon discovered, was packed with people just like him. "I need a break," he said. "I've been working twelve hours a day, seven days a week, for six months straight, and I quit because they weren't paying us enough. We were supposed to have one day a week off, but we didn't." He'd been working on a dredging barge creating The World, a miniature land of islands in the shape of a Mercator projection of the world's continents on which vacation villas for the rich would be built, with a crew of Iranians and Filipinos. "In Dubai I never saw an Arab," he said. "Indians, Bangladeshis, Filipinos, Indonesians only." Over the years he'd worked in Singapore, in Brunei, on oil rigs off the island of Kalimantan, and he straddled worlds. He was a Toraja, a once fierce race of seafarers who lived in stylized wooden houses with upturned roofs, carried out elaborate funeral rituals and interred their dead in family caves. "All of my family is in a cave," he said, "but we're running out of room. I haven't seen my family in five years." He fished out his cell phone, checked to see if it had a signal. "I'm worried," he said. "Not so excited. My village is very traditional and it will take me eight hours by bus to get there from Makassar. There is no electricity. No television. No mobile phone service—I have to go to town an hour on a motorcycle to check my messages. What am I going to do? Maybe when I'm old, like you, I will want to go back there, but not now . . ." He was used to the world at large now, wanted to stay in it, and he had no idea how long he'd be home for.

A few hours later I met Arthur, another returning worker. He had a narrow face, alive, brimming with enthusiasm. "There is much work," he said. "Too much to be free!" He was just twenty-four, returning to Ambon after seven years, his last job having been as an electrical mechanic for Shell/Petrobras in Brunei. And for seven years straight he had worked six days a week. "My boss loves me because I work, work, work!" His journey, too, was epic in its length, its passing between worlds. He had driven for two days from Brunei to Pontiniak, Indonesia, taken a ship to Jakarta, then five days to Ambon—nine days from start to finish, from a world of oil wells and technology and English to a village to see parents he hadn't seen in seven years. It was hard to imagine; I had trouble coming and going and being away for two weeks. What would it be like to be away seven years? And not just away, but away in a different world, speaking a different language?

We reached Surabaya that afternoon, and Mrs. Nova announced that we were going to *jalan, jalan*—the Indonesian expression for strolling around. She brushed her hair, placed a cap on her head and a pair of oversized sunglasses, and led the way, holding the hand of her five-year-old plank neighbor, while a young man who couldn't speak English brought up the rear. "My family is in Jakarta and my family is in Makassar and my family is HUGE!" she said as we wound through the heat and up the stairs and down the gangplank onto the trash-littered wharf. I had never encountered someone so bursting with enthusiasm, so trusting. "Surabaya! Wow!" she squealed, as we threaded through crowds and piles of trash and smashed concrete. "Wow! So beautiful! *Jalan jalan*! I'm hungry! Are you hungry, Mr. Carl? A photo! Bakso!"

We turned down a narrow alley lined with identical wooden carts, each with a two-by-four bench and jars of what looked like bright green and white worms. We walked up the alley and down the alley, Mrs. Nova peering at each cart, shaking her head, spitting out questions to the chefs. "This one!" she said, and we straddled the bench and in seconds four bowls appeared full of noodles and meatballs and hot peppers. "Bakso! You like bakso?" she said. I plunged in. Whatever it was, it was good, and we sucked our bakso down like it was candy. On some unspoken signal, the silent man paid, even though I whipped out a pile of bills. That, too, would happen over and over again—people far poorer than I insisting that they pay for everything.

When we got back to the ship, it looked like it was being attacked by ants. Another thousand people were fighting their way on board. I watched men shinnying up the mooring lines, human rats, a dangling, frenetic whirl of limbs up five stories to disappear in the throngs. If the *Siguntang* seemed crowded before, now it was packed. Every passageway and stairway was staked out with blankets and towels and scraps of newsprint. The decks inside, the decks outside—humanity covered every square inch of space. Children. Old men and women lying on the hard floor. The people outside had it best as long as the weather held. To descend the stairs into *ekonomi* was to get hit with a wall of heat and humidity and cigarette smoke. You could touch it, feel it on your face and hands. It almost knocked me backwards; made me want to flee. Massed human beings in tight quarters are not a pretty sight. They sweat, cough and hack. They snore and belch. They produce untold quantities of garbage and trash, from cigarette butts to eggshells to fish tails, which can't go anywhere, can't be hidden, and which slowly piled up and spread across the decks as the days passed. And we were lucky. The skies stayed blue, the seas calm. I could only imagine what it had been like on the *Nusantara*, which battled fifteen-foot seas for ten hours before it sank. Sickness. Panic. The garbage, shit, piss, and people rolling and pitching on an overloaded rollercoaster of death.

I escaped to the snack bar, but even that space was now jammed, Indonesians screeching on a way-too-loud karaoke machine. The *Siguntang*, I understood as the days passed, was a world in between worlds. Straddling worlds just like Arthur and Daud, connecting them; we were 3,000 Muslims and Christians and animists; some of us were from enormous cities like Jakarta, some from villages without power. One minute Lena would be in low-hipped jeans, applying eye shadow, the next she'd be wrapped in her shroud on her knees clutching her Koran, bowing up and down. I had traveled to Indonesia twice before, had been to Java and Bali, Kalimantan and Irian Jaya, but I'd never seen it before, not as it really was: this long, strung-out world of ocean and islands, of ancient kingdoms and cultures improbably united into a modern state, connected together by ship. To stand at the rail during port stops was to be swallowed up in watercraft, from tramp freighters to wooden Makassar schooners, thousands of boats weaving across blue sea.

We settled into a rhythm, every day heading east, east into the rising sun, after long, hot nights of pain and coughing and smoke, days of wandering and sleeping and talking as the conditions worsened. Once I was known, grown used to, an endless stream of strangers approached me, waved me over, bought me coffee and tea, called out to me. In my space on my plank, I was an old family member. Florinda fed me slices of fishy tempeh.

Mrs. Nova made sure I was hydrated. Lena, I suspect, prayed for my soul. To change my shirt, well, I had to do it in front of everyone. "Sexy!" cooed the middle-aged Florinda, conservatively wrapped in her robes and headscarf even in the sweltering heat. The bathrooms were so horrendous, I resisted the idea of taking a shower. But the irony hit me: the Indonesians were plunging into the malodorous room every morning to emerge shimmering and shiny and smelling like shampoo and toothpaste. While I was getting rank. So I plunged in, too, standing in line in the steam, showering, washing my hair in the cool water, brushing my teeth in the tepid tap water, pissing down the drain in the corner. The men in the bathroom nodded, made way for me, beckoned me into the stalls before themselves.

As the days passed, the conditions worsened. More garbage. More cigarette butts. Empty Styrofoam ramen containers and cans of soda, all flying off the stern, fluttering overhead—a wake of pure trash steamed off the *Siguntang*. Endless heat and humidity. There was no place to escape, no place for solitude, no place for silence; you could barely sit anywhere, stand anywhere, lie anywhere without another body touching you. One evening I trudged back from up on deck, stepping gingerly past people's sarongs on the floor and hands and heads, and came upon nine ebony-colored men with muscular arms gathered around each other a few planks down from mine. Three of them held crude, homemade ukuleles constructed of Masonite, thinly painted in whitewash. Clouds of cigarette smoke rose around them. Perspiration flew from their heads—it was 100 degrees at least, with not a wisp of fresh air. And for two hours they sang in rough, deep, mad harmony, songs of Papua and work and Indonesian folk songs, other men keeping beat with empty water bottles, roaches crawling on the ceilings, crawling on the walls, skittering by underfoot. They were coming off five months on a gas well in Brunei, heading home to Sorong, a journey from start to finish of almost twelve days. "Sit! Sit!" cried Jacobus. "We want whiskey! Where are you going?" Ambon, I said, and they broke into song, with a refrain of "Ambon Man" in English. Their singing was organic. Spontaneous. The raw energy of lions roaring on the plain, the best of human beauty in the midst of the worst shithole. After two hours they wore themselves out; Jacobus's fingers were bloody, he'd played so long and so hard. I lay down to sleep, the lights bright, my body a series of bruised points on the hard plank. And a few minutes later the inevitable happened: a roach dropped onto my face. I hardly moved; I reached up, grabbed it, and tossed it away. It was surprisingly soft and silky.

IN THE MORNING I found Daud gazing out to sea. A pod of porpoises sliced through the royal blue waves, leapt over the ship's wake, sped toward the ship, and cut abruptly away. Flying fish erupted from the sea, sailing across the surface to plunk back in fifty yards later. "Last night a woman in my area was hypnotized by a bad man," he said. "He talked to her for a long time and exchanged envelopes with her and when he left she was holding an envelope that was empty. She lost ten million rupiah"— about $1,000. I nodded, shook my head, sighed, and we silently watched the waves.

That evening, in the quickly falling twilight of the tropics, we approached Makassar, a long line of green hills rising out of the blue sea. The PA system crackled and boomed and I returned to my plank to find Mrs. Nova and Florinda and her family packing, and eight young men, tough guys, sitting on my bed. I climbed up, muscled my way in, and they barely moved over, and I realized again how protected I'd been the past three days. At about seven-thirty we docked and the crowds shifted, rose, hoisted, and dispersed. Mrs. Nova grabbed my pad and wrote her address and phone number under the header "Biodata," and urged me to come visit her family. Florinda and her family trooped off, replaced by the gang of tough guys, who stared at me, elbowed each other, and laughed. The ship's crew attacked the refuse, piled and strewn like the aftermath of Woodstock. They mopped and swept and carted, and most of it went right over the side. Thankfully, Lena was still to my right and she grabbed the hand of the little girl who seemed to belong to everyone, beckoned me to follow, and soon we were on shore eating a rich, brown-brothed soup made from intestines—a local Makassar specialty.

Late in the afternoon of the fifth day, as whales spouted off the bow and their big flukes slapped the sea, we sighted the green hills of Ambon. I was starting to crack; physically this had been my hardest journey yet. I had a hacking cough from the incessant smoke of unfiltered cigarettes. My throat felt like sandpaper rubbing together every time I swallowed. I was constantly hungry, the rice and fish tails and ramen unfulfilling. I was dying for the great riches of life: a long, hot shower and a cold beer and silence. And for a cushion; in the total absence of padding of any kind, it felt like my bones were pressing through my skin no matter how I turned or sat. In the middle of the night I was always waking to find a leg or arm draped across me, and the man to my right, who'd replaced Mrs. Nova, and I were engaged in a silent war. His knee kept dropping onto my leg. His fist flopped on my chest. I picked it up and laid it on him. It was *my* space, I kept thinking; it was all I had, and he kept intruding on it. In the bathrooms in the morning, politeness had evaporated; someone was always trying to butt in front of me. The crowds were so thick on the wharves, police with bamboo staves had to keep order, poking and whacking people into line. Lena and Florinda, Mrs. Nova and Daud were all gone; I had lost my friends, and my new conversations with new people seemed repetitions of ones already held. And conversation was lessening, anyway; people were receding into themselves. Or maybe it was just me. Maybe I was the one withdrawing, straining at the effort of connecting with people I couldn't really get to know.

As always toward the end of these journeys, I had the confused feeling of loss. As I watched the capital of the famous Spice Islands approach, grow larger, I felt desperate to get off and to be by myself. But the voyage was ending, and I still had more to know. I hadn't pierced farther into the world of my shipmates. Kind as they'd been, as much time as I'd spent with them, I still hadn't known them, and I knew I never really would be able to. As usual, though, a new place rose up to greet me.

TWICE IN THE LAST DECADE, in 2000 and 2004, Ambon had been racked with vicious sectarian violence between Christians and Muslims—thousands had died—and many of my shipmates kept saying I shouldn't be going there. We sailed slowly up a long bay between a rugged carpet of hills dotted with red tile roofs, the water green and calm, as glistening, silver-gray porpoises leapt among great floating mats of ramen cups and plastic wrappers and water bottles, and the nets of wooden fishing praus with outrigger hulls working in concert. In searing heat and humidity we docked at Kota Ambon, a ramshackle jumble of one- and two-story buildings and rusty corrugated roofs clinging to the hillside, the docks lined with even rustier tramp freighters and wooden schooners. The end always came too quickly; there was never any transition. I shouldered my bags and plunged into the thick crowds down the gangplank, to be plucked off the foreign street by a taxi driver.

OUTSIDE MY HOTEL I ran into Aristotle Mosse, a wiry, long-haired Indonesian who offered to show me around. Indonesia is the largest Muslim country in the world, and the Molucca Islands, a former Portuguese colony of which Ambon was the capital, were among the few places in the country where the population was equally balanced between Muslim and Christian. I knew the basic facts of the story—riots had broken out one afternoon, and looting, killing, and burning had followed for months. But I wanted to hear what it was like, what someone like Aristotle—a Christian—had thought and felt as neighbors who'd lived side by side suddenly went berserk with rage, killing each other. To me, at first glance, Ambon didn't look any different from any other small Third World city. It was bustling, dynamic, the streets and curbs crumbling, open sewers everywhere, but crowded with bicycle rickshaws and restaurants grilling chicken and pork and fish, and appliance shops stacked with stoves and refrigerators and street vendors hawking coffee and bakso. Aristotle saw it differently, as a city sharply divided. "This is the Muslim section," he said, passing a barrier that would have been invisible to me, but at which a red flag flew, into a part of Ambon that looked no different. Every city in Indonesia is full of half-completed buildings, but Aristotle pointed and I realized I was seeing concrete blackened by fire and riddled with bullet holes, thousands of bullet holes. "I was just in my house," he said, "and my neighbor came and told me people were rioting. I went out to the road and saw Muslim people take stones and throw them at Christians and Christians throw them back. There were hundreds of people. The police came and people ran. That building," he said, pointing to a vacant four-story concrete shell, "that was a Christian house they burned. I was afraid."

We came to another empty shell of a building, a former computer school on the first floor, with apartments above. "People ran into the building, upstairs to hide and get away. But the Muslims set it on fire and burned them." The fighting escalated, went on for weeks. No ships would come to Ambon, Aristotle said. It was difficult to get rice, to get kerosene to cook with. He couldn't work, no one could. "People were killing each other and I lived two hundred feet from the border," he said. "They attacked and we shot back; we had to guard all the time. We needed kerosene, so I crossed the mountain one day to find some. People shot at us. Everyone had guns. Finally I escaped to my home island of Babar for six months."

But why had it happened? How had it happened? What made people start burning and stoning their neighbors? "It was provocateurs," Aristotle said. "From Jakarta. They paid people to attack, to burn churches and mosques. We don't know who they were; only God knows their names." That was partly true; the Moluccans had long agitated for independence, and it was a fact that in 2000 the leaders of the radical movement known as the RMS—Republic of the South Moluccas—had hoped to take advantage of political instability in Indonesia, drive the Muslims out of Ambon, and declare an independent state. Yet that still didn't explain it to me. Someone could offer me all the money in the world and I still wouldn't start burning my neighbors' houses. Would I do it even if I was poor? I wondered. The hate and animosity had to be there in the first place; before the fire could be lit, it had to have fuel. I said that to Aristotle; I wanted him to articulate that hate, that anger, explain it. But he either dodged the question or just couldn't understand it. "We don't want to make a riot," he said. "It was just people giving money and guns."

We walked on. This church had been burned. That mosque burned. Those houses burned. "Before the war we stayed together," he said. "We weren't separate. Now we are separate; they stay in their community and we stay in ours."

I was trying to fathom it all, those feelings of hate so easily ignited between neighbors, as we wandered by the docks. I noticed something I hadn't seen when the *Siguntang* had docked: dozens of aged wooden ferries, far smaller than the *Siguntang*. "Where do they go?" I asked. He shrugged.

"Let's find out," I said.

We walked down a concrete pier, and I was mesmerized. They were forty, sixty, eighty feet long, clapboard and wood and corroded steel, and Aristotle asked for their captains. The *Amboina Star* was wood and steel, and beside her on the dock stood, it turned out, her chief engineer, dressed in oil-stained shorts and a ragged gray T-shirt. I questioned Aristotle in English and he translated for the engineer, who gave me an odd look every time I spoke. It was headed to Buru Island the next afternoon, to two villages, Lambrule and Leksula, a trip that would take eighteen hours. I was welcome to come; I should be at the ship by five tomorrow. Buru? I looked in my guide. There was one paragraph that said little: Buru had been the site of a famous Indonesian political prison. It mentioned neither Leksula nor Lambrule. Hotels? Facilities? English speakers? They were a total mystery. I packed my bags, jumped on the back of a motorcycle taxi the next afternoon, and headed to the ship.

It was damp, the air cloying and thick with the smell of smoke and fishy sea, the sky covered with low clouds, rays of sun shooting through onto pewter-gray water. Cocks crowed from the deck of a ship on the other side of the dock. A parade of men dragging two-wheeled handcarts loaded the vessel. Rebar. Angle iron. Pipes. Sheets of plywood and sacks of concrete and rice, boxes of cooking oil. A line of men, fire-brigade style, passed the goods inside, down a steep wooden gangplank, where they were lowered into the hold, below two long shelves that served as sleeping platforms that ran the length of the *Star*. Joppy, the engineer we'd spoken to the day before, led me to the top deck, along which a series of Hobbit-sized doors opened onto tiny wooden cabins. I shook my head and pointed to the main space of shelves below. Joppy looked at me and said, "There will be many people down there, and a lot of cigarette smoke."

I was startled; his English was perfect. No wonder he'd been looking at me so oddly as we'd talked through Aristotle.

"That's okay," I said. "I don't mind."

Joppy grabbed one of my bags, carried it down a ladder, found me a spot, and wrote out a ticket: thirteen dollars. "We won't be leaving until eight or nine," he said.

I asked him how he'd learned English. "I was an engineer on a factory trawler in Alaska," he said. "For two years." He had gone to sea at twenty-seven and spent a decade in the global economy, like Daud and Arthur on the *Siguntang*. He'd been to China, Panama, throughout the Caribbean, the United States, and Korea. "Sixteen countries," he said. But, it turned out, his English had been courtesy of the U.S. government. "I was arrested in a bar in Alaska. I spent six months in jail. I drank too much whiskey and there were girls there and I grabbed one," he said. "I don't really remember. There were no witnesses. It was a bad move; she was sixteen and the police came. I spent one month in jail in Palmer, Alaska, and then five in Seward and then, boom! They didn't charge me with anything and just put me on a plane and I was in Jakarta. I'll tell you a funny thing, though: in Indonesia you go to jail big and come out small, but in America you go to jail small and you come out big! There's a lot of food and nothing to do but sport and volleyball!

"Listen," he said. "If you need anything, you come to me."

On the top deck toward the stern the ship was open, piled with wooden pallets and a few old vinyl mattresses, and cracked plastic chairs. I plunked down and felt elated at the little ship and an unknown destination, and gazed across the bay, crowded with freighters and sailing schooners under the green mountains, as the hours passed and passengers slowly filed aboard. I smelled diesel fuel on the light breeze, listened to the roosters, the sound of foreign voices carrying across the water in the gathering twilight.

"Where are you going?" asked Dempe, a young law student from Ambon.

"To Buru," I said.

"But what town?"

I shrugged. "I don't know," I said; at that moment I couldn't even remember the names of our two destinations, or which one I'd told Joppy I was going to. Like when I had jumped in the car across the Amazon from Puerto Maldonado, I'd had no idea where I was going or what I would find when I got there, or how or when I'd be able to get back to Ambon. I was leaving the map, leaving it all up to fate. I carried no food. No bottled water. It was strange how good that always felt; it was freeing in some profound way, and made me feel strong. One thing I wasn't was afraid. Joppy was as fine a twist of fate as they came: I was in good hands.

"Are you going alone?" asked Dempe, furrowing his brow.

"Yes. Alone."

He looked at me; people were always fascinated that I was traveling alone, without family; it was inconceivable to them. They lived with multiple generations, slept crowded into beds and on floors in tiny apartments or houses, and they would do so their entire lives. For them, every night was like those nights on the *Siguntang* or the *Star,* crowded together, entangled in multiple legs and arms, always the heat of another human body next to them. I envied that, even as it repelled me—the idea was a central conflict in my life. I had a family, after all, and five of us had lived in a one-bathroom, three-bedroom house—but somehow I'd ended up in my own little apartment. I'd always found crowds compelling, I always liked feeling part of something, so why was I always running?

At nine-thirty the *Star*'s horn blasted, the mooring lines were cast off, and we slipped out onto the dark water. The ship was crammed—every space on the platforms taken. But big, open windows ran its length, and an eight-foot-wide doorway lay open in the waist, just two feet over the sea, and a warm breeze swept through. I sat perched at the doorway for an hour or so watching the sea pass, and then crawled up onto my platform, squeezed between two men, put my arm over my eyes, and fell asleep to the thrum of the engines and the roll of the sea.

Movement. Touching. Voices. A baby crying. Wind sweeping across me. It was 4:30 a.m., still dark, but I crawled off my shelf and Joppy offered me a burning-hot, syrupy-sweet coffee in a plastic cup so thin it was like paper. As dawn came over the ocean I realized we were motoring just offshore of a hilly green jungle, coconut palms and mountains rising behind. I had thought we were bound for two cities, but the *Star* was threading its way to every village along the coast, and for the next four hours we stopped every ten or fifteen minutes, bobbing a few hundred yards off the beach, as goods and people came and went on the *Star*'s beat-up outboard launch.

They were places far off the beaten track, almost out of this world. Just a tightly packed collection of corrugated shacks on a white sand beach, the shimmering onion dome of a mosque or the steeple of a church—never both—poking through the shacks. Blue ocean, cloudless sky stretching far to the horizon; uninterrupted green beyond. Groups of ten or twenty children played on the beaches, chased balls, jumped up and down, and shouted at the *Star*. Dogs barked.

"You have villages like this in America?" asked a man wearing a Pertamina oil company baseball cap on his head and a blue one-piece jumpsuit. He had thick, jet black eyebrows and a gray mustache over a pair of crooked white teeth, and he spoke formally, with what I thought was a Dutch accent, like many elderly English-speaking Indonesians who had been educated when Indonesia was a Dutch colony. His name was Santoso.

I looked at the village on the beach. Shook my head. "No," I said, "definitely not."

"A landscape like this?"

That was a harder question to answer; there were tropics in America, after all. But no, not really. Not like this, which I told him.

Santoso looked puzzled. Together we gazed at the sea and the shacks and the children. "But America is big and great, no?" It was an odd thought—that a great and big nation would not have a little village nestled on a beach in a vast jungle.

He wore a heavy gold ring with an orange stone as big as a quail's egg. I said I liked it. "You have no stones like this in America?"

The next village was called Wayalikut. "Have you written in your exercise book about the nice panorama of Wayalikut village?" he asked.

The day passed. Mile after mile of deserted green coast, thickly overgrown with palm trees and black sand beaches that became white in places, villages of fifty houses of rust and thatch. The crew cooked meals and fed me: rice and cabbage and bony dried sardines with a fresh, fiery paste of hot peppers ground out in a stone mortar. I'd told Joppy I was going to Lambrule, which was the first of our two official destinations. Over and over again people had asked me why, which I finally understood when we got there. Lambrule was no different from any other of the villages, except that it had a long concrete dock and some streets with half-finished concrete houses and a half-finished church. But no restaurants, no hotels; no stores or shops; just a pressing damp heat and a tangle of green vines and a single potholed street. *"Panas!"* everyone said to me—hot!

"I think I'll continue on to Leksula," I told Joppy, who introduced me to a policeman in shorts named Deddy. "He will show you around," Joppy said. "Don't be gone long, though." Deddy escorted me in the searing sun. He didn't speak English, so we walked in silence and almost nothing moved in the whole place.

Late in the afternoon we hit Leksula, and it was little different from Lambrule—just a minuscule village on an island in the middle of the ocean. Within minutes of our docking, Hendro showed up. He was twenty-one, wearing shorts, a camouflage-colored sleeveless T-shirt, flip-flops, and, as the village's known English speaker, he had been quickly summoned. "Let me show you Leksula!" he said, beaming, excited. As we walked down the long concrete pier, crumbling in places, a beached and ancient wooden ferry on its side in the shallows, the skies opened and warm rain came pouring down. Hendro didn't seem to notice, as the pier ended and mud and puddles began. The main street paralleled the shore, and we walked between corrugated and concrete houses, people huddling under porches and staring at me under the downpour. Nothing about the place really registered to me, at first. Just a heavy stillness. Hendro tapped my shoulder and pointed to a man in a doorway. "There is someone trying to say hello to you," he said. I waved. The man waved back. "Why don't you sleep in the village?" Hendro said.

"You can enjoy village life. It is much better and you will not go up and down like you will on the boat."

"Is there a restaurant or somewhere I can get a cup of coffee?" I asked.

"Closed," he said, "but we can go to my aunt's house." We stopped at a one-story concrete house surrounded by mud and chickens, with an open door. Removed our flip-flops and went in; the front room had a wooden and floral print sofa and two matching chairs, their backs covered with antimacassars, and a wooden coffee table. Portraits of stern-looking army officers gazed down from the walls. Hendro went into a back room, and a few minutes later a middle-aged woman came out bearing cookies and two cups of instant coffee. We were both soaked. Slowly a gang of children gathered at the door, peering in. Laughing. Calling out, "Hello, mister!"

"When I finished elementary school," Hendro said, "I decided I wanted to go to music school. I like music very much. I want to go to Jakarta, but I can't do it, I have no money. Now I just practice my music in the church; it is a symbol of God." He paused a moment and said, "New York is the biggest city in the world, isn't it?"

"No," I said, "not even close. Jakarta is bigger than New York!"

"Well, it's the most beautiful city in the world!"

"No," I said again, "there are many other cities that are much more beautiful. Paris. Rome. New York is very crowded."

He sipped his coffee. Thought. "Mister Carl, why aren't you an actor in Hollywood?"

"I never wanted to be an actor," I said, and asked if he had a girlfriend.

"No, but I would like one. I have no job, so I can't have a girlfriend."

When we finished the coffee the rain had stopped. Out we went again, and this time people flooded into the streets. Staring at me, waving, calling out hello. They were all in groups. Men held hands with each other, walked with their arms around each other. They squatted on the ground together, sat on walls together. A soccer game broke out on a muddy field. Always, everywhere, people were together; that's why my being alone was so hard to fathom. By now, everyone in town knew I was there, and suddenly I felt like one of the Inuit brought back to New York by Admiral Robert Peary after his polar expedition. I was seized with an urgent need for privacy. I wanted to be alone. Hendro took me back to the ship, where at the dock children were bombing off the pier, throwing each other into the ocean in their shorts and T-shirts, tumbling on the sand on the beach, playing with a joy and abandon long absent from the organized soccer fields and playgrounds of American cities. A crowd had followed us. Young. Old. Children. Men. There must have been twenty or thirty of them. They climbed on board following me, literally stood around me, surrounding me, watching me. I waved. They waved.

Joppy understood and opened a cabin for me, said I should sleep there tonight. It was tiny—two bunks not quite six feet long, the cabin only four feet wide. Instantly there were ten faces at the window peering in. I felt bad, but I did it anyway: took out my sarong and hung it over the window. The cabin was dim. Sauna-like. Airless. And it felt like the greatest refuge on earth. I was a freak in a village so far removed from the world it was almost inconceivable. No cell phones. No Internet. No roads to get here, no roads from here to anywhere else, just a big green mass jungle rising behind the village where, a man on the ship had told me, were "men without religion." It was hard to understand my own reactions, feelings. I wanted to embrace it, revel in it, take a little house and live here and get to know it. And once again I wanted to flee from the village as fast as possible. Part of it was simple: I'd been raised in such a different environment and I was used to so much personal space and privacy. But I couldn't help feeling there was something else, too, something deeper that I was just beginning to figure out—that as I pushed further out into the world alone and surrounded by otherness, amid people so deeply connected, I wanted that, too. The very gulf between me and everyone staring at me made me feel that much more alone and hungry for a genuine connection that I wasn't getting constantly moving through the world.

That night Joppy took me to dinner in town. We ate in a concrete room with a single bare lightbulb, rice and fish and cabbage and hot sauce. "When I was first arrested," he said, "the Seamen's Mission paid for a lawyer, and many people from a church came to see me. But then it stopped and I was alone. When I got out and back to Jakarta I made a promise that I'd never drink again. Bad things happen." That idea of aloneness again; Joppy had come back to Buru, married; now he had a family here.

After dinner we strolled up and down the street. The dark was deep, impenetrable beyond the weak bare bulbs of shops selling shoes and T-shirts and sarongs, and rice and mangos. Stars sparkled brightly overhead, millions of them. Girls walked arm in arm. Boys held hands. Suddenly I felt overwhelmed again, and it wasn't people staring this time. The night had given me a cloak of anonymity; people couldn't tell the strange "mister" was in their midst until I was nearly upon them. It was hard for me to imagine flourishing outside of a major city, and these days even a remote American farmstead was hardly remote, so many places interconnected by the web, highways, telephones; they were how I thought of and defined the world. But there were millions and probably hundreds of millions of people around the planet who lived in tiny, remote places like Leksula. Nothing but sun and sea and sand and jungle. And each other; people were so connected to each other in this little world. I was such a loose atom, ricocheting around the world. Walking with Hendro, he'd said, "This is my brother. My aunt. My cousin. My sister." Their world was this, right here. These shops. This sand. This harbor. These people. And Leksula was big; it had a concrete pier! The villages of Buru were tiny outlying worlds as removed from Facebook and the economic meltdown as Mercury and Pluto. That we were all out there simultaneously struck me as incredible. I myself had parroted the cliché that the world was getting smaller every day, but walking through the darkness of Leksula it didn't feel that way. It felt vast. Huge. And I was very far from home.

HENDRO WOKE ME up at 6:00 a.m., knocking on my cabin window, one eye peering through a crack that the sarong failed to cover. "My aunt wants to invite you for coffee, Mister Carl!"

I washed my hair and body in a bucket and we walked into town, children in red skirts and white blouses walking to school. It was so quiet, nothing but the sound of their voices and laughter. We walked through town and at a big, well-kept house,

Santoso—the man from the ship with the ring and Pertemina baseball cap—was drinking coffee on a wide verandah. He rushed out. "You must come and sit and meet my brother. He is the headmaster of the high school."

Hendro and I sat down at a table covered with a yellow plastic tablecloth, and sipped coffee with Santoso's brother and sister. Santoso reached over and held my hand. It was a disconcerting sensation, this strange man holding my hand in his. My American instinct wanted to pull it away; it went against everything I knew. But it also felt nice. Warm. Welcoming. It just *was*—the most elemental of human connection, laden with no expectations. An embrace, and no one else even noticed it. We said goodbye after coffee, and I followed Hendro through town. Birds chirped. The sound of voices on the breeze, since there was no traffic, no sounds of mechanization at all, and we came to a long one story building with jalousied windows, gardens. This was the high school, Hendro took me into the headmaster's office, the school's English teacher came in, and we visited on a sofa, Hendro and the teacher translating.

"How glad I am you have come to Leksula," the headmaster said, placing a hand on my knee. "What has brought you here?"

It had a formality, we were two heads of state meeting on some official state visit, two representatives from far-apart worlds.

"I am a journalist and I want to see the world," I said. "Not just the parts where everybody goes, but the faraway parts."

"And what do you think of it?"

"It is beautiful and quiet," I said, "and it feels very far from home, even though your school looks very much like a school in America." This last point was only a little bit of a lie—all schools did kind of look the same, after all. "And," I said, "I have been received most graciously with such hospitality."

He smiled. Nodded.

They took me for a tour; we peeked into tidy, spare class-rooms with students sitting at desks in rows, and passed two poor boys standing by a flagpole in the courtyard, each balancing on one foot. "They're bad," Hendro said. "Always late."

A horn sounded, the *Star* announcing its departure. I had to go. Again.

The teacher and headmaster shook my hand, thanked me profusely for visiting the high school and Leksula, and Hendro walked me back, through the tropical heat and stillness and dogs and little garden plots. I felt embarrassed by my celebrity and by the generosity and curiosity of Hendro, Santoso, and the headmaster. To me I was bringing so little to them, offering them nothing. Why show me the high school? Why take time out of his day to sit with me? Why hold my hand? Why be so kind to me? I bore no gifts. I could give them nothing. But Hendro spoke English, and spoke it well; the high school of-fered English—it was the language of power and of the world, of opportunity and the future—and I was its representative who'd just dropped in one afternoon out of nowhere on the *Amboina Star*. It was hard for me to imagine going so gaga over an Indonesian dropping into town, almost anywhere in America. It wasn't like we'd been studying Indonesian for years without ever seeing a real Indonesian. It wasn't like we'd all dreamed about going to Indonesia—Jakarta as the most beautiful and biggest city in the world! Hendro lived in a tiny village on a re-mote island, idealizing everything his village wasn't, and I was an emissary of that ideal. The whole concept humbled me.

"You must come back again, for longer," Hendro said, beaming, on the deck of the *Star* as we stood surrounded by twenty passengers. "When you come back," he said, "we can find you a house in the village."

SOON WE WERE OUT on the water again, nothing but sea and sky and crowded ship and village after village. This time a big swell was coursing in toward the beach, and the *Star* rolled heavily. A child vomited repeatedly, the puke running down his father's leg and foot, a man with teeth as black as old wooden boards from betel-nut chewing, as my fellow passengers stared listlessly in their nausea. Overhead, frigate birds circled round and round, and flying fish glided over the wave tops. "Up in there," said Alex, the second engineer, pointing to the verdant mountains of Buru, "there are cannibals." He touched his arm knowingly. "They eat you."

Toward dusk, great gray clouds moved overhead and we left Buru and headed out to sea and rolled and pitched in a darkness without stars, a wood-and-steel speck in a vast ocean. It was in conditions like these, on nights like this, that ferries went down and disappeared, lost forever along the capillaries of a still-large planet.

Mumbai: The city's cattle class train commute has put a big question mark over the future of a brilliant sixteen-year-old girl. Raushan Jawwad, who scored over 92 percent in her class X examination a few months ago, lost both legs after being pushed out of a crowded local train near Andheri on Tuesday.

—Times of India, *October 17, 2008*

SEVEN

The 290th Victim

"EVERYTHING IN THAT BOOK is true," said Nasirbhai. It was almost 100 degrees, the humidity of the Arabian Sea pressing down, and he was wearing a white dress shirt over a sleeveless undershirt, pleated black slacks, and black oxford shoes. Small scars were etched around brown eyes that studied me from a wide, inscrutable face; a big stone of lapis studded one finger, and a silver bracelet dangled from his wrist. He had a barrel chest and his hands hung at his sides, ready, waiting—never in his pockets. He looked immovable, like a pitbull, like a character from another time and place, and in a way he was. "That book" was *Shantaram*, the international best-selling novel written by Australian Gregory David Roberts, who'd escaped from prison in Oz and found his way to Bombay two decades ago, where he'd become deeply involved with its criminal gangs and Nasir—who always carried the honorific *bhai*, "brother."

"We met in the 1980s," Nasirbhai said, standing on a corner in Colaba, one of Mumbai's oldest neighborhoods and its tourist epicenter, the streets lined with vendors selling tobacco and sandals and newspapers and bangles, pedestrians as thick on the sidewalks as attendees at a rock concert. Roberts was famous now, a Mumbai legend, and through a friend of a friend had connected me to Nasirbhai, who agreed to take me deep onto the commuter trains of the most crowded city on earth, where the day's simple commute was a matter of life and death. "Traveling on these trains is very risky because they are so full," Nasirbhai said. "But people must be at work, they must not be late or their boss will fire them. They *must* get to their destination, so they lean out of the doors, hang on to the windows, climb on top of the train. They risk their life to get to work every day."

By population, the city—just nineteen miles across, with 19 million souls—was bigger than 173 countries. The population density of America was thirty-one people per square kilometer; Singapore 2,535 and Bombay island 17,550; some neighborhoods had nearly one million people per square kilometer. A never-ending stream of Indians was migrating to Mumbai, which was swelling, groaning, barely able to keep pace. In 1990 an average of 3,408 people were packing a nine-car train; ten years later that number had grown to more than 4,500. Seven million people a day rode the trains, fourteen times the whole population of Washington, D.C. But it was the death rate that shocked the most; Nasirbhai was no exaggerating alarmist. In April 2008 Mumbai's Central and Western railway released the official numbers: 20,706 Mumbaikers killed on the trains in the last five years. They were the most dangerous conveyances on earth.

As we threaded through packed sidewalks and streets toward Chhatrapati Terminus, still mostly known by its old British

name, Victoria Terminus (or VT for short), Nasirbhai talked
about his life and meeting Roberts. "I was a big man then," he
said. "Fighting every day. Drugs were my business. I sold hash
and brown sugar." Usually when he sold drugs to foreigners,
Nasirbhai did the deal and the transaction was over; dealer and
buyer went their separate ways. For some reason, however, he
and Roberts toked together. "I don't know why. Destiny. I loved
him. And then he started doing brown sugar and I hated him."
The rich smell of garbage and shit filled the heavy air, and
Nasirbhai guided me like a child, between lines of traffic and
careening buses. "If you're not like me you cannot live in this
city. You have to be tough." Roberts, like so many foreigners,
eventually disappeared, and Nasirbhai didn't hear from him for
fifteen years. He continued to live off the streets and deal drugs.
Then, in 2000, he was arrested. Set up. "I sold a lot of drugs to
Bollywood stars—I grew up with them, with superstars, including Fardeen Khan," the son of the late legendary director
Feroze Khan. For his deals, Nasirbhai used a taxi driver he
trusted. The driver had been arrested for selling heroin a few
days before, and, under pressure, had agreed to cooperate with
police. By the time Nasirbhai met Fardeen on May 4, 2001,
police from the Narcotics Control Board were waiting. "We
were just making the deal"—Nasirbhai had nine grams of
cocaine—"when a car came up in front and another in back.
They jumped out with guns. Fardeen hit the locks, said, 'What
do we do?' I said, 'nothing, there is nothing we can do. They
have guns.'"

The Bollywood star was released from prison in six days.
"His father got him out," said Nasirbhai, who spent eleven
months in Mumbai's notorious Arthur Road Prison. A few

years later, Roberts suddenly reappeared out of nowhere. A ghost, returned. And he wasn't running from the law anymore, smoking dope and shooting heroin in his veins. He was free, rich, and famous. "It was my destiny; I do not know what I did to deserve this. He told me to stop selling drugs and to reinvent myself. He paid for my house, my daughter's wedding, my kids' school, and now he pays me to work for him, only him. He is a man of his word and he saved me. First he became my friend. Then my brother. Then my boss and Godfather."

VT was like a huge funnel, sucking and channeling the hordes inside; sixteen ticket windows lined the walls, each with a line snaking fifty feet; all of India was here, lying on the floors, walking, running, selling, buying. The line moved quickly.

Nasirbhai barked a few words and out spit two tickets for fifteen rupees each—about twenty-five cents. We threaded and bounced through the jostling crowds, passed through a bank of inactive metal detectors into the vast departure hall, a vaulted, corrugated roof on cast iron pillars. Built by the British Raj between 1878 and 1888, it echoed Victoria Station in London. "I will show you my style of traveling," Nasirbhai said. "But first, chai." It was a constant ritual. Over the next three days, on seemingly every corner, every train station, Nasirbhai and I paused for the sweet milky tea, served in thin, hand-formed clay cups vigorously thrown to the ground or smashed into a bucket when we were done.

"Listen," he said, as we sipped our tea and a tide of people swept past, "It is very difficult to get inside a train, and once you get in it is more difficult to get out. Sometimes you have to get out three or four stations ahead because you won't have a chance later." Many Mumbaikers had commutes of two and three hours each way in and out of the suburbs. A long time to stand up, many had taken to riding the train the wrong way first, to the beginning of the line, where they might get seats. "But sometimes the train changes its route! They get stuck on the wrong train and have to start all over again! And sometimes you get so dirty from the train you feel ashamed. Sometimes it's so crowded you have to hang outside and there is a very small place between the train and the poles and you hit the poles and you're fucked. But what can you do? You must reach your job, man. It is fucking terrible."

We finished our tea, threw the cups on the ground, and strode down the platforms, six for the Central Line and one for the Harbor Line, some with waiting trains. Nasirbhai's eyes darted back and forth like he was scanning for roadside bombs. "Follow me," he said, dashing in the door of a waiting train and out the other side, to change tracks. "You've got to watch all the time. There is the right place to stand and the wrong place; you can get pinned with your hands up on the straps and you can get pickpocketed—people have a lot of practice. You have anything in your pockets? Camera? Wallet?"

I didn't; one of my cardinal rules of traveling was never to carry anything in my back pockets, and I kept my cash divided between the two front pockets, my passport and credit cards and most of my cash strapped to my leg.

"Be careful. You stay close to me. They will look you in your eyes. I meet them and say, 'Fuck you, man.' Do what I do, okay?" Sometimes, he explained, when it got really crowded he jumped in the cars reserved for handicapped riders. "And even that is crowded, jammed. People say, 'You look good, man.

Show me your [handicapped] card.' I say, 'You show me yours first.' Fights happen, man. People get killed for their seats." From his years on the streets Nasirbhai saw the world offensively, a place full of opportunists and thieves and danger lurking around every corner. He was a boxer on the ropes, his guard up every minute. The crowd was a current piling up on the platform like at the wall of a dam—saffron and crimson saris and men in blue jeans, and beggars shuffling on their knuckles. "With this crowd, the pickpockets come," Nasirbhai said. "They work the crowd. But listen, they don't have magic! They cannot stand far away and make your wallet or phone come to them. They must touch you. So never let anyone touch you anywhere in the world. The beggars are trained. 'Hello, hello,' they'll say, and they'll feel your pockets. They'll bump you once. You don't do anything. They'll bump you again, and you don't do anything—you think it's an accident. But they're watching your reaction; the third time they'll take your wallet or your phone." In the crowds, hanging on the straps, he warned, opportunists might try to block me with their elbows. But they'd never get Nasirbhai. "My eyes and my brains are how I make money. I can tell: he's a pimp; he's a robber. I have that judgment."

We pushed to the edge of the platform, the crowd building. Waiting. Anticipating. A train came. The crowd shifted; it was one entity. We shuffled to the left, we shuffled to the right. Where would the doorway stop? And before it did, sudden chaos—like the hike of a football on the line of scrimmage. One organism full of individual parts, we scrambled and pushed. The faces were hungry, desperate, and I grabbed the door's rail and pulled myself onto the train. "And it's early, man!" said

Nasirbhai, laughing, when we squished in. "Come, follow me." The vestibules were wide and big, but I followed Nasirbhai, squeezing past hot bodies, into the corridor between seats. The trains were industrial, no attempt made for comfort: metal floors, metal walls, metal benches facing each other in groups of two, bars on the windows, hundreds of handles hanging from the ceiling. Nasirbhai pushed me between the windows. It was his spot; there, standing with my ass in one person's face and my crotch in another's, my side to the wall, no one could pickpocket me, and fresh air streamed in through the window. Nasirbhai looked triumphant.

The train rocketed through Mumbai, north toward the suburbs. It stopped every few minutes and a mad rush ensued at the doorways. A stream of beggars moved through, including an exotic, sharp-featured woman with skin like mahogany and long black braids woven with marigolds and a red bindi the size of a quarter on her forehead. She wore a tight gold sari and a gold ring in her nose. Nasirbhai gave her a coin and I followed. She blessed us, touching our foreheads. There was something strange and beautiful about her. "A man," said Nasirbhai.

A man and little girl squeezed through and came to rest, standing, at the end of the bench. Nasirbhai touched the shoulder of the man seated on the end. He ignored Nasirbhai, who tapped again, harder, motioned with his hand to move. Nasirbhai had the look; you didn't mess with him. The man moved, the woman next to him moved, the whole organism squished more closely together to produce another six inches for the girl to sit.

Nearing Dadar station, we began working our way back toward the doorway. Nasirbhai pulled me tight against the walls;

we were in a dense crush, the doorways open, people hanging out. "You get ready," he said. As the train slowed, people ran up toward the doors, started grabbing the handles and swinging in—but there was nowhere to go, we were packed and already pushing out—and before we stopped the edges piled out, and we lunged and leapt onto the concrete. "I had a friend," Nasirbhai said, as we headed to a tea stand, "who chewed tobacco. He had to spit and when he leaned out to spit, his head hit a pillar and it was his last spit."

We moved to another platform over a bridge and steps that were shoulder-to-shoulder with people. Sometimes, Nasirbhai said, men just walked up and down the stairs in the crush feeling women. "They go up and down ten times. I don't understand it, but women, they get fucked. In India, if there weren't red-light districts, women would not survive."

We boarded again, this time staying near the open door. DO NOT LEAN OUT OF RUNNING TRAIN AS IT IS DANGEROUS AND CAN BE FATAL, read a sign. Which was like telling the ocean not to leak into a wooden ship. I leaned out, feeling a constant pressure on my back, a wall pushing against me that required resisting at all times. Electrical poles whipped by just six inches away. We cut through slums and past crumbling buildings, black with mold and dripping open pipes, makeshift tents of plastic tarp and string and old tires a foot from the train whipping by. Men and women dozed on charpoys—wooden beds—and cooked over open braziers two feet away.

At Thane station I noticed two battered and dented aluminum stretchers leaning against the wall outside the stationmaster's office. "We have an average of ten deaths a month within seven kilometers of this station," said Miland Salke, Kandivali's

deputy stationmaster, below a hand-lettered sign: LIST OF HOS-
PITALS AND UNITS IN THE NEIGHBORHOOD OF KANDIVALI. He
shrugged, waggled his head. Today, he said without emotion or
amazement, there had been three accidents. Just outside of the
station a man had walked up to the tracks and then, at the right
moment, laid his head down on the hot steel. He died instantly.
A suicide. At 1:00 a.m., nine hours before, the last Western
Line train of the night slid into Kandivali Station and cut a
fifty-five-year-old man into two pieces. He was trying to cross
the tracks. And a few hours later, as another Central Line train
pulled into Thane, the crowd ejected a young man out the door.
I could feel it, had just felt it as we'd pulled into the station like
a watermelon seed squeezed between your fingers. He, too,
died instantly.

It was now rush hour, and after another round of chai we
prepared for battle. Passengers ten deep waited on the platform
stretched out over 100 yards, the women—a riot of swirling
purples and blues and golds, of black braids and golden bracelets and bangles and nose rings—in their own group, angling
for the "ladies'" cars. A train came—they came in fast. It was
full, packed, not an inch to spare. The crowd became one again.
A thing. It moved forward. Left. Right. Slowly at first; you
couldn't know, after all, where the open doorways would pause.

Then, suddenly, an explosion, a riot, a volcanic eruption, a
struggle balancing on the edge of life and death.

The train was slowing. People burst from the doorways and
leapt into a crowd that was surging forward toward the very
same door. The struggle was short and violent; you pushed,
were pushed. Your body feels a crushing weight, a powerful
wave at your back. You cannot stop or even pause. But your feet

cannot move fast enough. You shuffle your feet forward, try to keep them under you. Your only hope is to grasp the door, a pole, a handle. Anything. There is punching. Elbows sharp in my kidneys. I see a man palm another man in the face. I am nearly at the doorway. The man in front of me falls—his body is being pushed, but his feet can't move fast enough—they get stuck at the step up onto the train. Another man falls onto his back—this is how people are trampled to death—and I am next. I grab the edge of the door to steady myself, to resist the surging weight and wall at my back, to pull into a place where there is no room. The men will be crushed. The crowd is a spasming muscle. One of the downed men shouts. Somehow, hands reach down and pull them up. A shoe is left behind; it will never be recovered. And then we're in. Tight, from hips to shoulders. I cannot move, but I must. To stay in the doorway is to risk death at the next station when the next violent pulse comes. "In ten years," Nasirbhai said, "you will need helmets and football pads just to travel to work!"

It was now dark, after 8:00 p.m., and I felt exhausted. "Come," Nasirbhai said, "I have some friends I want to see. They're all bad guys, but they're my family." We jumped off the train in the Muslim neighborhood of Mumbra, grabbed an auto rickshaw, and navigated through a swirling phantasmagoria of humanity. Goats. Donkeys. Beggars cross-legged in the streets as cars and rickshaws and motorcycles careened and inched around them. Women in full black burqas. Fish sizzling on grills and dangling carcasses and dust and noise. "Ten years ago there was nothing here; Mumbra was a village," Nasirbhai said. "There was a single bullock cart and you had to make a reservation if you needed it to take you anywhere." Now there

were one and a half million people living in four square kilometers.

We emerged from the rickshaw at a concrete apartment
building, and I followed Nasirbhai down an alley of rubble,
the building completely dark, without electricity. We wound
through narrow concrete halls and up concrete stairways, and
came to a one-room apartment full of shadows and dancing
candlelight. There was one chair, a television, a mattress pushed
up against the wall, and a poster of Mecca, and three men sat
cross-legged on the floor. One of them was old, with a single
tooth, wearing a skullcap, and was called Nima—grandfather,
said Nasirbhai—introducing me to his son-in-law's father and his
sons. As they talked in Hindi, someone brought out a chillum—a
hash pipe—and a ball of moist Kashmiri hash, which Nasirbhai
rolled and mixed with tobacco in the palm of his hand, back
and forth, back and forth, and packed it into the pipe. "I don't
drink or smoke anymore, since my mother died. It makes me
bad; I want to fight." He took a square of white muslin, wet it,
squeezed it, and wet it again and squeezed it tight and wrapped
it around the mouthpiece and we smoked, except for Nasirbhai,
the pipe passing around, as a little girl wandered in—the old
man's great-granddaughter—and plunked down in his lap and
two generations of the family got stoned together, and the hash
was good and sweet and the talk and language rolled and I wondered where I was and how exactly I'd gotten here and the world
seemed so varied and rich and beyond my comprehension. We
smoked a couple more bowls, the pipe passing round and round,
and by the time Nasirbhai and I were back on the train heading
downtown, it was nearly empty, just a big steel tube clacking
and rattling, the wind hot and smoky at the door, fires burning

on the tracks illuminating the dim shadows of hundreds of people walking and squatting in the night.

NASIRBHAI KNOCKED ON MY DOOR at six-thirty the next morning in order to hit the morning rush hour. "Come," he said. "I have been up since five and we must have breakfast and tea." We entered a café full of round wooden-legged tables topped with thick marble slabs, the walls covered with mirrors, the waiters all in dhotis and caps, with beards. "This place is very old," Nasirbhai said as we sipped tea. "It's been here since I was a boy and it is just the same."

We spent the morning fighting the crowds on the Churchgate line and, near noon, Nasirbhai took me to St. George's hospital, around the corner from Victoria Terminus. "Let's find some bodies," he said, "some victims of the trains, and you can see for yourself." That seemed weird and impossible, but he insisted, said he had a friend at the hospital who'd help. The hospital was a huge block of stone, built by the Raj in 1908, with arched windows open to the dust and heat. We stood in an open hall—hushed—as ceiling fans beat the humid air and the twittering of birds wafted in. A man sat in a wheelchair, his head swathed in bandages like a character in a movie; another man lay on a stretcher. Nasirbhai talked to people, stalked the halls and said his friend wasn't here—he had been injured on the train! It seemed a joke, but Nasirbhai didn't acknowledge the irony. "But don't worry," he said. "I am known and people will see me and come." Which people did, approaching him and whispering in his ear, until Nasirbhai barked "Come!" and took off out the front door.

We padded down the steps, walked around the hospital and down a cobblestone alley that turned into a crowded row of shacks and houses running alongside the hospital. Big black crows hopped and cawed; mangy dogs covered in scars, with drooping teats, lolled in the sun. Smoke. The reek of garbage. Geese and roosters pecked at the heaps of trash. We came to an eight-foot-high concrete wall, mottled black with mold and soot. A steel gate, crooked on one hinge, lay open. The flagstone courtyard of a small concrete building with a corrugated roof piled with broken chairs, the limbs of bare trees, a couple of rubber tires. Those big black crows everywhere. Watching. Waiting. Cawing. This was the hospital's mortuary.

Two men were sitting on a wooden bench. Nasirbhai strode up to them and spoke in rapid Hindi. "Sit down, Carl," he said, introducing me to Santosh R. Siddu and his son, Sanjay. Santosh, fifty-five, had a long brown face and a prominent, almost Roman nose, a thin mustache. He wore unhemmed plaid shorts, battered flip-flops, and a Nike golf cap atop his gray and orange-colored hair. His son was twenty-five, and sported a pair of hip, rimless glasses. Nasirbhai dug into his pockets and pulled out a chillum and a round pea of hash, and the Siddus passed the pipe around in the heat and sun and eerie cawing. When we were done Nasirbhai said, "They do the postmortems for the hospital and they will tell you anything; you can ask them anything and they will show you anything."

I followed Santosh inside: the room was twenty feet square, unpainted concrete, black with age and mold. Two marble tables stood in the middle; haphazardly spread across one of them, and on shelves in a corner, were plastic jars. "Spleen," Santosh said, pointing to one that looked like a sponge soaked in blood. "Intestines. Heart. All of these are filled with body parts." A white enamel tray held a stainless-steel hammer and chisel, a pair of scissors. They had dark stains, bits of something. I had a feeling of dread; it felt hot and cold at the same time. "We have a minimum of two or three bodies every day from the trains," Santosh said. "Maybe seventy-five percent are unknown, and sometimes the bodies are so destroyed we can't tell much. Sometimes suicide, sometimes they're drunk, sometimes they are old and get jarred so much in the crowd they have a heart attack." A goose honked and poked its head into the room. Death—raw, banal death—hung in the air. So much ceremony surrounded death, gave it meaning, raised it to sadness and glory, and nowhere was that truer than in India. Except this felt like I was seeing the man behind the curtain. One minute you were riding a train to work or to hang out with your family, the next you were cut up on a marble slab in a hot, dirty concrete room. Dead. No glory. No future. A piece of meat. Santosh poked around in a corner piled with papers and pulled out a log book. "Today Balkishan Kakoram. Forty-seven years old. Hindu. He was traveling and fell. He is railway postmortem number 290." That was, the 290th victim within eight to ten kilometers of the hospital this year. He had died an hour and a half before our visit. "The station sweepers take the body and the railway police bring it here." In the last twenty-four hours there had been four deaths. One had lost his arm, two their heads.

Santosh led me out of the room, to a tiny antechamber with a corroded steel door with a refrigerator-like handle. He pulled it open. The smell of death made me gag. I almost vomited. A dark room. Bodies lay on shelves. A crumpled, bent, contorted figure lay in a pool of liquid on the floor. Meat. Human meat caught in the mad wheels of the daily grind. A commute that chewed you up and spit you out, so mammoth an assembly line of human movement going so fast that not everyone could keep up.

The crows cawed. Santosh shrugged. "One of them, a man, his whole right side is gone; his liver is gone."

A call came; a doctor was heading over from the hospital to watch Santosh perform the postmortem on Balkishan Kakoram. He threw on a plastic apron and some rubber gloves and we went outside. He finished quickly. Fifteen minutes later he came out and we squatted in the alley and drank tea, and father and son smoked another bowl of hash. Three small boys played a game of cricket with a chipped bat against the mortuary wall. "He went for his job and didn't reach his office. The train came into VT station at nine-thirty this morning and he jumped off but he jumped the wrong way and his ankle got caught and he broke it and fell and hit his head." Father and son were close; they leaned on each other, bumped bodies, held hands, draped their arms around each other. And they lived next door to the gruesome place. "He fell hard; his brain was full of blood." Sanjay was twenty-five and would take over from his father, who'd been conducting this grim business for twenty-eight years. "I can do ten a day," Sanjay said, taking a long draw off the pipe. "But some bodies come in decomposed and there are many maggots and gangrene and my father has to do it. I can't. The bodies smell so bad I faint."

Another round of the pipe; Nasirbhai knew his stuff, knew how to make people talk. "But it is hard, you can't bear it," said Santosh. "Any normal person would faint within minutes."

"We drink together," said Sanjay.

"I must eat after a postmortem," said Santosh. "Meat. Lots of meat and drink!" They jostled each other, laughed loudly. But it was a mask. "Without drink," said Santosh, "you cannot do this job."

"When I travel on the train," Sanjay said, taking a long hit off the pipe, "I am very cautious."

IT WAS TIME FOR ME to leave Mumbai; I wanted more crowds and decided I'd push on to Bangladesh via a train to Kolkata. Nasirbhai said he'd get my ticket, and late that afternoon I hopped on the back of his motorcycle and we ripped through the streets of Colaba. Every streetcorner had groups of men and boys lounging, sitting on cars and motorcycles and curbs, and Nasirbhai roared from corner to corner, pausing, talking, introducing me. There was an army here, just sitting and waiting and watching, and soon Nasirbhai had them getting me a ticket. I paid in advance, and he said my ticket would appear at my hotel that evening. "Don't worry," Nasirbhai said. "You will get your ticket. They wouldn't dare not come through."

Which they did, and at five the next morning I threaded past rows of bodies wrapped in blankets and scarves lying on the sidewalk, to VT. The waiting room was a mass, a formless huddle of color and sleeping bodies. There were hundreds, all packed close into a square, touching; since Indonesia I had this increasing picture of the world as a place with masses and masses of people huddled together, touching, always touching each other. Nobody seemed to mind; they expected it, felt comfortable with it—craved it, in fact. I had asked for fourth class, but it turned out my ticket was in third, technically known as non-air-conditioned three tier, which was an open space of eight bunks. The train was battered, dented, scraped, with bars on the windows and swept clean, as all things in India are. I showed my ticket to people and they pointed me onward, until I found the right place, which was soon filled with five of us, as men chained and padlocked their bags to steel wire rings beneath the bottom benches. We pulled out at six on the dot and fifteen minutes later hit another station, where more people piled on, three women in yellow and purple saris, with a small barefoot girl, squeezed onto the bench next to me. A man asked to see my ticket; suddenly he started yelling at another man sitting on a bench with his legs extended. He yelled back; an explosion erupted; the man grabbed the seated guy's knapsack and threw it to the ground, grabbed the guy's lapels, pushed him violently. They both sat, fuming, and the young one said to me, in English, "This is ridiculous!" We passed fields, the shiny brown backsides of people relieving themselves, some of the 600 million Indians without toilets. Cattails. The sky white. Rice fields between dikes. A searing, dusty wind blew in through the window.

Someone shook my shoulder. I woke with a start, lost for a minute, unsure of where I was. The conductor, in a black blazer and white pants. "Ticket," he said. I handed it to him. He studied it. "Your ticket is not right!" He pointed to the man who'd had the violent outburst. "I will reaffirm and return," he said, marching off. Fifteen minutes later he came back. "Your ticket is affirmed," he said, "but it is not for here. You must move."

I pulled my bags from under the bench. People stared, as I squeezed and bumped through crowded aisles down six cars.

"Are you Washington?" said a man with a gray mustache, glasses, and gray pinstriped slacks, his bare feet wiggling in the air.

My ticket said where I lived instead of my name.

"You are late, but you are welcome!"

I squeezed in. Directly across from me sat a young couple, she in gauzy saffron sari and shawl that covered her hair, with a gold nose ring; he with a small beard and thick, heavy lips. They eyed me suspiciously, four brown eyes burrowing into me. The train rattled and shook, the noise roaring, wind pouring in, sometimes thick with the smoke of burning trash and burning fields. Goats munched on stubble. Cotton fields and bullock carts, a now blue sky, the endless fields and villages of mud brick of the motherland passing by hour after hour. A stream of beggars slid, skidded, and shuffled by. A man with no legs. A boy with no toes, his foot just a formless round ball. A man with no eyes in a soiled dhoti, led by a withered-looking woman singing a haunting melody. When the man with the mustache gave a coin, so did I. Chai sellers. Sellers of newspapers and magazines. I quickly became covered in dust and grime. At noon a man in a uniform came by and rattled away in fast Hindi. "Do you want lunch," asked Mustache.

"Yes," I said.

He returned a few minutes later with paper plates of dal and naan and a vegetable curry, but there wasn't enough to go around. Mustache insisted I take his. I tried to refuse, but he wouldn't hear of it. I tucked into Raymond Chandler's *Farewell, My Lovely*, even though reading on trains or buses often felt unnerving. Books sweep you up, take you away, transport you. I read Philip Marlowe's gritty tromp through 1930s Los Angeles and stopped and looked up and felt totally lost. I wasn't in 1930s Los Angeles or my living room or on my front porch. I was on a train hurtling through India. Suddenly I felt the dirt and heat and wind, and an utter aloneness, strangers crowded against me. It was one thing to be in it constantly, to be focused and present, another to forget it and myself for a few minutes, and then to be suddenly conscious of where I actually was—the puddles on the bathroom floor, so many eyes staring at me, all alone rattling through India. Which sent me into overwhelming feelings of alienation and disconnect, feelings that had been slowly growing with every mile, especially since Indonesia. Desperate to talk to someone, to touch, to feel love and human warmth—that was the flipside of my wandering. No matter whom I talked to in my travels, whether it was Moussa on the train in Mali or Fechnor in Mombasa or Daud on the *Siguntang*, I couldn't kid myself. They were fleeting connections, shallow and temporary and no substitute for the real thing. As the steel train clacked and shook and rattled and a man with a leg twisted at some impossible angle hobbled by on wooden crutches, I wondered what I was doing there. For the first time I wondered if I'd been fleeing from human connection itself. If that's why I felt happy on muddy dirt roads in the farthest Amazon—not the escape from bills and deadlines, the mundane details of everyday life—but from the emotional tentacles of human intimacy. Out here I could miss my family, my crazy parents and my friends. I could fantasize that I was a whole person who was just away for a job. There must be a reason, I had to admit, that I couldn't stay home, that I always sought another adventure, that the idea of spending five months away from home on the world's worst conveyances felt so good, that escape was so much part of my life. It was a stark realization. It hit me hard. It crashed down on me, swallowed me up. I scribbled in my notepad: I wanted to be known, not just for a few days by strangers passing me on conveyances. The truth was, I had a fear that if people really did know me, they'd flee, and I hadn't felt known or understood by anybody for a long time because I'd hidden myself from them, kept them away. I looked around. Poor old Fechnor in Africa, still sad over the charcoal seller with trading in her blood; he and I, we were both hiding in places where no one could ever really know us.

By nine that night I was rattled. I had been sitting bolt upright on a hard bench by the open window for fifteen hours. Every muscle and bone in my body ached. I was hungry. The woman across from me winced, rubbed her stomach in distress, picked her nose. Her husband spat out the window, a tiny drop hitting my face, showed her his gums. And I was cold now and covered with a layer of black dust, my hair stiff and gritty.

I thought of Santoso holding my hand on Buru and how good that had felt. Maybe it was all starker in places like India and Indonesia or Africa, where family was everything, where there was no personal space, where there was no being alone, where everyone felt deeply connected to their home. Could I reconnect?

Couples rarely publicly embraced in India; there was no such thing as a public kiss even in Bollywood. But the staring couple across from me sat close; her head lolled on his shoulder as she fell asleep to the shaking train and the heat.

Mustache peeled an orange, broke it in two, and handed me half.

Emergency crews scoured a turbulent river today for more than 500 passengers missing and feared dead after an overcrowded ferry capsized in southern Bangladesh. Strong currents hampered the search for the triple-deck ferry, which sank Tuesday night with about 750 people on board, where three rivers—the Padma, Meghna and Dakatia—meet. The ferry capsized as it approached a terminal at Chandpur, 40 miles south of the capital, Dhaka.

—New York Times, *Thursday, July 10, 2003*

EIGHT

I Can Only Cry My Eyes

"OH MY GOD! This plane is so old!"

"It smells like sweat!"

"I've got some perfume."

This plane was a Biman Airways Fokker F-28 headed from Kolkata to Dhaka, Bangladesh, and I was boarding in the midst of the Chennai American International School's girls' soccer team, a pod of energetic seventeen-year-olds in sweatpants en route to a soccer tournament in Dhaka. The plane didn't look too bad, I thought. The carpet was worn thin, my seatback didn't recline, the upholstery was horrid orange and green flowers, but it appeared as airworthy as any other. Sitting next to me was a young Bangladeshi with a bouffant, pointy black shoes, long sideburns, and an embroidered shirt with white snaps, who worked for Iran Air in Dubai and was going back home to see his family. His wife, as it turned out, worked for Biman.

I asked him how many planes Biman had. He had to think.

"Working? Six right now. They have many others, but corruption is the problem. But these Fokkers are good."

"Is it safe?"

He threw up his hands, tilted his head toward the sky. "God knows!"

I can't say I'd ever had much of a desire to go to Bangladesh, but its ferries were the stuff of legend. There were a lot of them and they sank. All the time. The statistics were horrific, some 20,000 ferries plying 24,000 kilometers of inland waters, only 8,000 of which were registered, and of those, only 20 percent were officially "fit to operate." More people died on ferries in Bangladesh than on ferries anywhere else—some 1,000 a year (between 1904 and 2003 there were exactly zero passenger fatalities on U.S. ferries). Between 1995 and 2005 a ferry sank nearly once a month, the vast majority from overloading and collision. On April 20, 1986, 200 died when the *Atlas Star* sank in the Sitalakya River. A month later 600 drowned when the *Samia* overturned in the Meghna River. The grim list went on and on, and often the actual death toll wasn't even known, since no one ever knew how many people were on the ships in the first place. Five hundred when the *Salahuddin-2* went down in the Meghna in 2003. Four hundred dead in the Meghna near Chandpur. The situation was so bad the minister of shipping had thrown up his hands and said, "Ultimately it's up to passengers to decide not to board ferries that are too crowded."

It was one thing to read about Bangladesh and those ferries, another to see it and experience it firsthand. After checking into my hotel, I persuaded the bellman, named Taz, to hit the docks with me—I had no guidebook for Bangladesh, no map, no idea of anything beyond the macabre numbers. Dhaka, though, was like the human equivalent of those *National Geographic* specials in which a camera is inserted into a beehive or termite nest to reveal a teeming sea of bodies, so many you can't fit them in your mind. I had never seen so many people—154 million in a landmass the size of Iowa, a population density of more than one thousand people per square kilometer. It was 15 kilometers to Sadar Ghat, the port, and it took us an hour and a half by taxi. "In a few years," said Taz, "we'll only be able to walk again; there are just too many cars." We sat parked in traffic without moving for ten minutes at a stretch. "Look at this building," he said, pointing to a hulk of demolished concrete. "It used to be twenty-four stories. But it was illegal, built too close to the road. The government said it had to be torn down, but the builder was a famous man and the prime minister said, 'If you pay me it can stay.' That's how things work here. But he wouldn't pay; I don't know why. So the army came and broke it. Fifteen people died in the breaking." We squeezed into and through the streets of Old Dhaka. A man, stark naked, walked by. Hand-painted wooden carts piled twenty feet high with barrels and boxes, PVC pipe. Tens of thousands of bicycle rickshaws, each a work of folk art, painted with elaborate peacocks, rockets blasting to space, Dollywood film stars with big beating hearts and enormous eyes, and plastered with old CDs and mirrors. Buses that looked like they'd been taken through a car wash that used sledgehammers, steel claws, and mud instead of buffers and water. Ancient wooden carriages drawn by two ponies and piled with people.

But the river. The Burganga River fulfilled my image of a romantic eastern port like nowhere I'd ever seen. You could almost walk across it on the thousands of wooden pinnaces powered by a single scull. Boats are form and function, their vernacular—if untainted by fiberglass, as these weren't—are design perfection borne of local water knowledge. Seventy-foot bulk carriers with high bows and waists nearly at the waterline puttered past equally graceful small wooden water taxis packed with women in blue and gold and red saris. Crumbling slums elbowed hard against the banks, 500,000 souls, our boatmen said, in the immediate area. Heat and smoke. Laundry drying on the concrete banks. Incomprehensible numbers of people. The streets had been choking and close and acrid with exhaust; the river was flowing with life, open, a breeze riffling silver-brown water. And, of course, big white steel ferries, human freighters really, that lined the banks by the hundreds. They were battered and dented and carried thousands. Three thousand in the smaller ones, 5,000 in the larger ones. They plied short passage routes and I wanted to go as far south as I could, so Taz and the boatmen directed us up the river, and we bumped against the most fantastic craft I'd ever seen.

The PS *Ostrich* carried an odd nickname—the Rocket. She was 235 feet long, thirty feet wide, a double paddle-wheeled ship weighing 638 tons and built by the British Raj in Calcutta in 1929. It was two stories of rusting, dented steel hung with burlap and an official capacity of 150 tons of cargo and 900 passengers, which regularly swelled to 3,000. A tall Bangladeshi wearing a plaid madras lunghi and a white muscle T-shirt showed us around. Long and low-slung, it had first-class cabins opening off an ornately carved wood-paneled dining area and lounge; second class was in the stern, each cabin with a small sink and two bunks; the masses slept on broad but shaded decks. We wound around a labyrinth of stairways and over rooftops to a concrete room in which sat five serious-looking men with betel-stained teeth, who discussed my passage to a place called Khulna, twenty-eight hours downriver.

"What food do you eat?"

"Any food," I said. "Bangladeshi is good." They nodded.

"Do you need a special room, or can a Bangladesh man share a room with you?"

"No problem," I said.

"OK," they said, "you are most welcome to come. We had a foreigner once who needed special food and his own special place. That is a problem."

The *Ostrich* was scheduled to leave at 5:45 the next evening, so I gave myself two hours to get to Sadar Ghat, but a block from the river the taxi stopped, totally surrounded by cars and rickshaws and pedestrians and horses and donkeys and motor-cycles. "I can't get any closer, boss," the driver said. I pulled my bags out, and was set upon as if I were a fumbled football by a dozen crazed porters wanting to carry my bags. I grabbed one, handed him my bag—two other guys pounced on him, trying to rip them off his shoulders, but we fought them off and plunged into the crowd. Down a set of muddy, trash-strewn concrete stairs, fires burning on the banks, and onto a floating steel pier, the ferries docked bow-in, a line of them stretching for two hundred yards. And across a wooden gangplank onto the *Ostrich*, which was now a teeming city herself, gorged with people. I picked my way over them and through them, up a narrow wooden stairway, to four wooden doors near the stern—my second-class cabin. I'm not sure why, but I'd decided to take a bed. It was a moment of weakness; I'd slept on a lot of floors, had been squished and elbowed for months and I wasn't in my twenties anymore. Or so I convinced myself. Looking at that steel floor, I'd forked over the cash for a bed. The man who'd showed me around the day before appeared; now he was wearing a red double-breasted jacket and black slacks. "I'm Ashisha," he said, "and I am the first-class steward. You are welcome to eat in first class if you'd like. And if you need anything, anything at all, then you just tell me."

Under a moon full and round and almost gauzy in the tropical night, the *Ostrich* shuddered and thumped, and we pulled out into the current. Boats were everywhere in the river, lit with flickering oil lamps. I leaned on the rail, and young men crowded around me, thousands of insects buzzing around the bare lightbulb on deck.

"Do you have an agent here?" asked a young man who introduced himself as Nipu Hossain.

"An agent? For what?"

"For tours, hotels, tickets. I can get those things for you instantly. And if you see something interesting, something you like, a sample of cloth, say, I can ship it. You and me. We can have a good business. You need a business partner."

"No thanks," I said, explaining that I was just traveling.

"Business can be good!"

"I'm sorry," I said, "I'm not interested in any business."

"This is very easy, and the profits can be large."

I looked him in the eye. "I'm not going into any business with you."

"Yes, I see," he said. "But the profits can be very good. All you have to do is to take my card and if you, say, have a friend who likes things and if you connect us, I will give you a percentage. As a gift!"

We slid past a mile of shipyards, steel hull after steel hull appearing as dark shadows on the beach, sparks flying from welders' torches, flashes of heat lightning in the blue-black sky. Nipu and Sunam Roy, twenty-five, taught me Bangla. *Ami cha chai*: I would like some tea. *Dhonno baad*: thank you. *Dam koto*: how much?

"We are so poor," said Roy, who lived in Chandpur with three families in a single room. "Culture is all we have."

I suggested we have some tea, and we walked into the center of the ship, jammed with huddled masses on the floor. At one end stood a counter piled with packs of cookies and chips and nuts, sodas, a kettle of boiling water on one side and a man sitting cross-legged on the top, in front of a wooden cash box. I asked for a cup of tea, and men moved over, making room for us on the single bench reserved for tea drinkers in front of the stand. "Foreigner," I heard, rippling through the crowd. We were tight, hip-to-hip and shoulder-to-shoulder on the bench, touching, always touching, in every passageway and in front of the snack bar. I asked about so many sinking ferries, and mentioned the statistic that a thousand a year drowned.

"It's not so many," said Roy. "And most get afraid and lose their senses. Are you alone?"

"Yes."

"Why? Where is your family?"

I tried to explain that I was traveling for work, but even that left them puzzled. I was feeling a little testy; it was hard to keep open to the crowds and the same questions all the time.

"Aren't you cold?" they asked. The night was balmy and warm, but they shivered. "It is winter!" they said.

The hours ticked by and the men pressed in. I was surrounded all the time, the questions thrown over and over again: Where was I from? Was I alone? Why? What did I think of Obama? Finally I escaped to bed.

At midnight I awoke to cocks crowing. At 5:00 a.m. my roommate's cell phone rang. At six I went out on deck, to a pink horizon, thick clumps of green water hyacinths floating in the khaki river. We turned up another river at eight, hard against wide expanses of swamped land in which water buffalo waded, past rice fields and thatched shacks, from which men, women, and children emerged to stare at the old steamer throbbing by.

The snack-bar cashier never moved, sitting cross-legged on the bar in front of his box all day and night, and he gave me a discount. In a corner a man stood talking into a microphone, his voice booming and distorted, the deck so crowded it was hard to move. A pair of teenage girls covered in black, only their brown eyes showing, sat on the tea bench, their eyes swooping over everything, and me, staring at me, elbowing each other, taking it all in. "That man is selling medicine," said a man with a long beard and skullcap. "Take it and you will feel better! I don't believe it, though."

His name was Hasan, and he'd just retired after fourteen years as a bellman at the Intercontinental Hotel in Riyadh, Saudi Arabia. "I will now go into the stock business," he said. "I will buy, hold, and then sell. In Saudi, it is a Muslim country. A woman can't go out without a head covering, but my country is a little bit more free."

"Which do you like better?" I asked.

"Well, we are a Muslim country so that is our way, but a little bit more free is good."

Around lunchtime, Ashisha appeared, inviting me into the

first-class salon. I felt guilty, but I went anyway, cutting through the massed humanity, the jumbles, opened a door, and passed into another world full of Western children playing Monopoly and men and women who looked just like me, playing guitars and munching on cheese and crackers under the veranda on the bow. The women's hair flew in the wind, free, bare arms outlined in tight, short-sleeved T-shirts. Barefoot. Suddenly I saw them through the eyes of the men and women in their flowing robes and head coverings—so free, so cavalier with their bodies, no wonder men equated that with "easy." The children shouted at the waiters imperiously and climbed on the rails like they owned the ship. Everyone had space to lounge and spread on the sofas and big, comfortable chairs. It was a different world entirely, and it shocked me. I had barely spoken to another westerner in a month. They were so easy, so relaxed, so unhindered; they were like candy, like a drug, like an unbelievable luxury; five minutes in their presence and I didn't want to leave. I wanted to sprawl on the wicker sofa, sip a glass of wine, nibble on familiar crackers and cheddar, watch the children, who reminded me so much of my own. I wanted to hug them and tousle their hair. I wanted to talk and talk and talk, about whatever came to mind, without carefully picking my words. But I had to leave. It was like when I was reading and suddenly looked up in the Indian train, and couldn't believe where I was. But this was worse. It felt heartbreaking. Instead of that wild feeling I got bursting into the Amazon, I felt weary and homesick. I wanted my own children laughing and playing Monopoly and my own friends drinking wine. I had to run away; if I didn't I would have been swallowed up. And this was the worst part: hanging out with them threatened my ability to tolerate the tea stand amid the

multitudes and the crushing solitude of the crowd and the unre-
mitting poverty, which I didn't even notice when that was all I
saw. Up in first class the contrast was too great.

I asked Ashisha if I might see the captain, and he took me up
a flight of stairs to the roof and a small wooden pilot house, and
introduced me to Captain Lutfas Rahman, wearing blue denim
jeans and jacket, buttoned up tight despite the ninety-degree
heat, sitting cross-legged on the wooden chart shelf. The pilot
house was simple: a big old wooden wheel and brass throttle,
replaced by two stainless steel levers when the *Ostrich* had been
converted from coal to diesel in 1995; a GPS and a compass. It
had no radar. I asked him if the *Ostrich* was a good ship.

"No!" he said. "An old ship! A paddle-wheel ship is useless
now; where in the world is a paddle ship used? Nowhere but
Bangladesh!" He almost spat the words out. Shook his head.
The *Ostrich* was owned by the government, which had no
money. At least, he said, it was safe; it was the private launches
that sank.

"I would like a new, modern ship. With a screw instead of
paddles." He'd been on the water a long time, starting as a
deckhand in 1976, and he saw his wife and children in Dhaka
every Sunday evening and Monday morning, before returning
to Khulna again. It was a good job, but the pay was bad. "In
Dubai I could make 150,000 taka [about $2,000], but here the
government gives me just 20,000 taka [$290] a month. And
there are no instruments on this ship so we rely only on my experience, and the rivers change all the time. I have seen many
cyclones in my life. I have seen man, cow, horses, floating in the
river going to the sea. I look and think, but I cannot help. I can
only cry my eyes."

. . .

I WANDERED out of the pilot house and sat on the wooden walk-
way across the *Ostrich*'s roof, my feet hanging off the side, watching the river flow past. It was late afternoon. Quiet. The river
silvery blue, the banks green and lush. The sun strong, beating
down; beads of sweat rolled down my back and my forehead. I
wasn't alone long, though. A young man climbed the stairs, saw
me, and came over. He wore blue jeans and a T-shirt, and had
a satchel strung over his shoulder. I braced myself for another
wheeler-dealer, but Rokibal Islam was different. He was just
nineteen, on his way from home to university. He was smart.
Bright-eyed. And he told such a sad story, a story so common in
places like Bangladesh. His father was the principal of the local
high school. "But he was very, very honest. He believed in honesty, always. He told us that money wasn't everything, that you
should not be greedy." But his honesty was challenged all the
time. "Always people wanted money for his promotion. But he
would not pay. They couldn't fire him, but they could transfer
him. So they transferred him all the time and he rode his bicycle to many different schools. Once he was offered a job as a forest supervisor, but it was a corrupt job and he didn't take it and
gave the job to a friend who is very rich now. He has four houses
in Dhaka City." Instead, his father died of cancer when Rokibal
was fourteen. "We were so poor," he said. "We had no money
for tutors and then we had no money for school, even." Rokibal
read on his own, studied on his own, at home. He missed a year
of school. But he muscled his way back, graduating third in his
class. And now he was at university and thinking of a master's
degree.

At first I'd been worried, when he told me how poor he was, that he'd ask me for money, for help with a visa; so many did and I could do nothing for them. I felt guilty that those requests annoyed me. But he never mentioned it, and as the day turned to dusk and the river became a world of shadows for a few minutes, Rokibal told me about dating and dreaming and struggling, opening a crack into his world. He had a girlfriend, sort of, that he called on his cell phone, but it was no more than a little bit of talking back and forth. He would eventually marry someone arranged by his mother. "Yes, of course," he said, frowning slightly. "There is no other way."

IT WAS NEARLY MIDNIGHT when we docked at Khulna. We squeezed and jostled through the *Ostrich*, out over bouncing wooden planks, and onto dirt streets, dark and rutted. I spent three days in Khulna and it felt like the end of the world. I didn't know what day it was, what day of the week even; I had lost track of them. I was feeling just more and more out there, somewhere, alone on the planet. Tourists didn't come to Khulna, or not many of them, anyway. My plan had been to take the Rocket to Khulna, then find a local ferry farther south toward the ocean, deeper in. I asked my hotel the name of the port and climbed in a bicycle rickshaw and off he pedaled. There were few cars, which made it quiet. Hazy. Cool, dust in the air, on the streets, the rickshaw, the storefronts, everything. Toward the river, we bumped slowly—the pedaler straining, sweating, slower than walking—over potholed dirt streets lined with trucks in swirling red and blue and yellow, and handcarts piled twenty feet high with barrels and PVC pipes. Cows and goats wandered and munched on garbage and piles of pineapple stalks and sugar cane. We passed open shops stacked with metal sheeting, and factories welding steel cabinets and bed frames, men in salwar kameezes and lunghis, and women in black burqas. Rubble and chickens and people, people everywhere, thick and pungent. Once off the rickshaw, though, I couldn't find any ticket office, anybody who spoke English and could help me. Launches lined the wharf, but no one knew anything—just stares and shaking heads from old wrinkled men with few teeth and brown, weathered faces stained with betel nut and paan. It was like I was in a dream, a nightmare in which I couldn't communicate, couldn't cut through the lines of human interaction.

Finally, giving up, I returned to the hotel and persuaded the bellboy, whose name was Milton, to go with me, riding in the rickshaw in his black pants, white shirt, and tie, riding hip to hip, 300 pounds now, the driver drenched and straining. When I suggested it might be faster to walk, Milton shook his head, said no. And at the river, Milton found three men sitting at a desk in a wall-less room, in front of a weatherbeaten log book. They talked back and forth in Bangla, their heads shaking. "They don't understand you," Milton said. "They are ill-educated. Ignorant. They don't know why someone wants to travel; why you're here." But finally it was revealed. There were no boats heading farther south, only a few short-haul launches going back the way I came; to get to Dhaka the *Ostrich* was the only answer, and it wouldn't be back for another three days, leaving at nearly 3:00 a.m. "How about the train?" said Milton.

The train station was next door, and we found a hulking man sitting at an old oak desk surrounded by ancient-looking equipment and huge bound ledgers three feet long. A train left nightly at 8:00 p.m.

I spent two more days in Khulna and I walked through the streets a celebrity. I couldn't make it more than half a block without getting stopped, engaged in conversation. What country was I from? Why was I in Khulna? Was Barack Obama a Muslim? What was my profession? Bangladesh was the friendliest, most curious country I'd ever strolled through. I drank tea on a shelf carved into a tree on a streetcorner, got taken into the offices of a frozen shrimp importer, was given a tour of the local university by a boy accompanied by two young women covered except for their eyes. Workshops lined the streets, industry was personal and everywhere. Anvils rang and showered sparks. Shops made tin pails. Welders, all barefoot, squatted on dirt floors in shops the size of one-car garages. "Please, just if by some chance you meet someone interested in doing business in Bangladesh," said Hossain Lukman, who stopped me on the street. "I know, I know, but you never know and you give them my name and contact information. We are a family and business is our business. We are honest and we can make a good business. Bangladesh is very poor but we work very hard." I could barely get a word in; my protestations that I had no interest in business went unheard. Bangladesh was a place of worker ants, filled with tens of millions of them, curious, willing to do almost anything, eager for just about anything. Lukman was twenty-seven. "This is the honor of my family to be successful; it is very important right now." The second I said the word *American*, people touched their hearts, nodded their heads to the side in reverence.

. . .

THE TRAIN BACK to Dhaka was uneventful, but awful. I sat upright all night as doors opened and cold, damp air blasted in through the open windows and the train shook and rattled and distorted music roared, and we slid and bumped into Dhaka at dawn.

I STILL HADN'T TAKEN one of the thousands of private launches, though, and they were the real death traps of Bangladesh. So early the next morning I made my way back to Suder Ghat and bought a ticket to Chandpur, where hundreds had died in numerous sinkings and capsizings over the years.

Nose-in at a floating steel dock floated hundreds of battered, bent, rusting white steel ships, the waterborne equivalent of the matatus in Nairobi, the commuter trains of Mumbai. "Chandpur, Chandpur, Chandpur," touts called, and I slipped aboard. The launches were all the same: one large, open deck lined with benches facing the bow and, above, an open, flat deck with tables and chairs welded to the deck. Sometimes these took 3,000 passengers; today there were only a couple of hundred. I counted thirteen life rings, and no rafts or lifeboats of any kind. A bronze bell on the bow rang and we pushed away, into the current and crowds of the river itself, under a hazy blue sky and a burning sun. Freighters and small wooden *nowks*, as the little pinnaces were called, hundreds, thousands of them filled with people and bricks and stacks of wood, some so overloaded that their topside rails were literally underwater. We passed miles of brick factories, barren expanses of sand around a tall cylindrical smokestack, each one an almost pharaonic scene of hundreds of bare-chested men and sari-clad women carrying buckets of sand and piles of bricks on their heads. It was the world unfiltered, raw, the water flat and greenish, perhaps half a mile wide.

As I was eyeing paper plates of some chickpea food that a boy was delivering from the deck below, a tall, boyish-faced man plunked himself down in the chair in front of me and introduced himself. Mohammed Amir Hosain, to be called Fardus. He wore green khaki slacks and a pink checked shirt, and he had a face as round as a ball. "Would you like some?" he asked, and whistled, calling the boy over and imperiously ordering.

"I am a soldier," he said. "I am strong! Where are you from?"

"America." The golden word.

"America is my hobby!" he said. "Would you like to have lunch with me when we get to Chandpur?" There was something about him. Kind. Open. I trusted him. I said I would.

Fardus whipped out two cell phones, placed a call, paused, said, "Fish or chicken?"

"Either one," I said.

The chickpeas arrived, spicy and covered with onions and peppers and lime juice. Fardus insisted on paying. I suggested tea, and soon after, it arrived; once again I wasn't allowed to pay. The sun beat down and the breeze passed and the engine roared, and every now and then a wooden launch appeared alongside and transferred a few passengers. As we neared Chandpur a woman covered in black, only her eyes visible, appeared. Fardus's sister. He introduced us and I went to shake her hand; it came out, hesitated, and withdrew without our touching. "In our culture, no touching," he said. "But it's okay." Chandpur looked like how I imagined Zanzibar had appeared in Richard Burton's or John Hanning Speke's time—a cluttered bazaar, a world of garbage and wooden boats, some under sail, women covered in black and naked children glistening and shiny and playing in the trash-strewn water. A narrow market of wooden stalls pressed in on a mud street. Fardus paused and bought apples and oranges; again he refused my attempts to pay. We crossed railroad tracks and cut up a lane between walls with doors and waddling geese, and all three of us piled into a bicycle rickshaw and slipped past small houses fronting ponds covered in duckweed. It was silent, no cars or even auto rickshaws, just the tinkle of bicycle bells, hundreds of them, and the sounds of voices, commerce, and hammering as we passed a row of rickshaw workshops. "That's the government primary school," he pointed out. "The mosque."

People called out to him. "America!" I heard. "My mother's sister," he said. "My uncle. My cousin." Fardus was home; everyone knew him and he knew everyone and every corner and tree and building. He started calling me "brother Carl."

We bumped down the road, the driver straining with the weight of all three of us. "My mother is away on Hajj, brother Carl," he said. "My father is dead. He was a textile worker. My father's coffin is behind there," he said, pointing down a lane. We passed men and women bathing in ponds, scrubbing and lathered in soap, dropped his sister off at a corner, and jumped off at a tree-shrouded lane paved in bricks. We hung a left down a dirt path, and came to a door in a wall, which passed us into a yard and a garden and a small corrugated-metal house. Fardus's uncle, who had a long, stately nose, was waiting in a blue shirt and a lunghi with his two brothers, aged sixteen and nineteen. "We must wash," said Fardus, who went inside and emerged a minute later shirtless and barefoot in a green plaid lunghi. "This is my favorite one," he said. In the corner of the yard stood a pump, and we squatted around the pump scrubbing our faces and hands with fresh, cool water and a bar of soap.

A man appeared—I never knew who he was—and scurried up a coconut tree and started hacking coconuts off with a machete. Fardus expertly split them and emptied the water into a plastic pitcher, and then we all drank the semisweet juice, and munched on the fresh pulp. We went inside the house: one room with a double bed, another, bigger, with a double bed and table and television and wardrobe and a brand-new computer— they had no Internet connection—the ceiling bamboo, the floor bare concrete, smooth and cool to my bare feet. In a portico outside was a one-burner stove and some buckets, a woman with big eyes and a gold nose ring squatting in the dirt, cooking. It was a strange thing, a strange time. Fardus's English wasn't bad for the most casual conversation, but beyond the basics we couldn't really go. His brothers and uncle spoke no English; I was there, in their house, in their lives, but there were great chasms of miles, distance, culture separating us. The food was served and only Fardus and I ate, the others sitting on the bed watching. It was delicious, though: huge piles of rice and chicken and fish, hard-boiled eggs, green spinachlike vegetables. We ate with our hands, Fardus urging me on and on, displaying a hospitality and generosity that felt overwhelming. Again, I had so little to offer; nothing, in fact, but myself. As always, my feelings were complex. Part of it looked idyllic: a quiet village, closeness of family and town, a place where you could be known and loved by everyone. And part of me knew the idea terrified me. It was the fundamental struggle of my life, between being connected and being separate, between being part of a group and being alone.

Fardus and his brothers were enamored of America, so I gave my spiel—that it was hard work there, often cold and lonely, that people worked and worked and sometimes never realized the American dream. Families weren't close; old people were institutionalized; people lived alone, not like this, in beds squeezed together. I pointed out their garden, their coconuts, their two bedrooms, their family close together. "What more could you want?" I said. "In America," I said, "it wouldn't be easy to have this."

It was wonderful, but awkward and exhausting, too. And I had to leave to catch the ferry back to Dhaka. Fardus insisted on escorting me. The brothers and uncle lined up, I shook their hands, they touched their hearts and we left, this time squeezing into an auto rickshaw with three others and the driver, all touching each other. "I am going to quit the army in January," Fardus said, as we drank a quick cup of tea at the docks. "I'm going to go to Romania and work as an electrical contractor. I will make seven hundred dollars a month, while here I make seventy dollars a month."

I said nothing, just nodded and tried to understand, to empathize, and then it was time and we hugged and he waved goodbye as the ferry slid out into the river in the silver light of the late afternoon. But I couldn't help thinking it was a mistake— of the awful winter in Romania, of Fardus, warm Fardus, far from his family and village and his father's coffin and brothers and uncles and water pump and coconuts and fresh spicy fish in a cold and grim Romanian apartment working for nothing. How much could he save? What were the chances of being trapped there for years?

The captain invited me into the bridge, which had nothing.

No GPS. No radar. Not even a radio. Just a wheel. And then I walked downstairs and lay on a bench, sleepy, full, full of Fardus's world and Bangladesh and the river and my own loneliness and my failure to go deeper. Again I thought perhaps I should have stayed in Chandpur: a house, try to build a life; no, even then would that be deep enough? The diesels thundered and dusk came and I read Rohinton Mistry's *A Fine Balance* and men came up to me and stared, and then darkness fell, and I thought of Fardus and his fine balance between hope and despair. We were two hundred feet from the banks, passing old wooden dories and wooden freighters, unlit save for small fires burning on them, each a world unto itself. This river, flowing to other rivers, flowing to the ocean; the Amazon, the Mississippi, the Casamance, all part of one world and all different and all the same. I wanted to look into every boat, every house. I wanted to touch each person, to taste every meal, to open them up and slip into each like a suit of clothes. But I couldn't. The world was too big. Too diverse. There were too many languages and not enough time; it was easy connecting with people like the families in first class. We had a shared language, technology, worldview. We all loved prosciutto and Picasso and lying on the beach in the sun and sitting with friends in a café. But to pass the days with the poor was something else. I sat up, gazed into the darkness. We slid past a boat with no lights at all, just a black shadow, its gunwales underwater, the dim outlines of figures standing at the stern. The deeper I pushed, the harder it became to know them, the more ignorant, curious and powerless I was. Each was a world unto its own that I could glimpse but never know.

A speeding Blueline bus on Sunday hit a tree in New Delhi, killing a woman and injuring 20 people. The accident happened when the bus went out of control on the Ashok Road in New Delhi. The privately owned Blueline buses, dubbed "killer buses," caused 120 deaths on the roads of the capital last year and the toll this year has reached 19 so far.

—Hindustan Times, *March 23, 2008*

NINE

What To Do?

CIGARETTE WRAPPERS and paan wrappers littered the dirt. Noise, the constant clamor of horns and voices that never stopped in India. Long coils of rope lay on the ground next to the bus, as turbaned men from Rajasthan climbed a ladder with huge boxes balanced on their heads. The roof was already covered in burlap sacks three feet high, and more stuff was being hoisted up every minute. A queen-sized bed with a carved headboard. A sofa. A whole world was up there. Beneath the bus squirmed a man in a white T-shirt, black with grease and oil. The oil pan lay on the ground. We were supposed to be leaving for Patna, the capital of Bihar, in thirty minutes, which didn't look too likely.

Bihar was India's poorest state, with an illiteracy rate of nearly 50 percent. It was rife with banditry, murder, suicide, road accidents, and corruption. I thought it might be interesting to take the bus right through its midst.

Avoid traveling through Bihar at night, warned the *Lonely Planet* guide to India.

"My god, why would you take a bus to Patna?" wrote an Indian, when I posted a query about safety and logistics on the guidebook's Thorn Tree bulletin board.

"You must not take the bus," said a taxi driver. "The train."

I wasn't too worried, though. As a native Washingtonian who felt quite safe when D.C. had the highest murder rate in the U.S., it never surprised me whenever the alleged horrors of a place failed to materialize. Still, I liked to be prepared. Airport security in Kolkata had taken away the knife I'd had since Colombia; I bought a razor-sharp, handmade one from a vendor on the street and had a tailor at an open-fronted shop the size of a telephone booth sew me a sheath that I could strap to my leg. And hailed a taxi for Babughat, one of Kolkata's bus terminals. Which, of course, wasn't a terminal at all, but a chaotic, trash-strewn strip of dirt along the Hooghly River lined with buses, each with a sandwich board advertising a destination. Most were served by multiple buses, Patna just one.

It only traveled at night, leaving at 4:00 p.m. for the seventeen-hour journey.

But no worries! Ranjit Pandit clapped me on the back, said he was the driver, and we'd be on the road by 4:30 p.m. Even better, the bus had cramped berths over the seats in place of the luggage racks, and I booked one.

The assistant driver squatted on the ground and had the whites of his eyes washed. The professional eye cleaner waved his hands theatrically like a magician, swept a black chopstick through his oily and dusty hair, and scraped the sticks, covered in charcoal and hair grease, across the driver's eyeballs. He waved his hands. The driver blinked, his eyes tearing. More flourishes. The eye cleaner twirled a swab of cotton around the tip of the chopstick, dipped it in a glass bottle, and swabbed that across both glistening, bloodshot orbs. It looked horrendous.

At five the horn sounded; miraculously the engine was back together. We all piled in and lurched through Kolkata traffic as the sun dropped, the window at my berth open, babies screaming, my stomach cramping for the first time on my journey. The air was acrid, smelling of diesel and exhaust and shit, a layer of grit and dust streaming in and covering me. The city looked like it had been scooped up into a big cup, shaken violently for a decade, and then dumped on the ground.

In the end, though, I had no complaints about my journey to Patna. The bus was full, the aisles taken by fifty-kilo bags of rice. The knife was unnecessary. I was, as usual, in a cocoon of generosity and watching eyes. Ranjit handed me a down pillow covered in red velvet; the wind (and dust) streamed in from the open window at my shoulder; we stopped every three hours for a break—twenty-five men standing (or squatting) in a line like some grotesque Roman fountain. The first stop almost made me retch. We stood in a line next to roadside stalls, a trillion insects flying and buzzing in the lights, pissing into a trench that had years of plastic water bottles, plastic wrappers, toilet paper, and reeked of shit and piss. Then I remembered doing the same thing in Peru, in the rain as we descended toward Puerto Maldonado, and I laughed; around the globe right at this very minute, probably, were lines of men and women pissing in mountains and on highways and in jungles next to battered buses.

This journey to Patna and back was Ranjit's life. He was thirty-six, earned 300 rupees (US$6.00) for each trip, seven days a week. I asked him where he lived. "Here," he said, patting the bunk across from mine, which he shared with his co-driver. It was a telling answer, for he had a wife and two sons in Kolkata. He saw them between morning and afternoon departures, but the bus to Patna was where he lived. "But you must come back to Kolkata and call me and bring your family," he said, writing his cell-phone number in my notebook.

We watched three Bollywood films on the twenty-inch TV bolted to the door between driver and passenger sections. "The hero!" Ranjit said, pointing to the hero. "That man," he said, "is about to get slashed with knives." A band of circling motorcyclists slashed the actor with knives. Then everyone broke out in song and dance, the lovers flitting among palm trees as the bus honked and inched past bullock carts and tractors. Ranjit knew every scene; he'd watched them all an untold number of times. But he delighted in them all the same, could barely take his eyes off the screen. The romance, the singing, the sudden outbreaks of violence, the family struggles and redemption, were formulaic, yes, but they spoke so clearly to Ranjit's soul that there was something comforting and amazing about it. Popular American films were all about alienation and individuality; even in romantic comedies the lovers existed almost in a vacuum rather than in the big Indian family.

We pulled into Patna at 10:00 a.m. I was so covered in dirt, I looked like Pigpen. But an elephant was walking down the street, and the city was a dynamic jumble of brokenness and blacktop covered in sand and cows munching in piles of garbage.

I didn't linger, though. It felt like I'd been on the road for a long time, moving constantly, barely a conversation with a native English speaker. I felt tough, road-hardened, able to endure anything and eat anything and talk to anyone. But there was a price: I was aching for connection; my family felt far away in time and space, and being already separated from Lindsey didn't help. E-mails were becoming more rudimentary, perfunctory. As for friends, e-mails from them had been slowly trailing off. I was just out there. Somewhere. I did have friends in New Delhi, though, and Thanksgiving was approaching; I was eager to get there. The Majhdad Express left at eight that night, and the train station was a carnival of all India: a couple with two monkeys on ropes, women with gold toe rings and silver anklets, wrapped in brilliant purple and saffron and sky blue. A man with his hands and forearms chopped off shook the stubs in my face. A small boy lay huddled on newspapers. A blind man led by a blind wife stumbled along with a tin cup. I sat on a concrete bench, squeezed between two men. Another came up, thrust his hips and shoulders against me, wedged himself in. A man with only one eye and a little girl in bare feet came over, pushed my shoulder with his hand, then pried them both in. We were completely squished together. It was beautiful and ugly and full of life, but also otherness, an otherness I couldn't hope to pierce. And the more I was in the middle of it, the lonelier I felt, the loneliness of the crowd exposing my solitude. I was like a walking ghost, a presence among the throngs, but unnoticed, unseen by them, too.

It got worse on the train. My plank was three tiers up, removed, swarming with mosquitoes. We rattled and roared and shook through the night, a cold wind chilling me to the bone and covering me with Mother India's omnipresent gritty dust. I passed the long night in a fetal position. Shivering. But a few hours later I was showered and shaved and deep in a sofa within

the comfort of my friends' silent and spotless New Delhi apartment.

THINGS HAPPEN when you least expect them. But, I suppose, you
have to be ready for them in the first place, even if you don't
know you are. My friends took me to a chichi dinner party at
a grand house with high ceilings and a roaring fireplace and
wine and a meal cooked by their chef, and the next morning I
could barely get out of my big soft bed. After months of street
food and the tap water of Mumbai and Kolkata and Dhaka,
Delhi's Belly had found me. A fever coursed through my body.
I ached, and the Cipro I popped hit back, covering my face with
hives.

Then terrorists struck Mumbai. Outside Leopold Café,
where I'd met Nasirbhai two weeks before, gunmen sprayed automatic gunfire and lobbed hand grenades. And at Victoria
Terminus, the locus for all our commuter train adventures,
more than fifty people were killed. My hosts disappeared; she, a
diplomat, became swallowed by the unfolding attack and hos-
tage crisis. Her husband, a journalist, jumped on a plane to
Mumbai on Thanksgiving morning, leaving me, again, alone.
"Go to the Thanksgiving dinner we were invited to anyway,"
my friend said in a call from the airport. "I'm sure it'll be okay;
just tell him the situation. And bring the case of beer I was supposed to."

I still felt a little sick, not to mention awkward asking a
stranger to let me come to his Thanksgiving dinner, but I made
the call anyway. The host replied with grace. "Everybody had to
go to Mumbai, so I'm not sure who'll even be here, but at least

there'll be plenty of food," he said. "You're most welcome to come."

Feeling like I had a stone basketball in my stomach, I lugged the case of beer into the Delhi night and hailed an auto rickshaw. It was far, the driver got lost, the temperature dropped; I froze as we wheeled and whined for an hour through the chaos, until he dropped me off at wide concrete house behind walls, and I stepped into the warmth of an apartment filled with the smell of turkey and the laughter of children.

"Hi," said an American woman with thick brown hair and big brown eyes, wearing a flowery dress and black tights and no shoes. "Who are you?" I'd been asked a lot of questions in the past months, but never that one. The world of expat journalists in New Delhi was small; everyone knew everyone else, and I was an alien. She was direct. Sparkling. Inquisitive. The dinner party was small, casual, and most of the significant others were gone, deployed to cover the carnage in Mumbai. We ate off plates on our laps and she blasted questions at me; I liked her curiosity. We talked about the future of magazines. What we were doing. She'd had a couple of my editors as professors at journalism school. I couldn't take my eyes off her, especially her hands. She was as tall as I was, both awkward and graceful, but her fingers and hands had a life of their own; they were the most feminine hands I'd ever seen. They floated and danced and drew me in.

When it was time to go, she called three taxis and three of us left the party. But there was only one taxi outside and I had the farthest to go, had no idea where I was. "You take it," she said. I said goodbye, and she started walking away. Suddenly she stopped. Looked at me, looked at the taxi. Took a step. Stopped.

It was tiny, the barest motion and expression, but I couldn't help thinking she wanted to get into the taxi with me.

Her e-mail arrived the next morning. She loved my blog, and I could tell she'd read every word. I pressed her for criticism; she was younger than I, a creature of the web. "You have to interact with your readers, your commenters, more," she wrote. "Your videos are too static." My stomach was feeling better; I was dying to go out, and wrote back that if she and her boyfriend were hitting the town any night, I'd love to tag along.

"I'm throwing a party on Monday," she said, "and you're welcome to come."

I got there late and was still the first to arrive. I came up the stairs onto a roof deck and she emerged, long brown hair wet and sweet-smelling, fresh from a shower. It was a moment. Wordless. I fumbled with a bottle opener to crack the wine while she stood close, too close, not close enough, just the two of us and those hands. After so long without a real connection to anyone, separated from my wife and living apart from my family for almost two years, the attraction couldn't have been more fresh or surprising.

NISA, AS AN EAR CLEANER I befriended later called her, and I met for lunch in a park a few blocks from her office the next day, had a quick drink that evening after work, and over the next days kept up a constant stream of texts, e-mails, and quick lunches and stolen drinks. We were connecting hard and fast and deeply, and I told her everything, my life spilling out like

Victoria Falls. And the more I told the more she listened, questioned, wanted to know. And vice versa: she seemed a whole unexplored continent waiting to be discovered. Travel had taken me out of my life, had shaken loose my already eroded sense of home. A further complication ensued: I needed visas to China and Russia, and a letter of invitation had to come from Moscow. The Russian one would take at least another ten days, a process that would eventually stretch to three and a half weeks. After months of movement, I was suddenly stopped, going nowhere.

A week after we met, we were spending long nights on Delhi rooftops drinking wine and talking, talking, talking and days in parks amid gamboling gymnastic beggars and on the crazy, crowded streets of Old Delhi.

And then, at a bookshop one afternoon, she reached up to a shelf and pulled out a book: *East of Eden*. "One of my favorites," she said. "Read it." I did, and it was all about men's complex but stunted emotional lives and I saw my life and my journey in every word. No book had spoken so directly to me since college. That we might, if we wanted to, tried hard enough, rise above ourselves and be strong enough to forgive ourselves. That we might rise above our own mistakes not because we must or because some deity commanded us, but simply because we could choose to. It should have been obvious, of course, but I'd gotten lost somewhere over the past decade, had done what many men did all too often: focused on work and let their wives take care of everything else, from friendships to social events to family. I was gone so much. If my sister or my parents wanted to organize anything, they called Lindsey. If I wanted to know anything about my children, I asked Lindsey, who also organized most of our social events, started new friendships. She held up our world, but it was a world in which I too often failed to contribute, literally and emotionally, and thus felt too often a stranger. Instead of admitting my distance from it, instead of trying to talk to Lindsey or anyone else about my unhappiness with the status quo, I just worked, running farther away. I'd lost so much of the intimacy and closeness I was envying in Indonesia and India and that I'd felt with Lily in Peru. But it wasn't hopeless. It wasn't the end. Every moment we had the choice to forgive ourselves and try again. And suddenly I didn't want to run anymore; I wanted to be those people on trains and ferries and on Buru, lying in tangled piles, holding hands instead of running. Travel—my journey—was showing me what I wanted, craved, giving me perspective for the first time in seven years.

I FELT LIKE I'd been scoured clean, sandblasted by the travel, and that's when I met Moolchand. I'd seen my first ear cleaner on the Rocket in Bangladesh, and the thought of some street person sticking sharp sticks into my ears horrified me. But I was fascinated by the tens of millions of street entrepreneurs, from ear cleaners to eye washers to shoe polishers to touts, who prowled the parks and railway stations and dusty corners of the world. I wanted to know them, and Moolchand caught me at a good moment.

He knelt beside me on the putting-green-short grass of Palika Park in New Delhi's Connaught Place and did his best to convince me that, no matter how clean I thought my ears were, they could use his skilled attention. "You will not believe it!" he said. "Pay me nothing and let me do my work and you will see, and then you can pay me. Whatever amount you wish."

There was something about him. I engaged, deflected, danced, joked "but my girlfriend loves to clean my ears, and if you do it, well, she'll be unhappy."

He slapped his leg and howled with laughter. "Your ears need to be cleaned by a professional!"

"Yes," I said. "But what about my girlfriend?"

"She won't give you any lucky-lucky if she can't?"

"Exactly," I said.

He roared again, pressed his case, and we laughed together, at each other. He had six children, rode the bus, the notorious Blueline, an hour and a half into and out of the city every day. That was it; I'd been meaning to ride the Blueline ever since arriving in New Delhi. A private line of battered buses, it was notorious for high speeds, plowing into people, driving the wrong way, anything to make time and make money. "Let's ride the Blueline tomorrow!" I said.

"Don't move," he said. "I'll get some chai."

We met again the next morning. We lurched and jolted through hours of traffic and, to be honest, my Blueline hours were pretty tame. Just crowds of people packed into slow buses. Once a passenger in another bus attacked one in mine through the windows from three inches away; and once we raced a bus going the wrong way up a divided avenue head-on against traffic, a tout hanging from the doorway waving at the swerving, oncoming tide. But we didn't crush anyone against a tree, run over any bicyclists, kill anyone. It felt good to be plunging into the world again, listening to Moolchand's life, one so typical in India.

He'd left his village near Khajuraho, a town notorious for its Kama Sutra sculptures, when he was ten, coming to Delhi with an uncle, and started shining shoes in the park. At fifteen his parents found him a bride; she was fourteen. He met her at their wedding, briefly, then returned to Delhi for three more years until she finally joined him. "We slept together and talked for the first time that night."

He'd been cleaning ears now for twenty years, had four daughters and two sons, had lost one child to starvation. "In my next life," he said, pressed against me on the bus, "I will not have so many. They are very expensive." He sent money home to his parents, shelled out 1,000 rupees—about twenty dollars— a month to the police, hustled seven days a week, cleaning the ears of sometimes two people, sometimes none, sometimes many in a day, and somehow kept his family clothed and mostly fed and usually in school.

We ate spicy something with chapattis off the street, strolled through crowded traffic and dust in distant Rohini, and he said, "Is it true that in America people kiss on the street?"

"Yes," I said.

"I have seen it!" he said. "I have seen tourists do it here!"

Then he asked me about lesbians. Did they really exist? Did women really kiss each other? They did and they did, I said. He was amazed.

We talked about women. He was stumped about something— foreign women, Western women, were supposed to be so easy. They wore tight clothing. They bared their shoulders. They met a guy in the movies and the next thing you knew, clothes were flying off and everybody was doing everything. But he hustled Western women all the time to clean their ears, and every once in a while he angled for a little bit more, but none of them would ever sleep with him. He didn't understand.

It was almost impossible to explain. As I usually did with questions and perceptions about America's beauty and bounty and easy riches, I tried to tell him that Hollywood was one thing, reality another. That, yes, it was probably a whole lot easier to sleep with an American woman than an Indian one, but that most women just didn't let it rip anywhere at any time. "Yes, but why do they wear such tight clothes? Why do they kiss and hold hands in public?" He just couldn't wrap his mind around the idea.

In the afternoon we headed back to Connaught Place and I told him that I'd be honored if he cleaned my ears.

"Wait," he said, smiling. He left, then returned with his baseball cap and canvas satchel and tools. Sat me on the grass, the sun streaming into my ears. Gripped my head firmly but gently and went to work. I had, in fact, just gone at them with Q-tips several days before. No matter. He knew his craft, and scooped and scraped—here I will not get too graphic—stuff from my ear canal that he wiped on his hands. And he noticed that my right eardrum was scarred, blown in an old diving accident.

"Doesn't that disgust you?" I said, as my ear wax collected on the back of his hand.

"Hold still," he said. "It is my work and it is nothing."

He wound cotton onto the end, swirled it around after the scraping, and rinsed out my ears with something. "Ayurvedic medicine," he said. And then polished them with mustard oil. "*Now* your ears are clean," he said.

Every couple of days I plunked down in the park with

Moolchand and the boys. We sat on the grass and drank chai.
To look at Palika Park was to see a small and overused urban
mound of grass dotted with trash and the red spit of paan chew-
ers, full of the kind of sad hustlers that you usually tried your
best to avoid, to not even really see.

I knew it well after a couple of weeks. There was order there,
an Indian cosmos. Everyone had a job, a trade, and each trade
came from the same area. There were the shoe shiners. The ear
cleaners. The masseuses. The touts, who earned 100 rupees if
you just went into a shop with them, and fifteen percent of your
purchase.

The shoe shiners were from villages around Khajuraho—
every single one. They knew each other, were born near each
other, knew each other's families. Their wives were plucked
from their villages. Ear cleaners all wore a round, red hat from
which protruded their sticks and swabs, and they were all Muslims. They were poor, but not alone; they belonged and knew
who they were and where they were from. Moolchand wore a
red baseball cap. He was an exception—he was Hindu, a shoe
shiner, who switched professions, hence the baseball cap, the
only ear cleaner from Khajuraho and the only non-Muslim ear
cleaner I ever saw. Maybe that's why I'd liked him. His small
stab at difference in a sea of tradition.

In May and June they all would go back to their villages for
two months with their families. Moolchand's family had six
acres, "but sometimes the rains come too much and sometimes
they don't come at all. What to do?" Today it was cold and
cloudy and the park seemed dirty, as if it really belonged to the
crows; no tourists today, they said. What to do?

One of the shoe shiners noticed a broken zipper on my bag.

He pulled it between his legs and went to work, with the attention to detail and care of which only a poor Indian seemed capable. I pulled and yanked and always made it worse; he slid and worked with his fingers, greased it with wax from his wooden shoe-shining box, sliced stray strings with a razor blade, and it was as good as new. The park hustler asked for nothing in return.

Moolchand lived in a single room with his wife and six children. "What to do?" he said, and smiled. "Tell your friends here in Delhi," he said, "that you know a good man for a job. I need a steady job. Cleaning. Washing. One thousand rupees a month." It was twenty dollars.

I'd been treated so well by so many people, poor people, in the past months. But with people like Moolchand I never knew whether we were really connecting or if their attraction to me, their openness to me, was because I was a white foreigner. Were they just hoping for visas? For jobs? Yet I also knew from my experiences on Buru, for instance, that it wasn't that alone. Could we ever really be friends across such gulfs of culture and wealth? There was no way to know in the limited amount of time I had; I'd been in Delhi for three and a half weeks, and it was time to go; my Russian visa had finally arrived from Moscow. I said goodbye one morning to Moolchand and the others.

"What to do?" he said. "When are you coming back to India? And what about Nisa?" Moolchand said, his brow furrowed in worry.

"I don't know," I said. I would need to deal with things at home before I could consider moving on.

Moolchand was quiet for a moment. "Next time you will

come to Khajuraho with me!" Moolchand couldn't imagine that I might never return.

"Yes," said the others, sipping their tea and smoking and chewing tobacco, "we will all go to Khajuraho."

I would like to go, I told them, honestly, and I shook their hands and walked away from a little world that was part of a much bigger one in a tiny park that I had gotten to know just a bit. Sad, a little, that there was still so much to know and that I would probably never get to a village that sent its sons out to be shoe shiners in Palika Park.

What to do! I had been hoping to get home by Christmas, had been saying I would, but because of the visa delay I wasn't going to make it. And I knew that whatever growing closeness I felt with Nisa, there was nothing I could do unless I resolved my situation, met the challenge of home head on. I had to go. And that meant Afghanistan. On a Saturday I went to the Ariana Afghan Airways offices to buy my ticket for Kabul. It was one tidy room with wooden desks, the walls decorated with posters of Afghanistan as tourist paradise. The shimmering blue lakes of Bamiyan. Rugged and charming peasants. No hint of a country under siege, one of the most dangerous places on earth. "The flight is on Sunday," said Rajesh Kumar, writing my ticket out by hand after I'd forked over a pile of cash, "but I am writing the ticket for Monday. We don't know when the plane will leave. Sunday I hope, but I can't say for sure. There is fog here, fog there." He shrugged his shoulders, wrote my cell phone number down. "I will call you and let you know."

"What time does it arrive?"

"I don't know," he said.

"How many airplanes does Ariana have?"

"Six," he said. "They are very old. But do not worry about their airworthiness, sir!"

I spent the rest of the afternoon and evening and into the night with Nisa. We walked. We talked. We ate. We roamed across Delhi on foot and in rickshaws. We drank chai in a room piled with marigolds in Old Delhi and too much wine on a rooftop terrace and could figure nothing out. She had a job in India. I had a family 8,000 miles away, wanted to be there for them. I could promise nothing and neither could she. "When you leave, let's not talk again," she said. "Unless. Unless we can. I'd rather risk everything we have now to have the possibility of what could be."

And the next morning we hugged briefly, barely—we were on a streetcorner in India, after all—and I climbed into a taxi and she a rickshaw and a second later I was alone again.

Four armed assailants kidnapped a German aid worker dining with her husband at a restaurant in Kabul in a bold midday attack, as the Taliban said negotiations for the release of 19 South Korean hostages have failed. Meanwhile, a suicide car bomb attack killed 15 people and wounded 26, including several women and children, in Afghanistan's southern city of Kandahar.

—Denver Post, *August 19, 2007*

TEN

Scariana

NIGHT AND DARKNESS, the airport dim, nearly empty. Outside I could see nothing but blackness. No cars. No buildings. No signs or streetlights or life. A driver from the hotel had been supposed to meet me, but no one was there and the airport had emptied out quickly. I was alone in Kabul, Afghanistan, unconnected to any organization, and I was scared. I tried to call the hotel, but my phone wouldn't work. I went into the darkness and got hit by cold, something I hadn't felt in ten months. Stood there a moment, trying to get my bearings. No taxis. Nothing. Just a huge, empty square paved in concrete. I went back into the airport, but a soldier with an AK-47 stopped me. "Taxi," I said. He didn't understand. We pantomimed a few minutes and he got it. Out there, he motioned. Just go. I had no choice. I couldn't believe it, though; the thought of arriving in Kabul and getting kidnapped right from the airport seemed ridiculous but also more possible than any Peruvian bus plunging off a cliff or Bangladeshi ferry sinking. I took a few paces, rifled though my bags, found my Indian knife, and slipped it up my right sleeve, the handle in the palm of my hand. A quick left-handed slash across the face, followed by the power shot with my right—that should bring an attacker's hands up, at least—and break his leg with my right foot, then run; I played the scenario out in my mind and walked on. And then felt foolish: a wall surrounded the airport, with a gate in it; beyond it waited a handful of figures in the darkness and a man yelled, "Taxi!"

I said "Gandamack," the name of my hotel. He had a beard, wore a black leather jacket, grabbed my bag, and led me to a Toyota minivan. I got into the front seat, said "Gandamack" again, and he nodded. But I knew nothing that night and I couldn't see much from the car. Brokenness. Dim streetlights. Sandbags and blast walls and razor wire and roadblocks manned by machine gunners. We stopped outside of a high concrete wall, a small steel gate. "Gandamack," he said.

I stepped out. A three-inch window slid open in the gate. Words in Dari. A steel bolt slid, the door opened into a walled enclosure. Two men, both holding AKs, one with a 9-millimeter strapped to his thigh. Twenty feet later, another steel door. It buzzed, and I passed into a concrete room three feet square, facing another steel door, a man holding an AK watching me through a window. When the first door shut, the other one buzzed, and I slid into a world of Christmas lights and the warmth of Kabul's parallel universe, a world of expat journalists and aid workers and diplomats drinking wine behind walls and guns.

I FELT EXHAUSTED AND ANXIOUS. The Ariana flight had been two hours late, the plane an aged Boeing 727. It felt crazy coming to

Afghanistan. The country was in turmoil, the Taliban regaining power every day; they were said to be encircling Kabul itself. And Ariana's nickname was "Scariana." It had a deliciously checkered history, and in college I'd read Robert Byron's 1937 travel classic *The Road to Oxiana*, in which he'd written, "I'd left England in August with two hopes: one, to see the monuments of Persia; the other to reach this town," this town being Mazar-i-Sharif. It was one of those names that stuck in my memory—exotic, far away, the epitome of romance. I'd wanted to get there ever since, and it lay in the north, traditionally anti-Taliban territory from which the assault after the September 11 attacks had been launched by the Northern Alliance with the help of the U.S.

The flight itself didn't scare me, although I'd heard nothing but horror stories from people who'd taken it. It was banned from flying into the European Union, and thus forbidden to most contractors and UN personnel even within the country. As the plane throttled up and the captain said over the PA system, "We wish you a pleasant flight to Kabul," I hoped it would be as easy to get out of Afghanistan as it was to get in. There was no turning around, no turning back; in a way I felt like I was for the first time really keeping some macabre promise about traveling to meet danger. It was a short flight, a leaping of time and space, from the chaotic but warm swirl of India to the extreme hardness and violence of a medieval state in the throes of a war, India green and fertile at takeoff, Afghanistan pure unadulterated brown and snow-swept, serrated mountain ridges, all in two hours. As I settled into my room and its cozy bed with down comforter behind layers of walls and guns and razor wire in a city where lived men who would slit my throat in an instant, I was alone but not lonely, for the first time in a long time. My phone pinged; an incoming text from Delhi: "Don't be sad. Be excited. You have adventure to find."

I had no idea what the future held for me. But I had a growing sense that I would know soon, and that it was this journey that was pointing me in the right direction. That clarity was in my power to have, and that I knew there was, in fact, an other side and I could get to it, find it.

I WASN'T SURE what the security situation was in Kabul, whether it was safe to walk around or not. In Delhi I'd had dinner with a woman who worked for the UN, who'd said she was forbidden to walk anywhere in the city; she had to be driven to and from work. Only months ago the five-star Serena hotel was attacked, gunmen running amok, spraying bullets. Around the corner from my hotel, two Americans working for DHL had been gunned down.

I taped my knife onto my right forearm with a slender piece of duct tape, the handle just protruding from my sleeve, grabbable, and walked out. Brightness of a cloudless blue sky, the high mountains of the Hindu Kush covered with snow surrounding the city. Choking smell from car exhaust and the diesel generators that lined the sidewalk of every storefront. Men wearing salwar kameezes, with keffiyehs around their necks; gnarled faces and beards, ancient-looking, as old and weathered and of the earth as trees, hills, mountains. Roadblocks. Brand-new green Toyota pickups carrying police with machine guns. I pieced together what I'd read about kidnappings: a car, always a car. Guns probably. Time: you had to be spotted, your location known, while the men and the cars and the guns came together. People were abducted from restaurants, from their cars at roadblocks or on routes they drove daily that had been scoped out over days. So I walked fast, crossing the street every hundred yards or so, switching, changing constantly. Kept my back to walls as much as possible. Walked against traffic in the street, so no car could overtake me from behind. I scanned constantly, like Nasirbhai. Plunged into the market of downtown Kabul, past ministries sheathed in high blast walls and razor wire, got nervous when I went into a store to buy an Afghan SIM card for my phone. The salesman had to copy my passport, fill out forms; the minutes ticked by. I stood in the corner opposite the door, my back to the walls, watching the door, my left side forward, my left hand by my right, with the knife. I figured there would be a gun; but I was worth more alive than dead, wouldn't be expected to resist, and was likely dead if I was taken, anyway. Maybe I was crazy. Maybe it would never work, but I was ready, ready to explode in violence: a fast and hard kick to the knees to bring their hands down, a vicious slash across the face, and go. There could be no delay—that was the first rule of self-defense. The moment one or more men came close enough to touch me—and I knew I'd know by their eyes— the moment that I saw a weapon or that a hand reached for me, that was the moment to seize the initiative and strike, like two cocks coming together in a cockfight, like a rattler lunging the second its threat is in range. A bomb was another matter. Bombers liked crowds and crowded marketplaces. In that case, there wasn't much to be done. Again, I just had to keep moving.

Crowds filled the streets, mostly men, but women in blue burqas ambled by and every now and then a woman in blue jeans and headscarf. But there were no other westerners; I didn't see a single one. In the throngs, among the storefronts selling cell phones and computers and office supplies, I could almost forget where I was. But the moment I looked up, a wall of brick and mud houses rose steeply up a hillside behind the road, a world without running water, power, or heat beyond coal- and wood-burning stoves. I walked for two hours; I wanted to stop and drink tea and sit and just watch, but I couldn't. The city felt simmering, anxious, waiting, fingers on triggers everywhere.

Christmas dawned bright and blue and cold, and that evening alone in my room I called home, watching my family open Christmas presents—a bundle of which I'd sent from India—through the wonders of the Internet. My computer's camera wasn't working, so, in a telling metaphor, I could see them and they couldn't see me. I was there and I was not there; I felt part of the morning, got to *ooh* and *ahh* at the presents and laugh and shriek, but then with a push of a computer key I was gone, a world away, alone again, missing them and wondering and hoping that once that screen went black I wasn't forgotten. And I knew that for all of my efforts to send gifts and call home and be there, I wasn't, and that was no one's fault but my own.

THE NEXT MORNING I met Najeeb, a fixer meeting with a photographer in the hotel, and asked him about taking a bus across the Salang Pass and northern Afghanistan to Mazar. He wore a tweed sport jacket and slacks, looked like a professor. He thought a long time in silence. "I think it is possible," he said, speaking slowly. "Maybe a seventy-five-percent chance you will be safe. But this is a serious question and I have to give you the right answer. The question is the driver. If you find the right one, who works for a good company, then they will guarantee your safety. If not, sometimes the driver will call their friends. And the Salang Pass is full of snow right now; last week people were stuck there for three days."

Najeeb had a friend, he said, who might be able to go with me, and an hour later Khalid Fazly showed up. He was young, twenty-five, with alert, bright green eyes, spoke perfect English, wore striped slacks and a long black peacoat. We drank tea outside in the cold under a warm winter sun, as Blackhawks and old Russian Mil helicopters clattered and thumped overhead.

You should not have walked so long downtown, he said. "It is too long to escape attraction. A German was kidnapped one month ago from where you were." In Afghanistan I was less a man than a big jewel, a glistening diamond, almost unimaginably valuable. "Don't take any taxis," he said. "The driver might call a friend and betray you." Khalid said he'd ask around, suss out the safety, and get back to me. Which he did, a couple of hours later. "I think it'll be no problem," he said. He'd talked to a bus company, felt it was safe. But, he said, I had to get a salwar kameez, a local Afghan costume. I could not stand out. We'd leave in two days.

MEANWHILE, I WAS CURIOUS about Ariana, so I called its president. And got through to his assistant, who scheduled a meeting the next morning, and I ended up in a labyrinth of security, totally lost. A soldier with green eyes flecked with gold led me down dirt roads, a canyon between concrete walls topped with coils of razor wire and sandbagged gun positions, to a dilapidated three-story concrete building painted a once-bright but fading blue. Guards frisked me and didn't find the knife, now strapped to my leg, and I went through an unheated hallway staffed by an old man with a tattered blue notebook. Up three flights of stairs lay a doorway that said PRESIDENT.

Inside, sofas full of waiting men in suits, carpets, warmth. A tall Afghan in a brown corduroy suit and an electric orange tie stood up, introduced himself. Mohammed Omar, the president's assistant. "I'm so sorry," he said. "I tried your mobile many times. The appointment has to be postponed until eleven; President Karzai called and he could not refuse."

I hung around in the dust and cold outside for an hour, returned, and Mohammed ushered me into a spacious office with a big map of the world on one wall. Oriental carpets covered the floor. Moin Khan Wardak's desk was the size of a car, covered in glass and piles of paper. Wardak wore a blue three-piece suit. He was big, burly, clean-shaven, with short-cropped black hair. A servant brought trays of raisins and almonds, cups of hot tea. The story of Ariana mirrored the story of Afghanistan. Once upon a time Kabul had been a city on the rise, and Ariana had been partners with Pan Am, beginning in the 1950s. It had a fleet of DC-3s, DC-9s, Boeing 727s, a big DC-10, routes to Paris, London, Frankfurt. But things turned ugly as civil war broke out and Ariana flights had a habit of being hit by rockets or crashing into mountains. The Northern Alliance captured a plane in Mazar and sold it to Iran. An insurance company grabbed a plane that had been hit by rocket fire. In 2000, to escape the Taliban, two brothers hijacked a 727 with 180 people aboard, which ended up in London, after stops in Tashkent and Moscow. The U.S. bombed three 727s and a Russian-made Antonov. By the end of the Taliban era, Ariana had no planes left. None. "We lost everything!" he said. India donated three aged Airbuses to restart the airline, and now Ariana had five Boeing 727s flying and one leased Airbus based and maintained in Germany, allowed to fly to the EU. The phone rang.

"You are asking for five lakh and ten lakh; how much in dollars? If you kindly send me the invoice I will transfer the money, but you need to release the engine! I will pay, I promise!" He hung up, shook his head. "We have an aircraft stuck in Ankara and it needs an engine and we have a deal with Air India but they won't release it!

"*Inshallah*, we are growing day by day." He'd been a pilot for twenty-four years, had flown with a beard "down to here," he said, holding his hand by his chest, during the Taliban years. "There were no nav-aids in Afghanistan, not a single one. Now I have an instrument landing system in Kabul and runway lights in Kandahar." Pilots had flown with handheld GPS units. Which was scary, considering Kabul was surrounded by 13,000-foot mountains. And even now, he admitted, "Kabul is a very dangerous airport, especially at night and in bad weather, and the runway is only 6,000 feet long."

I MET KHALID at 5:00 a.m. wearing a gray salwar kameez, a ratty ski cap, a keffiyeh wrapped around my neck, and I hadn't shaved in three days. I felt like a clown, but Khalid was encouraging.

"You don't look like a foreigner," he said. "You look like an Afghan!" The morning was still pitch black, freezing, stars sharp like strings of Christmas lights overhead. Most of Kabul had no power, nothing but dim shapes of mud and brick piled on top of each other, a world of shadows and darkness and, I imagined, huddled bodies inside. Three buses were waiting at a muddy parking lot in the darkness on the edge of the city, a vendor selling tea and bread in the glow of a kerosene lamp. Formless women in burqas. Men in flowing green robes and lamb's-wool caps, and in leather jackets. For the first time in Afghanistan I felt hidden, safe. No one noticed me in the dark and in my clothing. And, I realized, out here, away from hotels and ministries, there were no gunmen, no barricades, and their absence felt safer.

"One year ago," Khalid said, as we stood drinking tea in the dark, "there were many women walking through town. Now, almost none. The security has gotten much worse." The latest security bulletin, in fact, posted in my hotel was twenty pages long. Taliban were encircling the city from the south, east, and west, were infiltrating it, and had been spotted at the gates. The north, we both hoped, would be safe. But Khalid's life was on the line here as much as mine, or more. When I asked him if he was nervous about his safety he said, "Only when I'm with you." If we ran into trouble, after all, I'd probably be kidnapped. But he would be killed.

We boarded and pulled away a few minutes after six, rolling and bumping through the dark, silent, and sleeping city. Paused at a checkpoint—big speed bumps, soldiers, guns—then picked up speed, the driver hurtling into the countryside, careening around corners, through a world of brown fields, brown mud walls, brown mud houses, toward the sharply rising wall of the jagged and snow-covered peaks of the Hindu Kush. A man walked up the aisle, handing out plastic vomit bags. The sun poked over the horizon, and the murmur of prayers echoed through the bus. Khalid passed his hands over his face. "I've prayed for a safe trip."

We hurtled around curves, hit the mountains, and started climbing. Up, up, and up again, the two-lane blacktop running alongside a river, as we headed toward the Salang Pass, a tunnel built by the Soviet Union in the 1960s at nearly 13,000 feet. Brown and barren, houses turned from mud to stone. Cubes of rock clinging to steep scree, a hard, cold, barren landscape that turned to snow quickly. At places, muddy, icy shoulders and vendors selling tire chains out of rusted shipping containers. Men and women coughed—the coal and wood stoves, the generators, the cold—everybody, it seemed, had a hacking cough. Then just snow—we could have been winding through the Rockies. And Khalid told me about surviving through the Taliban, his three arrests. Once he'd been with his mother and thirteen-year-old sister, who was not wearing a burqa. The Taliban stopped them, his sister must be properly dressed. "She is too young," said his mother. "There are none her size." The men didn't care; they beat her with a flagpole on the street. Once Khalid was picked up on the street for not having a beard—he was still a teenager—and taken to prison. "I was scared," he said, "because they had no record of who was who, and I didn't want to be lost and forgotten with the political prisoners." He was just plucked off the street; no one called his family. After five days the guards asked if any of the prisoners knew how to cook. Khalid raised his hand, said, "'I am a good cook!' But I didn't even know how to cook an egg!"

He cooked potatoes for his jailers the first day, beans the next. At least he was out of the cell, had some freedom of movement. The fifth day a bus brought a load of prisoners from the north. Khalid went to the bus driver. "I am here just for shaving my beard," he told the driver, "and now I am free, so please take me with you when you leave." Okay, the driver said, but I can't guarantee what will happen at the gate.

"Don't worry," Khalid said.

Before they got to the gate, some Taliban jumped on the bus. "Give us money," they said. Khalid can't remember how much he had, but he gave them all of it, and an hour later walked into his house, almost a week after being taken.

We hit the tunnel, which had seen violence for years, as the principal route between northern and southern Afghanistan. Mujahideen had ambushed the Soviets in the area repeatedly; even now the hulks of tanks and APCs littered the sides of the road. The Northern Alliance had blown up both ends to keep the Taliban from heading north. Minefields lay everywhere. "Almost died here once in a car accident," said Khalid, as we entered a dim, dark, dripping world, the road covered with hard ice, the air thick with exhaust from cars and trucks inching through, bumper to bumper.

On the other side we emerged into intense sun and started descending on switchbacks, swerving around slow-moving trucks and into an ancient and untouched land. We stopped at around 9:00 a.m. at a long, low, concrete building, a restaurant. It was cold inside, unheated, a knee-high platform covered in dark red and brown Afghan carpeting running along the walls and in the center of the room. We sat cross-legged on the platforms, and boys ran back and forth, bringing us aluminum trays of lamb kabobs and tea and flat, warm Afghan bread. The meat was salty and tender. Nobody seemed to notice me. No one had guns. No women—I wondered where the women on the bus were supposed to eat. I was just here, deep inside Afghanistan. A fly on the wall.

We drove on. The land flattened; we sped through broad valleys of brown, a place called Disho, the fields dusted with the barest green lace. Mud brick compounds. Round cow patties drying on the walls like hubcaps on the junkyards of D.C.'s New York Avenue. Donkeys and children playing, and scarlet blankets drying on dusty shrubs. Huge piles of hay. It struck me there was no trash on the ground. None. No plastic water bottles, now ubiquitous throughout the world. Which meant that here there were few manufactured things, few things bought in stores. Bumped through Baghlan Province and the city of Pul-i-Khumri, where the bus suddenly ground to a halt and couldn't be restarted. I started to get up when Khalid warned me about Hekmatyar and that I should stay still and quiet. Then he started praying, and I broke into a cold sweat.

We were on a slight incline. A crowd of men pushed the bus backwards and the driver popped the clutch. It roared to life. Sputtered. My heart spasmed. Started again, and stayed rumbling. Everyone poured back on, and off we went.

It had been ten minutes. It seemed like a lifetime, and a few minutes and miles later the fear was a memory. Gone. Didn't seem so bad. Which is the way it always seemed afterwards, despite how close I'd been playing it. The ferries, the planes, the buses on cliffs, it all seemed like nothing. The more I did it, the more natural it seemed. But I was riding a narrow line, especially here in Afghanistan. What if I was kidnapped? Disappeared. Poof, off the radar I'd go. Would I think it had all been worth it? Would my children ever forgive me, or would they think I'd died doing something I loved? Would anyone even tell Nisa? Death was so banal, so unromantic. Walking to the edge of the cliff could feel glorious, but when was the last step? The step into the abyss? You couldn't tell until you got there, and that was the problem; I never knew if I was standing right on the edge or miles from it. It made me feel alive; that edge was a powerful aphrodisiac, and weeks without it at home made home seem quiet and boring. But its pursuit always came with a price. It separated me from everyone else in the normal world; no one could understand what I'd been through, done, unless they'd done it too. Unless it was a regular part of their life. And not just my friends, but the people I loved. My family. It was selfish. A selfish secret that I carried around, that I couldn't share even when I tried to. I remembered once coming home from southern Sudan, and Lindsey was angry that I hadn't called her. And just plain angry, which I couldn't fathom. "I'm home!" I said. "Why are you mad at me? And how could I call?" I'd stammered. "I was in a war zone with drums in the night and men dying of gunshot wounds and starving children and there wasn't a phone for hundreds of miles!"

"How can I love you when you're there?" she finally said. "How can you love someone who might be killed or kidnapped or die in a plane crash and puts his family through that pain and worrying?"

But how could you not live that life, taste that taste, after you'd had it? The bus rolled on and my fear was a memory already, mitigated and rounded, its sharp edges sanded off. That moment was there, though. That moment of fear. Of intensity. Of feeling so afraid that I knew I was alive and didn't want to be dead, and that I loved my family and missed them, even as I knew I had to straighten everything out and change my life. And that that was what travel was all about, showing you things in a starker way than you could ever see them at home.

Past Pul-i-Khumri, the landscape became desert. Just sand and brown and flat. No bushes. No trees. No rivers. Whole villages of brown sand castles and, nearby, mass graves where the Northern Alliance had killed thousands of Taliban and buried them where they lay. And poor Khalid, he had girlfriend troubles, like everyone everywhere, but it was worse in places like Afghanistan and Bangladesh. "I am in love, but no one can know," he said. She went to school with him. Somehow he got her cell phone number. Called her. Don't call me, she'd said, when she answered. But then she'd called him back. "We see each other at University and we go to a park, but sometimes the police stop us and ask if we're related. We can kiss and touch a little, but nothing below the waist. Our parents cannot know, hers especially. She would be beaten and forbidden to leave the house. And they might come and hurt me." It wasn't hopeless, though. If he told his parents he had seen her and wanted to marry her, he said, they would go to her parents and suggest it, say that she was suitable. "And then she'll put pressure on her family, indirectly, to agree."

Khalid, too, was mystified by Western women. Once he'd worked with an American journalist and invited her back to his house for dinner. His parents, of course, were there; they were always there. In a strange reversal of Moolchand's unsuccessful assumption that Western women were available for easy sex, she'd told him she had been shocked, that she thought he lived alone and would never have come to his house if she'd known his parents were there. "I didn't understand that at all!"

THE BUS DRIVER had been screaming along for hours, and we arrived at the gates to Mazar-i-Sharif an hour early. We stopped, the driver laughing and talking. "He says," said Khalid, "that he's driven too fast, that he'll be fined if he arrives too early, so we have to wait." Husks of Soviet APCs lay around; a few soldiers with AKs got on the bus and looked us all over. No one noticed me, and finally we started again and a few blocks later Khalid and I jumped off the bus at a dusty crossroads in a gauzy afternoon, the sky white. We walked down a cobblestone street, turned a corner, stumbled down rutted dirt roads, until we found an unheated concrete house behind high walls—the hotel.

An hour later we were in a dusty brown field among two hundred horsemen—known as *chapandaz*—in knee-high leather boots and fur caps (and a smattering of old Soviet padded tank helmets) with high-pommeled saddles, surrounded by thousands of spectators for Mazar's weekly Buzkashi spectacle. It was a wild free-for-all of macho horsemanship and brute strength and power, as each man tried to drag a hundred-pound calf carcass into the *daira halal*—a circle chalked in the dirt. The horses reared and pawed the ground and sweated and foamed at the bit, big, powerfully muscled beasts bred for the task. The men whipped them and fought them and fought each other and whipped each other in clouds of dust under a warm winter sun, as men and children—there were no women—crowded the field and ran for their lives when galloping horse muscle swept through them. There were no boundaries; imagine a football game in which the spectators littered the field and stood around the huddle. Live music throbbed amid the smell of hashish and horse, and the announcer proclaimed the proceeds for each round in dollars—$50 or $30 or $130—and the great, threatening Afghans pulled me out of harm's way and tucked me behind them whenever the mass of hooves and whips and yells swept over us.

It was serious business, said Aqamurad, thirty years old, astride his $20,000 mount, after the matches. "The best horses here," he said, sweeping his hand over the field, "are worth $200,000. They surge for the circle; they know it, they go right there. They do not need to be pushed." He was a horse breeder and trainer, and he drove his horses hard every day except Saturday, and made sure they were warm twice a night. Some of the chapandaz rode their own horses, like Aqamurad, and some were paid to ride the horses of rich businessmen.

It was getting dark, a dusky world of white sky and heavy dust. There were no horse trailers here. For blocks in every direction the streets were scattered with booted horsemen and sweating horses clip-clopping home, a world where everyone looked like they'd been grafted from the gnarled roots of the very first tree. And I felt safe and free for the first time in Afghanistan, as Khalid and I settled down over an enormous pile of mutton in a chilly restaurant open to the street.

. . .

EVERYTHING ABOUT MAZAR was different from Kabul. The edge was gone, the fear and pathos of a city under siege. Mazar felt normal. Few roadblocks, gunners, sandbagged emplacements, blast walls, and razor wire. And yet the handful of expatriates living in the lodge who worked for the United Nations were forbidden to walk the streets, had to be driven from lodge to work and back every day. They were prisoners of their office and hotel, which seemed awful as Khalid and I ventured out the next morning. A cold wind blew, and fog lay heavy. It was all white; white sky, white haze—I couldn't make out a horizon. We wanted to fly back on Ariana to Kabul but needed tickets and found a faded blue painted concrete building on an unpaved street, a row of muddy shoes outside the door. We shed ours, walked into the frigid unheated building, nothing but empty passages and a row of men sitting on a sofa in the hall. Upstairs, down a dark hall, lay the scheduling office. "We don't know," the man said. "Maybe there will be a flight tomorrow, maybe not, and the time is not exact." Khalid persisted, asked more questions, was directed up another flight of stairs to an office where we found Ariana's communications manager huddled around a kerosene stove. "There is only one scheduled flight a week, on Fridays," he said. "The rest are Hajj flights and if there's room, they'll take you. But no one knows anything; call me after eleven."

We walked through teeming Mazar. "Indeed, the whole town has been smartened up lately," wrote Robert Byron. "The bazaars are new and whitewashed, and their roofs are supported on piles which let in light and air underneath. In the new town, where the hotel and Government offices stand, the roads are edged with neat brick gutters." Things had changed. Mud and dust, the curbs broken and crumbling, the city as raw and broken by decades of war as the rest of the country. Cars shared the roads with pushcarts and donkeys. Nut sellers fanned charcoal braziers, the storefronts open in the chill; everyone cold and underdressed. "Come," said Khalid. "I will show you something," as we came upon a fantasy of minarets and tiles in blue and yellow and purple set within a courtyard—the shrine of Hazrat Ali, the tomb of Ali ibn Abi Talib, the fourth caliph and the cousin and son-in-law of Muhammad, which Byron described as "a cross between St Mark's at Venice and an Elizabethan country-house translated into blue faience."

It was why Mazar existed in the first place and why Byron had come here seventy-two years before. Although most Shiites believed the caliph's grave lay in Saudi Arabia, Ali himself was said to have appeared in a dream to the mullah of nearby Balkh in the first half of the twelfth century, and confirmed that his grave lay in what became Mazar, and a shrine was built there in 1136. Genghis Khan had been here, destroying the shrine, and it had been rebuilt in 1481, making Mazar a place of pilgrimage. We strolled into its outer gardens, amid pools of water and swans and thousands of white pigeons that alighted on the hands of delighted children with crusts of bread, a place full of men and women that felt, for the first time in Afghanistan, still. Peaceful and calm. Outside the gates was struggle, a constant struggle with cold and heat and between men and women and Afghanistan's ethnic identities and for survival. "Shall we go inside?" Khalid asked.

"Is it okay?"

"I don't know," he said. "Probably not. But don't say any-thing to anyone; don't talk, and just follow me and stay close. No one is staring at you. It is the way you walk; you don't walk like a foreigner."

We passed through a low wrought-iron fence. An old man with a beard and deep lines in his face stood guarding hundreds of pairs of shoes. We slipped ours off, and padded down a red carpet leading to the mosque. Inside, it was hushed, filled with soft murmur. Rays of light streamed in, a world of carpets and huge wooden doors, and a low table behind which sat a row of mujawers—the men who clean and care for the shrine. Khalid approached. Knelt before them. I followed, imitated, feeling completely exposed, my heart beating. He passed his hands over his face, as if wiping away dust from his eyes and cheeks, made a quick motion with his hands over his chest. I didn't have a clue. The mujawers watched me. An American in the holiest shrine in Afghanistan in a mutton-stained salwar kameez, wearing a North Face ski hat. I vaguely imitated Khalid as best I could. They held their hands out. Khalid passed some money their way, and I did the same. We stood up and he whispered, "We have asked for forgiveness." No one seemed to see through me. In the center of the mosque stood a glass cube the size of a ga-rage, surrounded in wood filigree—the tomb. Men and women pressed fingers, faces, bodies against it, circling it, and we made a circumnavigation and then left. I felt like Richard Burton in Mecca, and guilty and exhilarated and a little mystified, and ashamed that I knew so little, understood so little about some-place and something that was so important to so many people.

We ambled through the growing fog of Mazar. Sat on a cor-ner and drank pomegranate juice while Khalid had his shoes shined by a freezing, shivering boy with no socks and a runny nose. Beggars, old men and women, held their hands open to Khalid, who always gave, and they gave back. "I will pray for you so there will never be restrictions on your way of life," said one man. We entered a candy store. Walls and aisles filled with homemade sweets of sesame and cardamom, carrots and cashews. We ate samples, sweet and nutty and milky, and Khalid filled two shopping bags. "I have a big family!" he said, eyeing the cold white sky outside. "I hope it doesn't snow, because we will be stuck in Mazar." Even without snow falling, Ariana remained opaque. We called five times between ten thirty and three, and each time were told to call in an hour. The plane hadn't even taken off from wherever it was, still had to get to Mazar. If it got here, Ariana said, it would turn around fast and leave. Tickets could only be bought at the airport; we'd have to go and wait and hope. "This is Ariana!" said Khalid. "It is the most unreliable airline in the world, and so badly managed!" I thought of Ariana president Moin Wardak, sitting at his warm desk in Kabul. We hunkered down by the propane heater back at the lodge in Khalid's room, watched American wrestling on the tube, and considered the problem. We could go to the airport and wait. The plane might come, but it might not. If it didn't, it might not come the next day, either. And if it did arrive, it might not leave—it was already getting dark, the cloud ceiling was low and getting lower. It was an easy choice: in Afghanistan the bus was more reliable than flying. And probably safer.

WE ARRIVED IN KABUL and flagged a regular yellow taxi. By now my beard was five days old and my clothes stained with mud and mutton grease. On the Salang Pass we'd been stopped in a massive traffic jam of buses and trucks and cars, skidding and sliding and putting chains on, and a man had walked up to me and started barking in Dari. Khalid exploded with laughter. "He thought you were the bus driver!" Which made him feel safer now that we were back in Kabul. And after hugging good-bye, I changed hotels to a smaller, cheaper one with less security, run by an Afghan family, my room heated by a woodstove, all of which made me feel more secure, less of a target in a much less obvious place than in the well-known hotels that stood out like big red bull's-eyes.

AND I WALKED, my initial fear of the place not wholly gone but considerably lessened, getting my hair cut in a barbershop, and entering an open-fronted kabob restaurant with a ceiling hung with salted haunches of beef, its walls sporting a wolfskin and the head of a deer. There I met Ali Musabah, a bull of a man with the worst cauliflower ears I'd ever seen, wearing blue jeans and a leather jacket. "I am a wrestler," he growled in husky English. Afraid of saying I was an American, I stupidly told him I was Canadian, a lie that I regretted instantly and couldn't pull out of. "I am moving to Canada!" he said. "With all of my family. I hate Afghanistan. It is violent. Full of guns and kidnapping and bombings and bad men. Afghans are mean like Americans, who are not good people. When I get to Canada, God willing, I will call you." He brought me a heaping plate of fatty, gristly mutton and bread. "The fat is good!" he growled. "Eat it; this is my gift, my hospitality." I asked him who he'd vote for in the coming election.

"Nobody. There is nothing good here. I will not miss it at all. I will never marry here." He sat with me, guarded me, peppered me with questions about Toronto, which I tried my best to answer, having been there once, desperately wanting to confess my lie. Ali refused to let me pay a cent for my meal, or for the meals I ate there over the next three days.

The Kabul Lodge was nearly empty, and I woke up to falling snow and my bed shaking—a small earthquake. At breakfast I met the lodge's only other guest, a tiny French woman with jet black hair and a sharp, exotic face named Marie-Elise Palmier-Chatelain. She taught nineteenth-century history at a university near Paris, and had been traveling throughout Afghanistan, Pakistan, and Yemen on and off for three years. Alone. She made me feel like a rookie. We compared knives; she had a six-inch switchblade and confessed to having carried a small automatic pistol in Yemen. She'd taken the bus all over Afghanistan, was headed straight into Taliban country in a few days. Had ridden on horseback from Pakistan into Afghanistan. She had balls of steel. "Come," she said. "You will like this." We donned our costumes—she in a long black abaya with a black headscarf—and set off through muddy streets, the sun now out and melting the inch of snow on the ground. Hailed a taxi and jumped out in a throng of thousands thick in the streets which led to narrow passageways of mud and ageless wooden shops selling brown-speckled white pigeons with thin gold bands on their legs, and parakeets and red-legged fighting partridges. Smelling of spices and smoke, the bird market was supposedly a no-go area for foreigners, but it was rich and ancient feeling and alive, and I wished times were different and I could spend days there getting to know it without worrying about being blown up or kidnapped.

Marie-Elise said no one noticed her—and she sure didn't look Western—but she was wrong. Everyone noticed her, stared; it was the way she walked. Sure-footed. Fast. Head up. Pushing through throngs of men, a sense of power no Afghan woman would ever dare display in a public market.

I was out of time, though, and I had a flight to China to catch. I was searched and searched and searched again, working my way through layers of security to the airport, the gate packed with Afghan and Chinese traders, who elbowed and fought their way to the bus that took us to the plane. At the stairs to the jet, the same aged Ariana Airlines 727 that had brought me to Kabul from New Delhi, I was frisked again.

My seatmate was a Singapore Chinese living in Beijing who owned a company working for the American military at Kabul's Bagram Air Base. "War, insecurity, unease," he said, "wherever those are, the army spends more and that is good for me. And your new president is sending more troops! Business will be even better!" For so long, he said, everyone had been leaving China for someplace better. "Now," he said, "it's the other way around. Everyone wants to get to China!"

Three hours later we slipped and slid down the steps into the zero-degree cold of Urumqi, China. I had turned twenty-four in China, in 1984, and I hadn't been back since. Then, the wide avenues of Beijing had no cars. No signs. Just people walking and riding bikes in green and blue Mao suits. Five hours before, I'd been walking in a collapsed city with intermittent electricity and half the population hidden inside burqas. Airplanes were like traveling capsules, cans of preserved culture. The plane was mostly Afghan, and suddenly I was disgorged into a taxi blaring hip-hop—"I want your body" thumped the music—

and we were rushing along freeways bathed in neon, and twisting through streets lined with modern glass high-rises and I was blinking my eyes at the affluence and style of once-provincial Urumqi—women in knee-high leather boots with four-inch heels and tight blue jeans and twenty-four-hour ATMs and hipster dudes in black Chuck Taylors and earrings. The cold, the sudden affluence and style—I had been in India, Bangladesh, and Afghanistan for almost seven weeks—and the blatant sexuality made me reel, and again that dislocation in the world swept over me. I felt totally displaced. It was New Year's Eve and the texts rolling in from family and friends could barely assuage my loneliness, as I sat at the hotel bar drinking a scotch amid glitter and Christmas trees and a few waiters singing to a karaoke machine. I was heading home, I realized. I had thousands of miles to go, still, but from now on I'd be traveling east toward the western United States, and there was still so much I hadn't seen, so much I didn't know. For the first time since I'd rolled away on the bus out of D.C., I was going toward something, not away. But what was home anymore? Did I even have a home to return to? I thought of Moolchand. What to do? I took another sip of scotch and went to bed.

A speeding passenger train en route to a Chinese coastal resort jumped the tracks and slammed into another, killing at least 70 people and injuring hundreds in the worst rail accident in the country in a decade. In January a high-speed train ran through a group of maintenance workers, killing 18. China . . . is expanding the system to accommodate what is the world's most dense passenger and freight network.

—Sunday Times, *April 29, 2008*

ELEVEN

Hope and Wait

EVEN AT EIGHT in the morning it was as dark as a cave in Urumqi. And freezing, the streets slick with ice, frozen gobs of spit dotting the sidewalks and streets like gross polka dots. When I left Delhi I'd inadvertently tossed my guide to China. Chinese were like Americans—they thought they were the center of the universe (the Chinese name for the country, Middle Kingdom, said it all)—and few Chinese, at least in Urumqi, spoke English. "Few" being an understatement. No one spoke English. At all. And I had two things I could say in Chinese: thank you and hello. My hotel was twenty-four stories of glass; for the first time in months I was in an affluent, totally modern world, yet I felt cut off. I had to improvise the moment I tried to take a taxi to the train station. I drew a picture of a train. Said "choo, choo, tchka, tchka," and somehow ended up at the train station, a massive square Stalinist building that was packed—a line of shaking, freezing people jumping up and down like engine pistons, running out its doors and snaking down the stairs.

I pushed on through and found eighteen ticket windows, each with a line hundreds, maybe thousands deep. Melted snow and spit covered the slippery floors. Which was the right window? I couldn't tell. Was I to wait for hours and then get to the wrong window?

I needed help. Maybe my hotel? I tried to get a taxi. Drivers shook their heads when I tried to get in. Men and women aggressively pushed me away and jumped in. Finally I pushed back, and jumped into a front seat. Handed the driver the card with the hotel's name and address. "Uh-uh," he said, shaking his head, grunting, spitting out something. I got out. Tried again. Finally found a driver who took me. The desk clerk summoned a woman who spoke some English. There was another ticket office, she said. Nearby. I wanted to get to Hohhot and she wrote the name in my notebook. In the end it took me four trips to two stations to get a ticket to Hohhot, there to catch a train toward Mongolia. The language wall was total; it was like trying to communicate with fish in the sea.

An hour after boarding, a woman in a blue conductor's uniform came to me and unleashed a torrent of indecipherable words. Thank you, I said. How are you? It was all I could say. She stomped off, returning with another conductor. He unleashed the same torrent. Thank you, I said. How are you?

He tried harder. She tried harder. Thank you, I said. How are you?

They left, returning a few minutes later with two passengers who spoke some English. "Where are you going?" they said.

"To Hohhot," I said, showing them my ticket.

"Yes," the men said in harmony, "but where are you changing trains?"

"Changing trains?"

"This train does not go to Hohhot. You must change trains."

"I don't know," I said. "You tell me where!"

They conferred. "Wu Wei," the men said, the conductors nodding. "You must get off in Wu Wei."

"When do we get to Wu Wei?" I asked.

By then I had my trusty pad and pen. The woman grabbed it, wrote "13:10," and presented it to me.

I had, somehow, ended up not in the lowest class, hard seat, but in hard berth—six platforms in a spotless train with down comforters and down pillows. There was nothing I could do, no conversation. Every once in a while the people near me jabbered at me. I nodded. "Thank you, thank you," I said. "How are you?"

I got off the train in Wu Wei and I didn't even know where Wu Wei was. It was freezing, maybe ten degrees. The train station stood elevated overlooking a square with a tall pole on which galloped three black horses. It was still. A few shops lined the square and one six-story, modern cube of a building. Wu Wei was deserted. I showed my ticket to a line of policemen in blue uniforms in the unheated station. I had no idea what they said. I unleashed a torrent of English.

A policeman grabbed me by the arm, led me outside, into another room, the ticket room. He marched to the front of the line, much was spoken, a ticket spat out. I drew a clock, pointed to my watch. "17:48," he wrote.

I followed him back to the station. He shook his head, pointed . . . out. To the square. I shook my head. Showed him my bag, asked if I could store it. He shook his head, said words I couldn't understand, pushed me toward the square. No, I didn't feel like taking a stroll with my bags, so I went back into the station. Where I sat for four hours freezing, amid peasants with ruddy cheeks and silver teeth. I made friends with some. I showed them photos of my children stored on my cell phone. A woman gave me an orange so cold it was hard to hold and partly frozen. I paced. I read. The time drew near. I had two scarves around my neck, gloves, long underwear, a ski hat, and I shook. But there was no train. I took my ticket back to the police. One of them, a woman, suddenly spoke: "Tomorrow," she said.

"You speak English?" I said.

"Yes," she said. "And your train is tomorrow evening."

Four hours freezing for nothing! The modern building was a hotel, and not a bad one. I squawked like a chicken. I drew a picture of a steaming cup of coffee. They nodded. I felt my communication skills were improving. Soon after, I got a glass of warm milk and spareribs.

That night I called home for help. My youngest daughter was in her second year of Chinese; Lindsey bought a guidebook and they sent me a few words and phrases, which I copied into my notes and I thought I might be able to take a bit of control again.

I SPENT THE NEXT NIGHT on the train in a hard seat. Every seat was taken, and some people had to stand. Frost and ribbons of ice an inch thick coated the window. I sat as upright as if on a pew in church. My fellow passengers snored, stared, and ate enormous quantities of sunflower seeds. My neck ached; my knees cried; my back throbbed. I had no idea where I was; I could talk to no one, decipher nothing. This was my moment of triumph: I had come three quarters of the way around the world. I had braved the rivers and mud roads of the Amazon and the desert trains of Mali and the ferries of Indonesia and Bangladesh. I had walked through the markets of Kabul. For the first time I felt helpless. As lost as lost could be. If I pushed aside the purple curtain and wiped the ice rime off the glass I saw nothing but blackness and snow. A baby wailed and I could not sleep. I felt totally cut off; connecting to the world, the thing I wanted most of all and that I'd been getting better and better at as the months passed, was impossible. My fellow passengers showed no interest in me. I thought of the scene in Tobias Schneebaum's *Keep the River on Your Right* in which, after four days of walking alone in the jungle, he came upon a band of naked Akarama Indians, a warrior tribe so fierce and feared that he'd been warned that they'd probably kill him on sight. Instead, though, the Akarama, after silently watching his approach, leapt up. "All weapons had been left lying on stones and we were jumping up and down and my arms went around body after body and I felt myself getting hysterical, wildly ec-static with love for all humanity, and I returned slaps on backs and bites on hard flesh, and small as they were, I twirled some round like children and wept away the world of my past." I had been feeling that more and more, in Indonesia and Bangladesh and sitting on the moist grass of Palika Park with Moolchand; that love for humanity which sometimes made me, yes, ecstatic and both liberated and connected. It was a feeling I seldom got at home, where I was known as a bit of a curmudgeon, but out in the world I so often felt new, fresh, like I could see each blade of grass and stone on the sidewalk, and feel open to whoever crossed my path. Out in the world I saw every human being as good and fascinating. As worth knowing. At home I too often ignored people and felt apart from everyone. Out on the road I had this driving desire to connect, and often I did, in part because people could read that openness I so rarely had at home. In China that seemed gone entirely, like a dream. Was it simply the language barrier? Or something else, something within me? Probably a bit of both. Here in western China the language and culture gap was huge, but I also realized that with every mile I was inching closer to my starting point, away from the new and back to the past. I felt scared; what if everything I had learned— evaporated upon my return? How could I find the courage to make that life real again?

An hour out of Hohhot we stopped and a young couple slid in next to me. He wore tight black jeans and a cool black sweater with a silver zipper. I was in a daze. "What's your favorite number?" he said, apropos of nothing, in excellent English.

I perked up. "My number?"

"Yes, you know, like one, two, three, four . . ."

"Six," I said.

"Dude, it's good!" he said, holding up his hand with the pinky and thumb sticking out. "Six and eight are lucky! We are students. I am a counter! I work with numbers."

"An accountant?"

"Yes! That's it! An accountant."

"What's your favorite sport? Do you like the NBA?"

I nodded. "Can you watch the NBA in China?" I said.

"CCTV 5!" he said. "Dude, it's the all-sports channel!"

That was an hour out of Hohhot, though, and soon I was off the train, walking through the streets until I found a hotel. Then back to the train station to puzzle out my next leg, toward

Mongolia. The lines were epic. Which window? I couldn't tell. I waited in one. I drew two clocks, with one through twenty-four. I wrote the word for *tomorrow* next to the word for *Erlian*. "*Erlian, ming tian*," I said boldly when I got to the window, courtesy of Charlotte—Erlian tomorrow.

"*Mayo*," said the woman, don't have. I drew a calendar. I pointed to the day. "*Mayo.*" I shrugged, pointed to the date again. Out spat a ticket. For Sunday, five days later, too long to stay in Hohhot.

Somehow I found the bus station. Somehow I bought a ticket to the Chinese-Mongolian border town of Erlian, leaving the next morning at eight. Most of the phrases my daughter Charlotte had given me I couldn't make work—intonation was so important in Mandarin, nothing but gibberish came out of my mouth. I trooped back through the cold to my hotel. I went to the restaurant. "How are you?" I said. "Thank you." I ordered, pointing to a photo in the menu of what looked like rectangular strips of meat and green string beans. My dinner came: strips of pure fat in hot peppers and garlic. Like bacon without the meat. The texture was hideous but it tasted really good.

I fled to my room, through a phalanx of waitresses and desk clerks who said, as I passed, "How are you? Thank you!" And then they giggled.

In the morning I shouldered my bags and strolled into the frigid streets of Hohhot toward the bus station. I had no idea where I was going, except toward Mongolia. I had no idea when I'd get there. There was some question about whether I needed a visa or not. The Mongolia guidebook said I did; various websites said I didn't. But I was buoyed by thoughts of Moolchand and Fardus, their eternal optimism, and I'd just finished all

1,886 pages of the Chinese English-language edition of Alex-andre Dumas' *Count of Monte Cristo*, whose ending words were "Wait and hope."

I skated onto the bus and off we went. My seatmate wore silvery shining satin slacks and had long sideburns. "How are you?" I said. He looked at me like I was from the Stone Age and said nothing.

We climbed and swirled up into brown mountains covered in snow, and an hour later emerged on high rolling plains. Sun. Big sky with a boundless horizon. Strange motel-looking places in the middle of nowhere with yurts instead of cabins. Acres of twenty-foot-tall imitation dinosaurs striding across the steppe.

We made a bathroom stop. The men's room was a work of art. An outdoor trough encased in frozen piss five inches thick gleamed a faint yellow. Five holes in the floor five feet above the ground revealed amazing free-standing sculptures of frozen shit that rose two inches above the holes themselves. It was so cold it didn't even smell.

In the early afternoon we left the highway and headed into a town, stopped by a restaurant. Everyone piled out. A lunch stop! I stood around. I went into the restaurant, but no passengers were inside. Maybe it was just a bathroom break. I waited. I got cold. It was freezing. I got back on the bus. I sat. After twenty minutes the driver came up to me and erupted in Chinese. I heard the word Erlian. "Erlian!" I said. "Yes, I'm going to Erlian."

"Erlian!" he said. "Erlian!" Then I understood. We had, in fact, arrived. Mongolia was here, somewhere.

I saw a hotel. It wasn't a hotel, but the bus station. "Mongolia!" I said at a ticket window. A ticket spat out. An hour later I

sat on a small, ramshackle bus with no heat. Women piled in
with duffel bags and more duffel bags, five to a woman; they
were traders. They filled the seats. Frost covered the windows.
A man boarded with a truck tire. Another man thrust a car
bench seat covered in faux leopard into the aisle. We took off.
Hit the border, as imperial as any I'd ever seen. Sky, snow,
steppe, and a massive marble building with mirrored glass shining in the sun. I went in one side, came out the other. Another
hundred yards and we hit Mongolia. The affluence, the sparkle
and shimmer of China, evaporated.

The border checkpoint was dim, old, dusty. I filled out a
form. Visa number: I had no visa. Hotel: I had no hotel. Flight
number: I was on a bus, so I left that blank, too.

I waited and hoped in a very long line.

My border agent was beautiful, with eyebrows finely arched
and plucked. Pink lipstick. Long black hair in a ponytail. Green
camo fatigues. A huge gold badge. "What bus number?" she
said.

"I don't know," I said. "The bus from Erlian." How many
buses could there be?

"What bus number?"

"I don't know."

She unleashed a string of words to the people behind me in
line. They shrugged; none of them were fellow passengers.

Five times she asked me and five times I just said I don't
know. She looked at me. "What hotel?"

"I don't know," I said. "Zamyn Uud." That was the city we
were going to.

"Zamyn Uud Hotel?" she said.

"Yes!" I said. "That's it. The Zamyn Uud Hotel!"

She wrote. But it was the visa, or my lack of it, that I was worried about. She opened my passport. Thumbed through the pages. Looked at me. "What bus number?"

I shrugged. She wrote something down. Picked up a stamper and, clunk, stamped my passport. Fifteen minutes later we were in Zamyn Uud, Mongolia, on the edge of the Gobi Desert.

There was nothing in Zamyn Uud, Mongolia. There was dirt and ice and snow and three restaurants and a train station, a lot of yurts, a couple of general stores. It was 42 degrees below zero Fahrenheit. A pool table lay dead in the town square, its felt covered with a layer of white. On the edge of town stood two boxcars, from which frozen horse hides, like sheets of plywood, were being unloaded onto trucks. My hotel, which was not the Zamyn Uud Hotel, had no hot water. When darkness fell the sky was nothing but stars, a dusting of snow sparkling like broken glass. I felt far away from everything. Nisa called from Delhi, sobbing. Lindsey sent me a note that hinted of a new, budding relationship; apparently I wasn't the only one who felt we had grown apart. On my way to the restaurant for dinner I ran into wandering yak. And found a man lying on the snow. He wore a fur cap and knee-high leather boots and had gold teeth and his legs were scrambling but he was getting no-where. He could not rise. He was hopelessly drunk. I did my best to lift him to his feet, but he was big, solid, and he clutched me tightly, weaving, slipping. He had no gloves. We slipped and slid and skidded to a bench in the square, by the pool table dusted with snow, where I left him. I wanted to hang out, to talk, to just sit and watch the world and meet people, but that was impossible when it was 42 degrees below zero. People rushed past in thick winter coats; if I paused for more than a moment the cold cut through my clothes as if I was naked. What would have happened to Schneebaum's adventure if those Akarams had ignored him?

In the restaurant it hit me: I was starting all over again. I knew not a word of Mongolian, and the menu was in Cyrillic. Bring me anything, I motioned. We struggled. Being me in such situations was like being a wiggling minnow on a line cast from a dock; if there was an English speaker within a half-mile they'd find me.

So it was: "What is your problem?" said a man who swept in through the thick blanket covering the doorway. "Meat," he said. "In Mongolia we eat meat."

"Perfect," I said. "I want meat."

He barked an order, sat down with me, and we shared a beer. His name was Tsedee. He was in his late twenties and spoke Mongolian, English, German, and Russian.

I saw my opening. Tsedee was driving to Ulan Bator in a twenty-ton truck hauling propane. It wasn't exactly playing by the ludicrous rules of my crazy idea—there was no history of propane trucks blowing up in Mongolia—and I'd been taking buses, boats, trains, and planes that you could buy a ticket on, but I wanted more. More adventure. More risk. More conversation. The train from Zamyn Uud to Ulan Bator didn't promise anything new. I filled his mug. Looked at him. Said, "I have a strange and serious question for you."

"What?" he said.

"I want to ride to Ulan Bator in your truck."

He looked at me. "The road is very bad," he said. "Not a little bad, but very bad. It is very rough. It is freezing. The truck's heater is broken. It will take thirty-six hours to drive 350 miles. It is like torture."

"Perfect," I said. "Can I come?"

He looked me up and down. Said, "You will see camels and yurts and the Gobi Desert." Took a swig of his beer. "Yes."

I waited for three days, the last in a one-room house with two beds and no running water, heated with a coal stove, while Tsedee waited for his Chinese propane man to call him on his cell phone; and I worried that it would all fall through and that I would freeze to death.

The truck stood outside, wooden beams under its front axle, with no left front wheel. There would be Tsedee, a driver named Batbillq and me. Batbillq didn't want me to come. "Too cold," he said. "And there is no room." I climbed in the truck. A single bench seat and in the middle, where my legs would be, an auxiliary heater balanced on the floor, connected to the electrical system with bare wires. The cab was a mess. Oil-soaked rags, trash, furs, a toolbox, were haphazardly strewn everywhere. It would be tight. But Tsedee texted me that night, finally: "You are welcome to ride with us and I am in Erlian and will be back tomorrow afternoon."

"*Bayarlalaa,*" I said to Tsedee. "Thank you." And the next morning I went to breakfast. "*Bi husej buuz baina,*" I said. "I would like some meat dumplings."

WE DIDN'T LEAVE until almost 10:00 p.m. that night. In the cold of forty below zero, everything was sharp. Tsedee climbed into a long-haired fur jumpsuit that made him look like a Yeti, and pulled a jacket over that. Batbillq had felt boots an inch thick. I had basic hiking shoes. The moon, one day from being full, was big and luminous and so clearly defined it looked like you could slice your finger on its edges. It hung over the darkness of the desert, glowing just enough to see a horizon that didn't end. The wind cut like a razor; it sliced and burned, and ran through four layers of polar fleece and down like I was wearing a cotton T-shirt. The snow, blown across short brown grass, was so dry it was like talcum powder. Tsedee had been right; it was torture. We lurched and jolted at five and ten miles an hour over a frozen, rutted dirt road that turned into no road at all, just tire tracks across the desert, and that punched my kidneys like George Foreman. The sclerotic auxiliary heater pumped its best, though my feet got cold after an hour. The cracked windshield fogged.

We had three flat tires. The first came around midnight, and quickly felt like a nightmare. The tires were big, heavy; they had tubes, and we had to patch the first one, which we did in the glare of the headlights. It took almost two hours. We drove on. Passed nothing; no other cars or trucks or yurts or camels. Not a bush. The second flat hit at first light. We fixed that one. In late morning we ran out of gas, and that really might have killed us, because the heater, such as it was, wouldn't work if the engine wasn't on, and a wind had kicked up. But, strangely, the engine died literally across the dirt from a gas station in one of the few villages we passed—a jumble of small wooden houses in the middle of nowhere. Still, it was an ordeal. Batbillq had to hike in the wind to the pump and we had to lift the cab up three times while he fiddled with the engine to get it going again as the cold sliced and cut. We drove for thirty-six hours straight. I watched Batbillq fall asleep at the wheel and drift off the road and I didn't have to say a word, because there wasn't really a road and there was nothing to hit, so we'd just drive until he woke up and headed back to the path. We did take one break, pausing for three hours in the middle of nowhere—an unbroken horizon stretching in every direction—for lunch and a brief nap. Tsedee rummaged behind the seats and produced a propane tank, a single burner, and a pot. Batbillq wedged himself in a corner and started snoring, while Tsedee boiled *buuz,* meat dumplings, in milk and salt and water. The broth was full of fat and oil, salty and rich, and we gobbled it down.

WE DIDN'T TALK A LOT. Or maybe we did, and thirty-six hours was just a lot of time. I learned a bit about the gas business and growing up in Mongolia. Gas was cheaper in China than in Russia—which had a road from Ulan Bator—so Tsedee made the trip a couple of times a month. He'd been raised by his grandmother, had been sent off to school in Moscow at fifteen, had spent a couple of years in Berlin. He was smart, worldly, ambitious; with his language skills and willingness to make these epic journeys, I imagined he'd be rich in no time at all.

I learned how cold cold could really be. We came across only one camel, sleeping on its knees by a yurt, and we saw a lot of tiny mice and several antelope bounding across the headlights. On the second night we had our third flat, and this time had no more patches, no more spares. We stood around the tire in the dark, scratched our heads. Took the wheel off and tied it to the truck and just climbed back in. "Ha! Ha! Ha!" laughed Tsedee, slamming the door shut. "We will just pray we make it with only nine tires!"

Had it been months ago, I would have asked a lot more questions, but I'd now traveled three-quarters of the way around the world. I'd already been across South America and Africa, Bangladesh, India, and Afghanistan. Instead I just settled in, cranking the bad tire back into its place with a wrench in the darkness and dirt and cold, munching on my buuz, watching the nights and day pass by in a country that had one-half a person per square kilometer. It was a measure of how far I'd come, how deeply I'd gone, how long I'd been away. I was stripped bare, totally open to the world and at home with two descendants of Genghis Khan and the truth was, I was a little bit bored. It was time to go home. Time to complete the circle. Travel was only worthwhile when your eyes were fresh, when it surprised you and amazed you and made you think about yourself in a new way. You couldn't travel forever. When you stopped seeing, when you lost your curiosity and openness to the world, it was time to return to your starting point and see where you stood. In everyone, I suspect, lay a tension between the need for otherness and home. We all want security, we all want adventure, the familiar and the new always jockeying for control. But when otherness began to be normal, home itself begin to seem like the other, perhaps even the exotic. Even Schneebaum had finally stumbled out of the world of the Akaramas and back to New York, "going out to look for the same self that I always was." Thesiger and T. E. Lawrence left behind their beloved Arabia for London. Plus, I had been avoiding things for far too long. I needed to start making amends.

After a night and a day and a night of nothing, the lights of Ulan Bator appeared as if we were coming in from the sea. It was 7:30 a.m. and dawn was breaking in a world of steam and ice, not unlike a morning in March when I'd arrived in Toronto after my first all-night bus ride. I could barely keep my eyes open. We stopped at a corner, and in a flash Tsedee shook my hand and was gone. We drove a few more blocks, to the gas depot, and as Batbillq shimmied over a wooden fence to unlock the gate, I shed the big felt boots he'd loaned me, grabbed my stuff, and hailed a taxi.

FROM ULAN BATOR to Vladivostok by train took four days. Long days of rolling, rolling through snow and naked brown trees and under white skies, and over frozen rivers, a landscape without end that never changed. "Nature," Albert Golod said, gazing out the window at it. "Russian nature!" He was seventy, strong and straight, both paternal and childlike in his quest to show me the delights of Russia. He was on his way to a sanatorium in Vladivostok for three weeks, and had long white hair and a white beard. He spoke Russian, German, Hebrew, and English, and he'd had two careers, first as a radar engineer and later as an archaeologist working and living in Tajikistan. He insisted I visit with him over tea and cakes, briefly every evening. "This is Russian tea," he'd say. "This is a Russian cake." Then he'd send me on my way again.

After the green warmth of the Amazon, after the passion and colors of India, after the blue seas of Indonesia and the hot crowds of Bangladesh, after the danger and exoticism of Afghanistan, the Russian landscape seemed oppressive, Russians proud and incurious. There was nothing glorious or grand about it save its length and breadth and its snow and unending cold bleakness. Yet Golod wasn't the only one who looked at it with awe, with yearning. A young soldier talked to me one afternoon and the first thing he said was, "Look! Russia is so beautiful!" I looked. Snow. White sky. Bleakness.

There was also nothing dangerous or crowded or dirty about it, which was disappointing to me. The Russian visa I'd waited for in Delhi expired by the time I got to Ulan Bator, and there, if I didn't want to wait another three weeks, my only option was a transit visa, and a prepaid train ticket. I asked for a third-class seat, but there were no seats at all on this train—it was only compartments.

Still, this was a piece of the Trans-Siberian Railway and, as Peter Fleming wrote in 1934, en route from London to China in *One's Company*: "Everyone is a romantic, though in some the romanticism is of a perverted and paradoxical kind. And for the romantic it is, after all, something to stand in the sunlight beside the Trans-Siberian Express with the casually proprietarial air of the passenger, and to reflect that that long raking chain of steel and wood and glass is to go swinging and clattering out of the West into the East, carrying you with it." I loved that description, even more because I was standing Fleming's image on its head, heading east from the East itself, all the way across the Pacific toward home and the West. But the whole journey had felt that way, a raking chain of steel and wood and glass and rubber and aluminum snaking from Washington and wrapping around the world.

The train rolled on. One afternoon I was dragged into a compartment steaming and sweaty and packed with seven men. They were hooligans, tough guys. "Vodka!" they shouted. "Russian vodka!" Empty bottles slid across the floor. A greasy chicken carcass dripped on the little table. They had full sets of gold and silver teeth and were covered with tattoos—spiders on their hands, crosses inside the spiders' abdomens. It was like being in a rugby scrum. We were packed in that compartment and they pawed and hugged and clutched each other and me with drunken abandon, and a physicality that American men are too insecure ever to display. They held my hand. Draped arms around me. Hit me and hit each other. It was full contact and the vodka shots rained and chicken parts flew and Patap, his eyes on fire, his metal teeth glinting inches from my face, gripped my hand and kissed it and put it to his forehead and punched me in the thighs, hard, and talked, talked, talked in my face. I punched back. And I talked back; we spoke without understanding but every word hit home. We were sure of it. Yes, yes, yes! The steward tried to drag me out; he was worried. "Bad men," he said. But nothing could be done. We were a tangle of bodies and sour breath and simmering brutality inches from getting out of hand and I don't know how long it lasted. I lost track of time. We pushed and shoved and Patap flipped and waved his sharp knife and poured another shot and thrust a piece of chicken skin at me and finally, somehow, I ended up in my own compartment utterly spent, dizzily gazing at a landscape that looked bleak enough to kill a smile. As I lost consciousness I heard thumps and barks; the gangsters were still at it, hugging each other and beating each other up.

Time never really came back to me. There was Moscow time and Vladivostok time and the time where we were at any given point and one day looked like the next, and in the darkness of an early morning we slid into Vladivostok. It was time to go, time to walk out of the jungle. I crunched across the snow and hailed a taxi to the airport.

BRANDON [Manitoba]—*Screaming passengers fled in terror from a Greyhound bus as an unidentified fellow passenger suddenly stabbed a man sleeping next to him, decapitated him and waved the severed head at horrified witnesses standing outside. The apparently unprovoked assault left 36 men, women and children stranded Wednesday night on the shoulder . . . watching while the bus driver and a driver of a nearby truck shut the crazed attacker inside the bus with the mangled victim. Reports Friday said the suspect tried to eat parts of the victim.*

—National Post *(Canada), July 31, 2008*

TWELVE

Same, Same, but Different

"DEATH!" THE HEAVY-METAL refrain crashed through the terminal, pumping out of the "Rock-On Greyhound Multimedia Center," as a man in a black T-shirt with pasty skin and long, greasy hair pushed buttons and dollar bills into the machine. A guy in a hoodie and goatee slumped on the metal wire bench. A fat woman in a T-shirt and sweatpants dragged a kid across the linoleum like he was a piece of luggage. Of which there seemed to be little; mostly plastic garbage bags stuffed full at the last minute, as if by people on the run. Six a.m. in the Los Angeles Greyhound terminal and I held a ticket for four buses and seventy-two hours across the U.S.A. It all seemed incredibly familiar, of a piece. Bogotá. Quito. Lima. Dar es Salaam. Nairobi. Patna. Hohhot. Another bus station, another three thousand miles. But different, too. I could hear conversations, ask for things, decipher it all, and it didn't look romantic. No sweet milky chai kiosks. No wooden bakso stands. No smell of shit. No smell of smoke. No monkeys or feral dogs or women with

gold nose rings and bangles or wearing felt hats. No fresh torti-
llas. No food at all, except for vending machines full of Snickers
and Fritos and twenty-ounce blue energy drinks.

It all seemed a little crazy, hard to grasp, process. A day before I'd stepped off a train in Vladivostok in snow and ice, still
hung over from the vodka hug-fest with the silver-toothed
gangsters, India and Afghanistan just over my shoulder, on my
mind, and then, wham, a taxi through warm L.A.—"Fuck,
man, look at that traffic!" said the driver, who'd emigrated to
the U.S. from Jordan when he was sixteen—and I was plunging
into a place I hadn't seen in months. As a T-shirt in India read,
"Same, same, but different."

Since the beheading on Greyhound in Manitoba, Canada, in
July, knives on board were no longer cool, and we were cursorily
frisked with a metal-detecting wand as we boarded. By now I
knew what to do: I placed a bag on the seat next to me and
feigned sleep, my mouth open and droopy, to discourage a possible seatmate. On buses the difference between comfort and torture lay right there; in fact personal space was the key to
everything, no matter what country you were in or what conveyance you were on. The most dangerous, most rickety bus in the
world could be a pleasure—as long as it stayed on the road and
no one cut your head off—if there were extra seats, if it didn't fill.

"My name is Tom. I'll be your driver to Las Vegas. We'll
have a thirty-five-minute break in Barstow at the Greyhound
steak house. You know what that is, right? McDonald's!" And
then he rattled off "the rules: No smoking. No alcoholic bever-
ages. No profanity. Any aggressive behavior, physical or verbal,
will get you thrown off the bus!"

Welcome to America.

Tom fired the engine up and we rolled out, past the warehouses and chain link of downtown L.A., onto the 405 and then east up into the desert, America huge and spread out and vacant-seeming. The streets felt empty. Where was everyone? Except for Siberia and the Gobi with Tsedee, even the great empty swaths of Afghanistan and Africa and the Andes always seemed dotted with a donkey cart or a peasant tending an alpaca. A voice cut in. "I'm on top of the world and making money like there's no tomorrow!" It was a man three rows in front of me, talking on his mobile phone. Loud. As if he were alone in a room. "I was blessed with superior intelligence and I start law school in four days and I have an MD, so soon I'll be a JDMD; isn't that awesome?" He hung up after ten minutes, dialed his doctor. "Yes, this is Drew Fenton and my social security number is . . ." I couldn't believe it; he yammered the digits and went on and on, made call after call, an ego that seemed insatiable. "What's your financial situation?" he asked someone else in another call. "Watch out; that guy treats me like a bank!" I wondered whether it offended me only because I could understand the language, the words.

We hit Vegas that afternoon, and America seemed like the saddest place I'd seen in months. The worst, most dangerous conveyances in the world always had a mix of people on them, people bursting with life and color and friendliness. In Peru or Mali or India or Bangladesh everyone was poor. The few rich people flew; everybody else took a ferry or a bus or a train and they prepared for the journey with their carefully wrapped boxes and containers of rice, and the stream of fresh food offered for pennies was ubiquitous. Except for Drew Fenton, the loudmouth on the cell phone, Greyhound was the dregs of

America, the poorest of the poor. My ticket from L.A. to D.C. was more than two hundred dollars; surely I could have found a flight for more or less the same. In America if you had an Internet connection and you wanted to get somewhere you found the lowest fare and flew, but the people on the bus were people off the grid. "We're busiest around the first of the month," said the driver. Which meant that its passengers traveled on government checks or whatever they could scrounge. A man boarded in Vegas with nothing but a plastic sack of Coke cans and he hadn't showered in days, along with a skinny, sickly woman with a neck covered in tattoos. No one carried food; they ate french fries and Big Macs at McDonald's. They were pale, had crooked, broken teeth. "Ready to Go Home?" read a poster in the Vegas station. "Don't Runaway Love, you're not on your own! Open your eyes and come back with me," read the poster, imploring teenaged runaways to seek help and call an 800 telephone number. I thought of Moolchand, poor as dirt, buying me tea; of Fardus, feeding me fresh coconuts from his yard and dreaming of Las Vegas. But this *was* Vegas. This *was* America, the dream itself! And it looked like a place cracking, peeling, coming apart at the seams. Who would invite me to their house for lunch? Who even had a home? When we'd passed temples on the Blueline, Moolchand had prayed; Khalid prayed constantly, for me, for our safety; the men and women to whom he gave money gave us prayers back. Moussa had made tea in the vestibule of the train in Mali, and handed it all around to whoever wanted a cup. Rokibal in Bangladesh had wanted to know everything about me, and Ranjit, the bus driver in the poorest state of India, had given me his red velvet pillow. Wakiba and

David had begged me to come home with them after twenty hours of fighting Nairobi traffic, and fed me in a house that had no kitchen and no bathroom. The conditions were deplorable sometimes. Dirty. Hot. Crowded. Groaningly uncomfortable. Dangerous. But all those people had been so filled with generosity and spirit, curiosity about a stranger, and they all in some way had felt connected in a way they didn't even realize to a larger society, culture, family. But the people around me seemed alone, disconnected; what bound them to each other? To America? What *was* America? We were a bus of lost souls in a country that itself seemed without a soul. Wherever I'd been in the last few months, people had asked me about Obama; he'd been inaugurated a few days before and here I was, finally in America, and no one on the bus mentioned him.

We made a quick stop in Vail, Colorado, where I'd lived for eight months when I was eighteen as a ski bum, and I clambered out of the bus to stand in the snow for a moment to remember. Suddenly the doors swung shut with a sigh of air and the bus started forward. I rushed and banged on the door. The bus halted and the doors swung open and the driver barked, "I didn't tell you you could get out!"

We stopped an hour later so he could put chains on the rear wheels for the trip over Vail Pass. I got out again, and a second later he jumped in and started forward again. I ran up to the doors and he barked again. "Ain't leaving, dammit, just moving forward a bit. What's your problem?"

In 50,000 miles no one had spoken to me like that. I lost it. "Why are you being such an asshole?" I said.

"Stay away from me!" he yelled. "I don't like you!"

. . .

WE PAUSED IN KANSAS CITY at 9:00 p.m., a light snow falling, and perky Suze Orman lectured us about cutting expenses to amass six months' savings in a down economy, from the wall-mounted flat-screen TV. "I know how to cut expenses!" said a man next to me, with a few days' growth on his cheeks, wearing work boots and a denim jacket. "I have a great idea. I'll say to my four kids, we're going to alternate eating. Your mom and two of you will eat on Mondays, and then me and the other two will eat on Tuesdays." He was a truckdriver who'd just gotten laid off when he'd rolled into the depot in Kansas City that day, and he was headed home to Florida on the bus. "Retirement? A 401k? I've got two plans: the good one and the bad one. The good one is to win the lottery. The bad one is to work until the day I die."

The miles and hours passed in a blur. By now I was used to the physical discomfort; it seemed like nothing, though the constant diet of Big Macs and fries was getting old, and my country felt so sad—there wasn't any other word for it. "I just have to get down to Tennessee and to court, and then I'll come back," said a fat man in white socks and shorts, though it was seventeen degrees outside and 3:00 a.m., in the St. Louis station. "Hoping I might get a job around Indianapolis or something."

"What's the court case about?" I asked.

"Wrong place and the wrong time, that's all," he said, picking his teeth, as the television overhead blared, "What if I told you there was a way to make money on your own terms? It's been right under your nose your whole life; the question is, are you ready for it? To take advantage of the enormous profits of the stock market, no matter where it's going!" I couldn't believe it; the stock market had fallen by 60 percent, had collapsed, and here was the same old song, and I wondered if anyone was buying. Not the guy next to me, at least. "Might as well just go to Vegas," he said. "All one big fucking gamble."

I loved the idea of being surrounded by otherness, but this was an otherness that I wanted to push away, not delve into, not subsume myself in. I imagined Moolchand or Moussa as bottomless pools leading me to India or Mali themselves. But my fellow Greyhound travelers felt like dead ends. I didn't want to feel that way about America; I'd been imagining coming home and seeing it in a new light, shiny and clean and easy and modern, and familiar and welcoming, and I hadn't noticed any of this on the China bus to New York or the Greyhound to Toronto so many months before.

We were waiting in line to get back on the bus, and I had to run to the bathroom. I asked a man who'd been on since L.A. if he could watch my bags. His wire-framed glasses were crooked; he hadn't shaved in a while, and he carried a garbage bag. But he just looked at me. Stared. "No," he said softly. "I can't. I just can't do it."

We boarded and headed toward Pittsburgh. A woman sat next to me and started texting with people in a sex chat room over her cell phone. "I got 8 inches!" "Please can someone help me, I want to so bad," wrote "lookin4luvlesbo," as we hurtled down the great American road.

Another voice from across the aisle. "The baby died! No he totally dead, you know, and that's what I'm sayin. Sounds like bullshit to me. She don't got no job and can't do nothing but sit and cop an attitude. She told me the baby died but there's no way that baby was six pounds and there's gonna be no body, no funeral, nothing. We gotta go down there and figure out what happened to the baby. It's the ugliest thing I ever seen."

WE PULLED OUT OF PITTSBURGH at midnight and I was headed home. I couldn't quite fathom it; I was so close, yet I also felt still very much out there, riding that unbroken chain, and I felt closer to New Delhi and Kabul in a way than I did to Washington. Get off the bus, find a hotel, plan my next leg. No. Not anymore. This was it, my last night on the road. I had a feeling that my life had changed. That I had, slowly but surely, inexorably, reached not an end but a starting point. A beginning.

Escaping into the farthest corners of the world had always felt good to me. Part of it was just adventure, the excitement of plunging along a muddy road in the Peruvian Amazon or jumping aboard a ferry with no idea of where I was going. I took it for granted that no assignment was too long or too dangerous—that the most intense ones were the best ones—and that my family would be there for me when I got back. That my wife would love me. That my children would miss me and hug me when I walked in the door again weeks or months later, and no one would ever feel abandoned and that I'd feel as much a part of their lives as if I'd never been away. That's what I'd always told myself.

But as the bus rolled down the highway toward home in the middle of the night, I started thinking about the price I'd paid. Going away, living the life I'd lived, had cost me. It was one thing to go away on a four-day business trip, another to be on a ship at sea in the Pacific for two months—and to leave three weeks later for another fourteen days in New Zealand, as I'd done, gone for more than 120 days that year. On this trip alone I'd been traveling for 159 days. My marriage had crumbled and I'd let it, even though I had told myself I was trying to save it. I'd let the duality of my life grow, without stopping it; while I constantly kept moving, Lindsey and I had barely taken a vacation together, just the two of us, in fifteen years.

All those people I'd met on the road had made me think deeply about travel and human connection and escape. I had always prided myself on the connections I made while traveling, from the nutty Swiss guy in Mombasa to Fardus in Bangladesh to Moolchand in New Delhi. But all those interactions were fleeting, shallow—I couldn't kid myself that they had been otherwise.

In places like India and Indonesia, where people almost always travel together and I was a freak alone, I had finally started to understand the value of deeper connections, especially as I cruised through the night toward home in this bus of lost souls. Only connect, wrote E. M. Forster—one of those famous literary lines that's now a cliché—and as humans that's what we all craved perhaps more than anything else. To be known, to let your guard down, was scary; how ironic that so many of us fled instead, that we didn't allow ourselves the very thing we wanted in our deepest souls. The lure of foreign countries and cultures has always been escape, but also transformation, redemption, discovery. People who felt like they didn't fit in had long sought escape in the exotic, but maybe that was because in those foreign lands they didn't have an excuse—they could never be really known in the first place, never have to take that risk of opening up and trusting. We passed another McDonald's and I thought of my father, who'd never remarried after divorcing thirty-five years ago. Today he was living in Thailand with a woman whose command of the English language was shaky at best, and it was his longest relationship in years. Did they get along because they connected so deeply, or because they barely connected at all and she couldn't ask him any of those pesky emotional questions? There'd been a time when I'd had all of those connections at home, but I'd let them lapse, had cruised through a great chunk of my life without thinking about it, working as if on autopilot, until it was too late.

In the end, I thought, as we pulled into Frederick, Maryland, at four in the morning, escape was less the answer than its opposite—that wrapping yourself in the cloak of otherness for a brief time was a form of hiding behind a costume. That being the lone Western face in a crowd of attentive exotics was no substitute for love and its sometimes daunting and irritating bonds.

Maybe there were certain kinds of journeys, assignments, I didn't have to take anymore. The really long ones alone. The ones to war zones or frozen, windswept plains in northern Greenland in which food ran low and the tents blew down and the intensity was so high that they separated me from the world. I thought of Afghanistan. Things were heating up there, and I'd read in the paper of firefights reported by writers and photographers on the front lines. For a moment I felt jealous of them; *I should be there!* I thought. But they'd all pay a price for those stories, those experiences. At its most expensive, some would die or be kidnapped, leaving behind spouses and children. Even if they returned safely, though, they would be people apart,

people carrying experiences that were hard to share with anyone who hadn't done that same thing.

We pulled out of the station and the bus stopped. Lurched
forward and stopped again. A smell of smoke, of burnt rubber,
wafted through the coach. The driver got out, came back in,
got back out again, and came back in. "We have what's called a
breakdown in service," he announced. "The brake lines is
froze. I've called the company and they'll send another bus,
eventually."

Forty miles from home, it had come to this: the only conveyance in five months of traveling that had failed to get me to my
destination was a Greyhound bus. We were supposed to go
from Frederick to Baltimore, then on to D.C.; who knew how
long we might wait? And I was so close. I called Lindsey, woke
her up. Asked if she could pick me up. "I don't want to," she
said. "Can't you take a taxi?"

Which I did, nestled in the back of a Chevy Caprice a few
minutes later, speeding in quiet and warmth down the inter-
state toward home. I had been looking forward to the bus pulling into the station, the hydraulic swoosh of the doors opening,
and stepping out into the dawn of where I'd started, greeted by
my children, Dad stepping off the bus triumphant after so many
miles around the world. Instead, I climbed out of the taxi at
5:00 a.m. in front of my empty apartment.

Only this time it was okay. I had seen the world and myself
afresh. I had left in order to find my way home again—and I
had, even if it was a new and different home. The journey had
shown me all this. As a young man I pursued opportunity and
career and adventure; I couldn't see any other choice at the
time. It was only later, with success and when a price had been

paid, that I could reckon the cost, acknowledge it. I had to forgive myself and start again. I remembered that train rumbling
into the station in Mali and thinking, *How in the world can I
throw myself on that scarred, battered thing?* Sometimes you just
had to close your eyes and board, to travel to things and not just
away from them, and of course I could see that because finally I
had, in fact, gone away on this journey. I walked up the stairs
and through the door, and slipped into bed, the world and my
life jangling in my head.

APPENDIX

I asked Fred Kilborne, a veteran insurance Actuary in San Diego, California, to calculate the actuarial risk of my 159-day journey. Here are his findings:

MORTALITY RISK ON THE LUNATIC EXPRESS—
OBSERVATIONS

1. The attached tables indicate that, if Carl had taken both of his trips 1,000 times, he'd have about a 50% chance of being killed en route. This follows from the combined cumulative risk of 481,070 per billion trips, according to the tables. The mortality risk can also be expressed as 5% per hundred such combined trips. This strikes the observer as being extremely risky, relative to traveling the 50,000 miles at home in the U.S., but a good deal short of being flat-out suicidal.

2. The entire exercise rides, of course, on the selection of the

index factors. Reasonably good statistical data was available concerning the risk of getting around in the United States, and the blended risk of one death per billion miles traveled is supportable. Some data is available for international air travel, and the selected indices are probably conservative (i.e., they may be high). Only sketchy data could be found, on the other hand, for such conveyances as ferry and matatu, and the index selections were highly subjective and may in some cases be greatly inadequate. Consider, for example, traveling by bus in and around Kabul. The assigned index of 96 is very substantial, but are we really satisfied that traveling a million miles in that vicinity would bear only a 10% chance of being killed? I'd be inclined to yield my seat to Carl.

3. The tables address only mortality due to accidents on the given leg and conveyance. Some consideration was given to the risk of terrorist attack in Afghanistan, but none to the chance of being stabbed by a crazed fellow matatu rider in Kenya or being consumed by a crocodile after slipping off an Indonesian ferry. Death could also result by reason of contracting leprosy in India or mad-cow disease in Canada. There is also a force of mortality at work on all of us even if we lie in bed at home, of course, but we won't blame that on Carl's trips.

4. We've discussed only mortality risk so far, but the actuary (if not the adventure traveler) must also consider morbidity and robbery and all manner of untoward events. I pointed out to Carl that he might have been sickened by the peanuts on the flight to Bogotá, or broken his leg jumping onto the train to Dakar, or been kidnapped for ransom while strolling in Lima, or convicted of espionage in Ulan Bator, or

mugged on the bus to D.C., and more, and worse. It turned out that he had already considered some of these events and was nonplussed about the others. This in turn led me to conclude that "The Lunatic Express" was an apt name for Carl's trips.

ACKNOWLEDGMENTS

I traveled alone and wrote *Lunatic* alone, but neither would have been possible without the help and support of many people.

For her unfailing love and friendship over twenty-seven years and too many months away, I cannot ever thank Lindsey Truitt enough. I wouldn't be who I am, have the family I do, or have been able to flourish as a journalist without her, and without her support and hard work. Lindsey also thought of the name; it's fair to say that without her *The Lunatic Express* would not exist.

For their love and patience over too many assignments, I thank Lily, Max, and Charlotte; I love you without reservation.

I owe a huge debt to my agent, Joe Regal, for professional and editorial insight over two books and a decade.

Lunatic would never have been more than an idea without Charlie Conrad, my editor at Broadway, who took a risk and jumped on *The Lunatic Express* from the start, and whose editorial guidance made a much better book. For helping shepherd *Lunatic* from raw manuscript to final book, a huge thanks at Broadway to Jenna Ciongoli, David Wade Smith, Julie Sills, and Laura Duffy.

I thank Alex Heard for sending me to the Congo and with whom subsequent conversations planted the seeds that led directly to my book proposal.

For reading early drafts of *Lunatic,* and for their friendship, I especially want to thank Clifton Wiens and Keith Bellows.

For their friendship, encouragement, and patient listening, I thank Scott Wallace, Lisa Ramey, Liz Hodgson, Nick Kuttner, and Geoff Dawson.

For their support over the past few years, keeping me busy, I thank Susan Murcko, Adam Rogers, Jim Meigs, and David Dunbar.

I'm extremely grateful to veteran actuary Fred Kilbourne for the painstaking job of calculating the risk of my journey; I know it was more work than he thought.

In Lima, Peru, a huge thanks to Tyler Bridges and Cecelia for their care and feeding, and a few days of the comforts of home.

For their hospitality in New Delhi, I thank Jeremy Kahn and Victoria Whitworth; sorry I stayed so long!

And last, but in no way least, *The Lunatic Express* never derailed, sank, or plunged off a cliff because of Melissa Bell. Her keen editing made *Lunatic* sharper, tighter, and more nuanced than it ever could have been without her. I owe her much, and many thanks.

ABOUT THE AUTHOR

Carl Hoffman has driven the Baja 1000, ridden reindeer in Siberia, sailed an open dinghy 250 miles, and traveled to sixty-five countries. When he's able to stay put for more than a few months at a time, he lives in Washington, D.C., where his three children make fun of him on a pretty constant basis. He is a contributing editor at *National Geographic Traveler, Wired,* and *Popular Mechanics,* and his stories about travel and technology have also appeared in *Outside, National Geographic Adventure,* and *Men's Journal.* He is also the author of *Hunting Warbirds.*